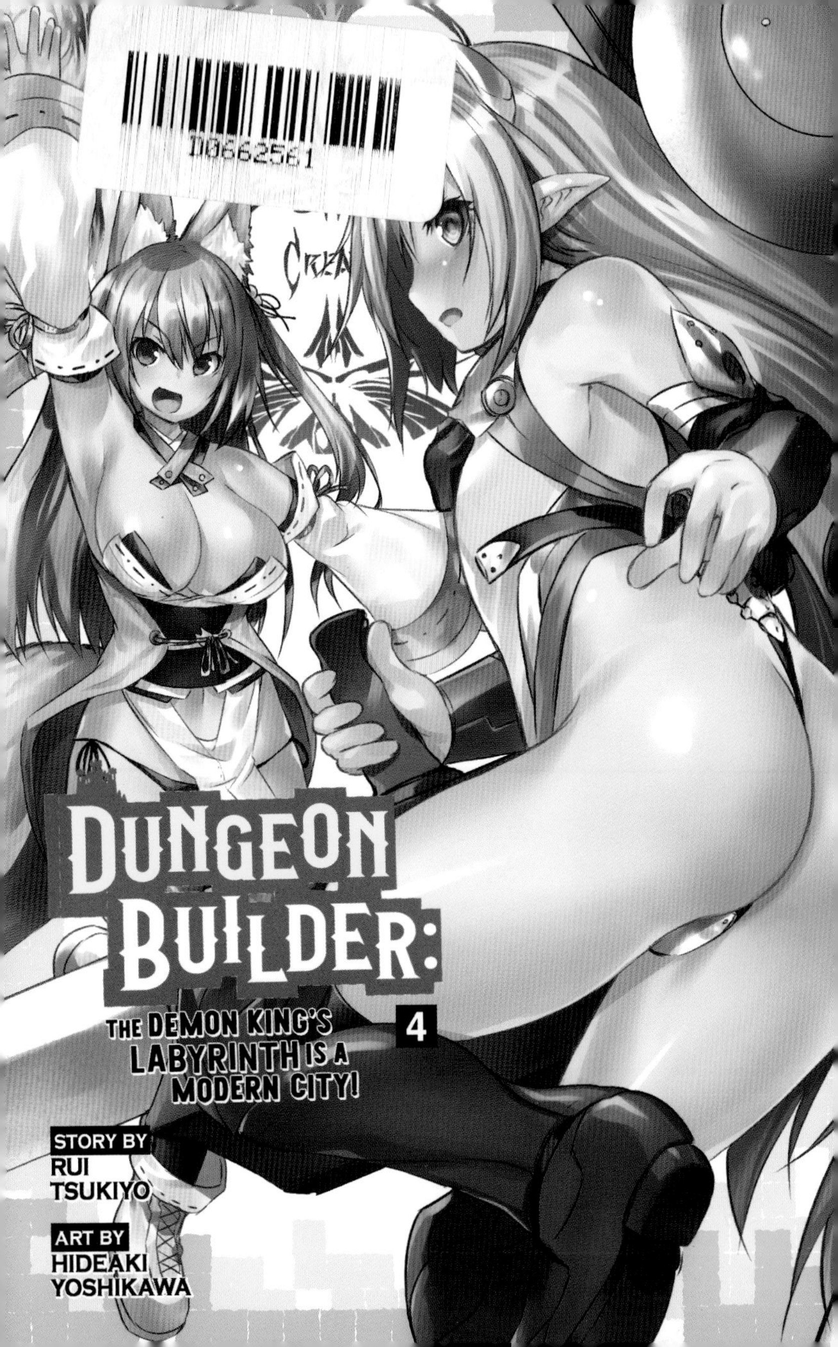
DUNGEON BUILDER:
THE DEMON KING'S LABYRINTH IS A MODERN CITY!
4
STORY BY
RUI TSUKIYO
ART BY
HIDEAKI YOSHIKAWA

DUNGEON BUILDER

THE DEMON KING'S LABYRINTH IS A MODERN CITY!

VOLUME 04

CONTENTS

ART BY HIDEAKI YOSHIKAWA   STORY BY RUI TSUKIYO

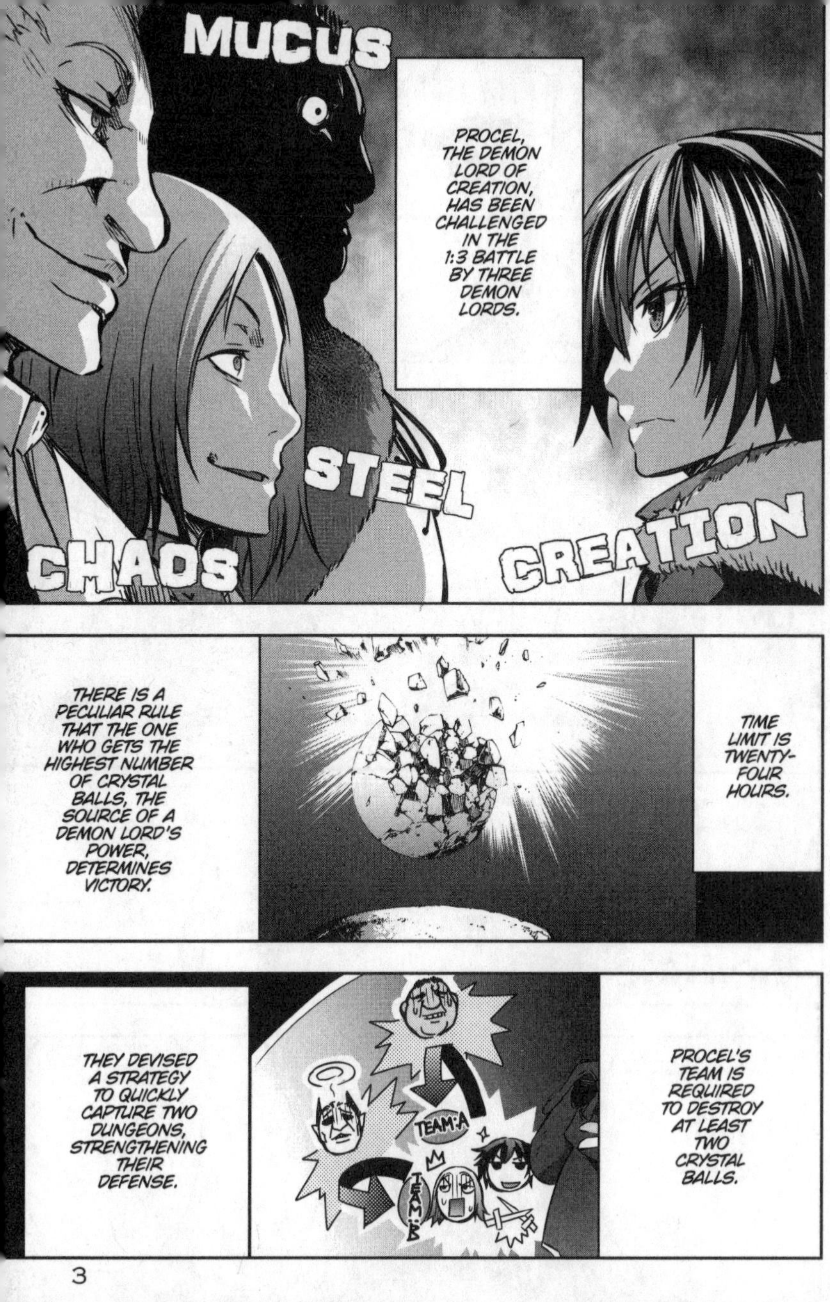

PROCEL, THE DEMON LORD OF CREATION, HAS BEEN CHALLENGED IN THE 1:3 BATTLE BY THREE DEMON LORDS.
MUCUS
CREATION
STEEL
CHAOS
TIME LIMIT IS TWENTY-FOUR HOURS.
THERE IS A PECULIAR RULE THAT THE ONE WHO GETS THE HIGHEST NUMBER OF CRYSTAL BALLS, THE SOURCE OF A DEMON LORD'S POWER, DETERMINES VICTORY.
PROCEL'S TEAM IS REQUIRED TO DESTROY AT LEAST TWO CRYSTAL BALLS.
TEAM:A
TEAM:B
THEY DEVISED A STRATEGY TO QUICKLY CAPTURE TWO DUNGEONS, STRENGTHENING THEIR DEFENSE.

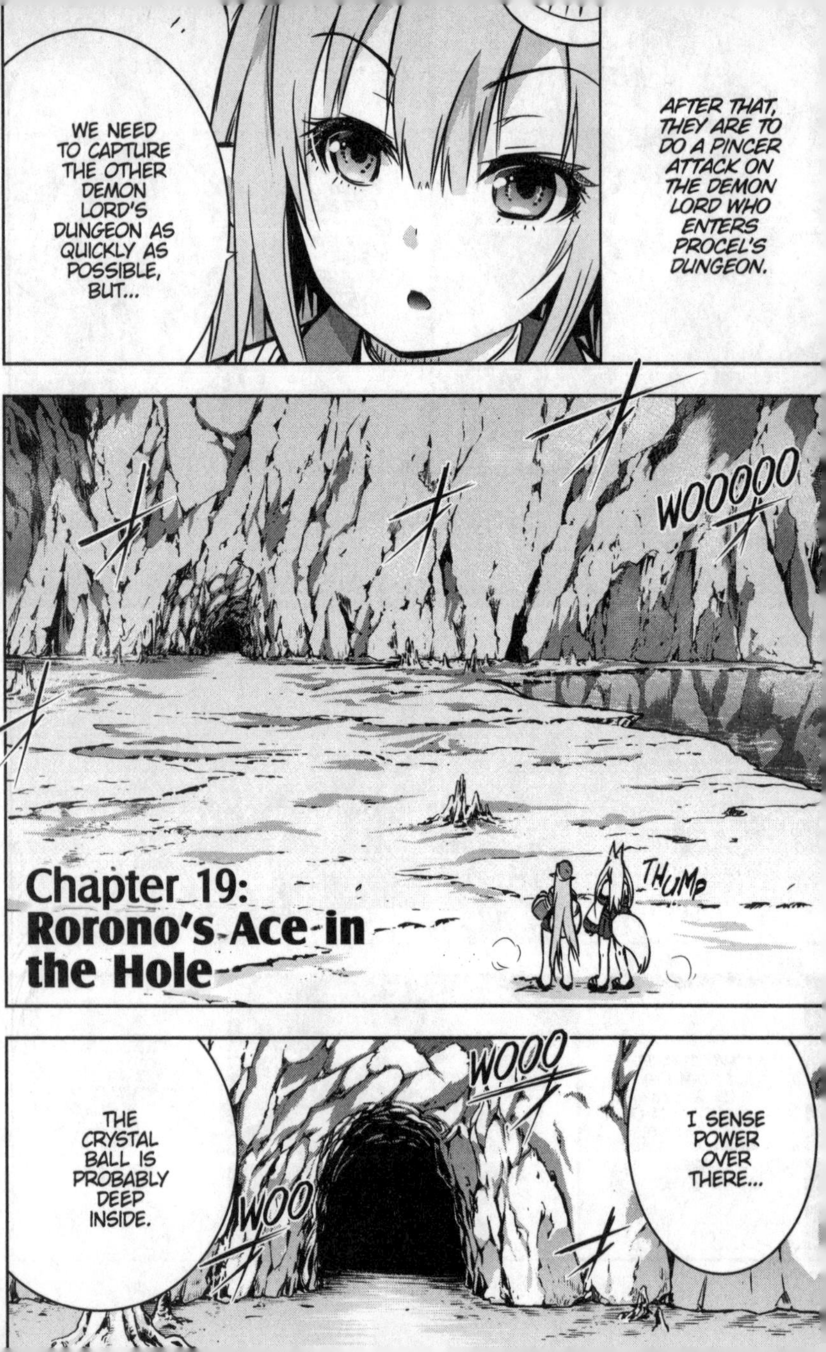
AFTER THAT, THEY ARE TO DO A PINCER ATTACK ON THE DEMON LORD WHO ENTERS PROCEL'S DUNGEON.
WE NEED TO CAPTURE THE OTHER DEMON LORD'S DUNGEON AS QUICKLY AS POSSIBLE, BUT...
WOOOOO
THUMP
Chapter 19: Rorono's Ace in the Hole
I SENSE POWER OVER THERE...
WOOO
WOO
THE CRYSTAL BALL IS PROBABLY DEEP INSIDE.

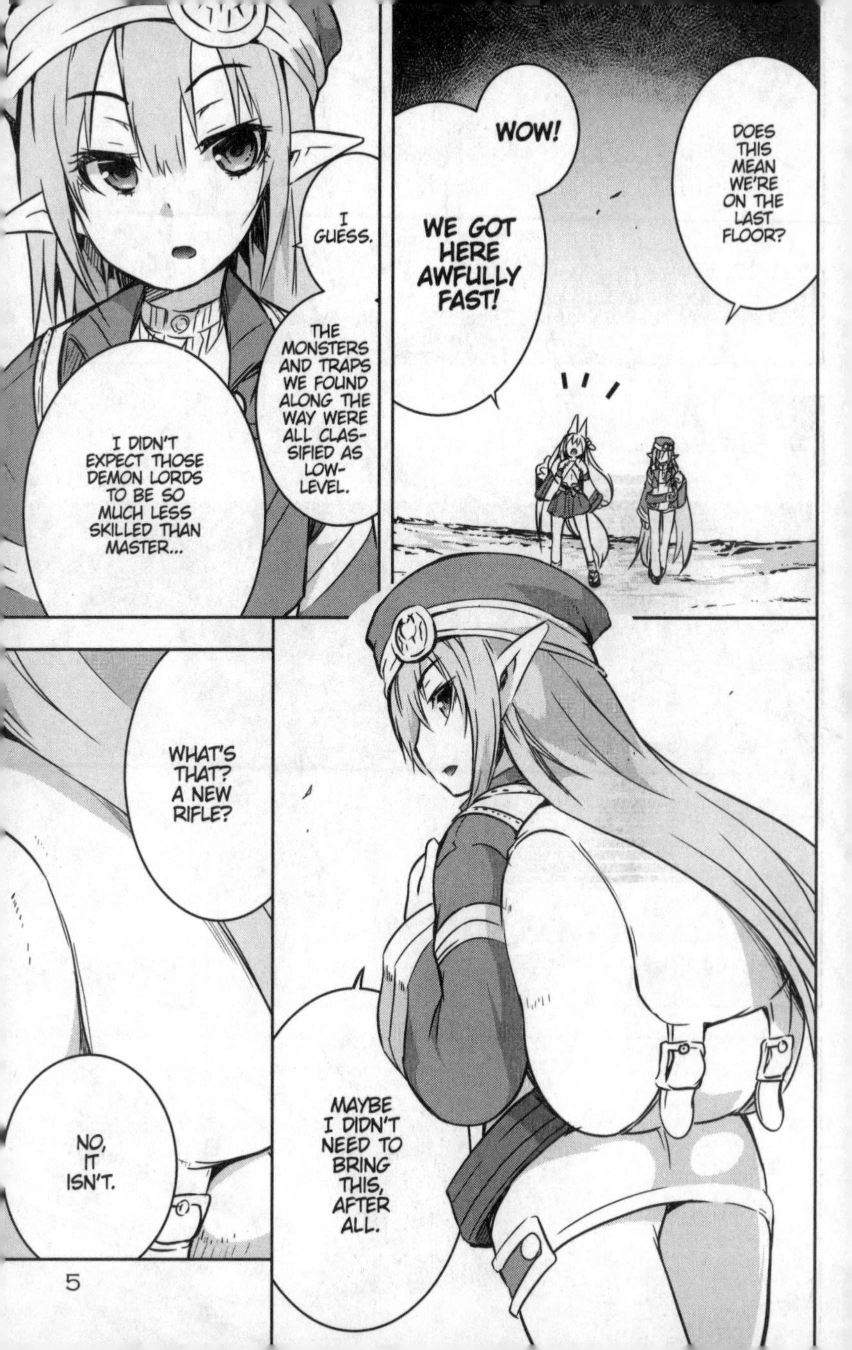
DOES THIS MEAN WE'RE ON THE LAST FLOOR?
WOW!
WE GOT HERE AWFULLY FAST!
I GUESS.
THE MONSTERS AND TRAPS WE FOUND ALONG THE WAY WERE ALL CLAS-SIFIED AS LOW-LEVEL.
I DIDN'T EXPECT THOSE DEMON LORDS TO BE SO MUCH LESS SKILLED THAN MASTER...
MAYBE I DIDN'T NEED TO BRING THIS, AFTER ALL.
WHAT'S THAT? A NEW RIFLE?
NO, IT ISN'T.

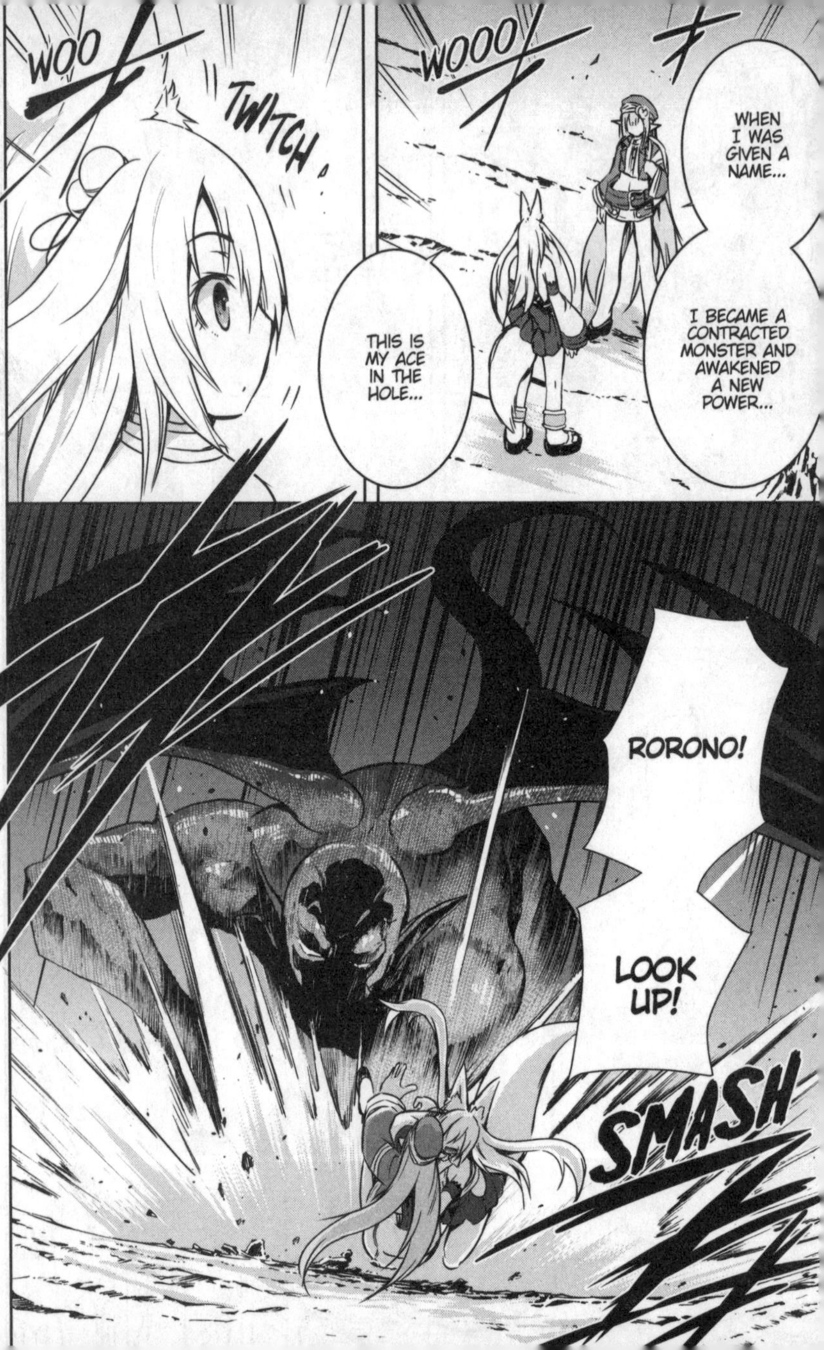
WOOO
WHEN I WAS GIVEN A NAME...
I BECAME A CONTRACTED MONSTER AND AWAKENED A NEW POWER...
THIS IS MY ACE IN THE HOLE...
WOO
TWITCH
RORONO!
LOOK UP!
SMASH

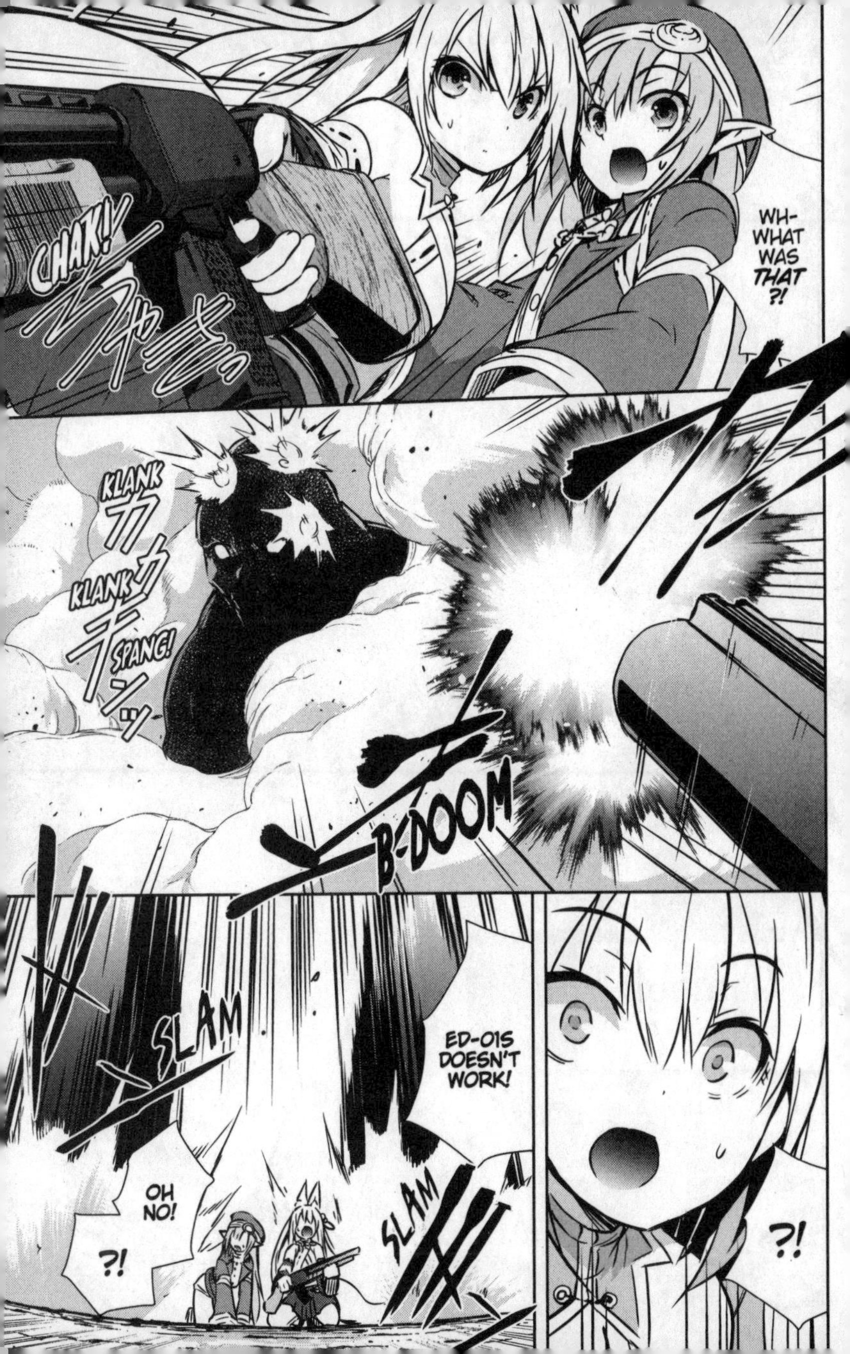
WH-WHAT WAS THAT?!
CHAK!
B-DOOM
KLANK
KLANK
SPANG!
?!
ED-01S DOESN'T WORK!
SLAM
SLAM
OH NO!
?!

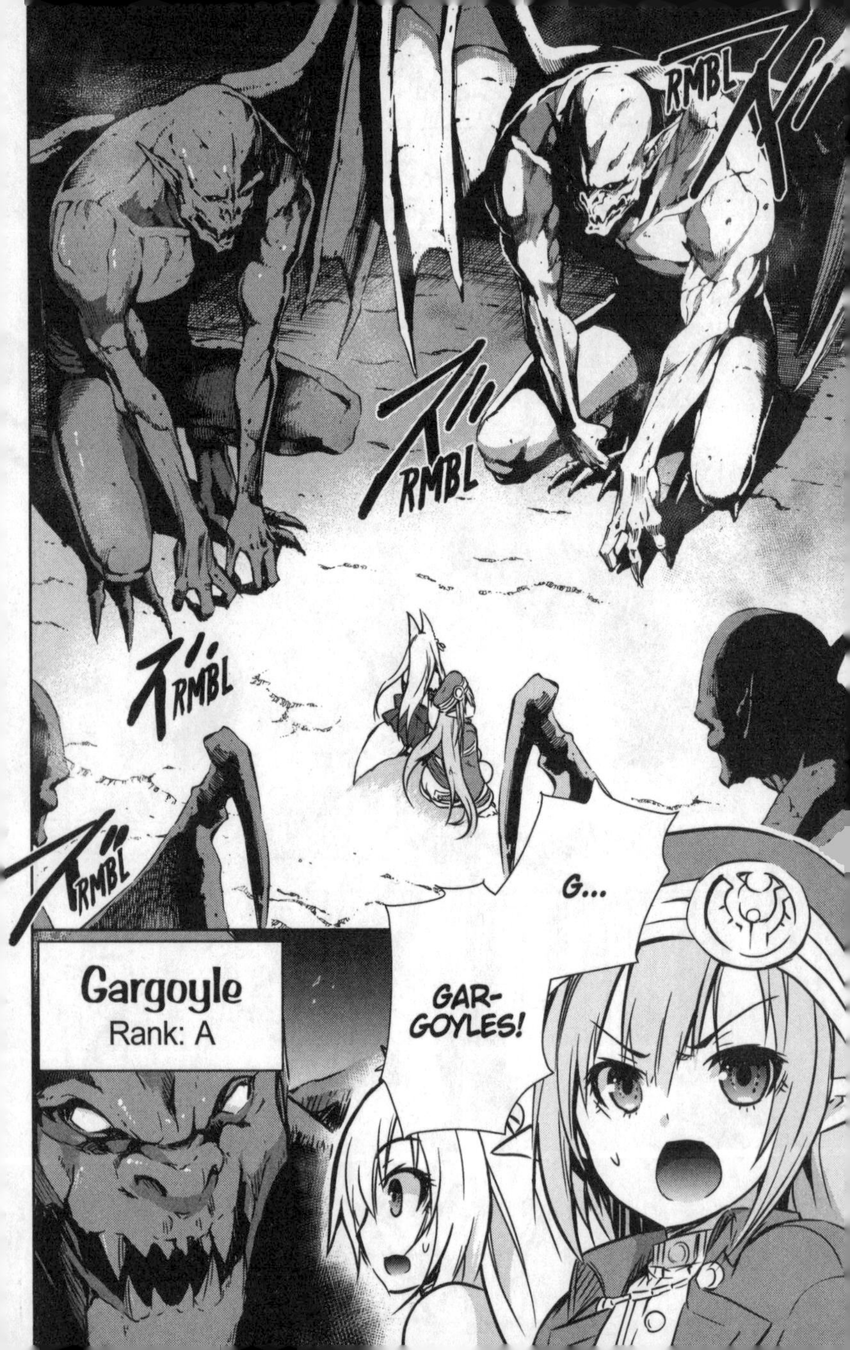
RMBL
RMBL
RMBL
RMBL
G...
GAR-
GOYLES!
Gargoyle
Rank: A

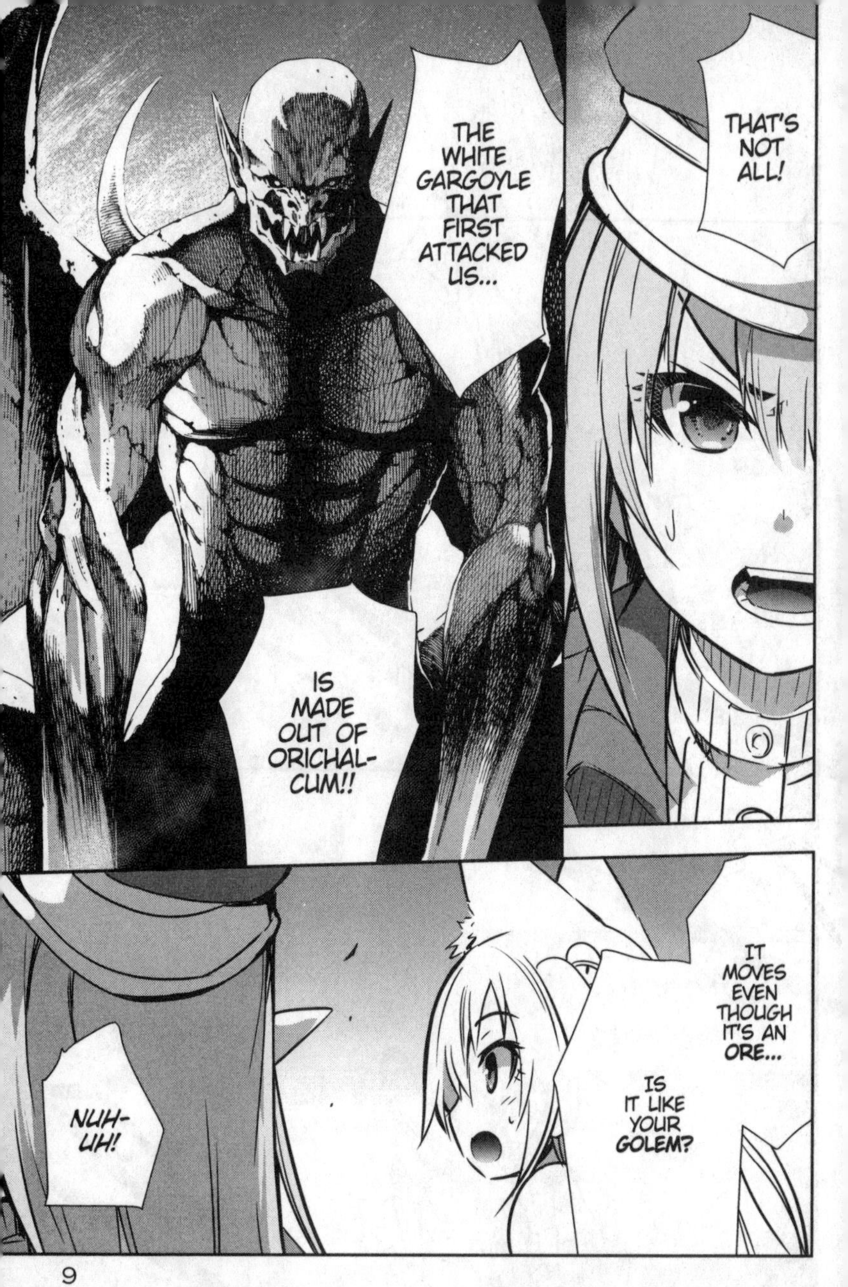
THAT'S NOT ALL!
THE WHITE GARGOYLE THAT FIRST ATTACKED US...
IS MADE OUT OF ORICHAL-CUM!!
IT MOVES EVEN THOUGH IT'S AN ORE...
IS IT LIKE YOUR GOLEM?
NUH-UH!

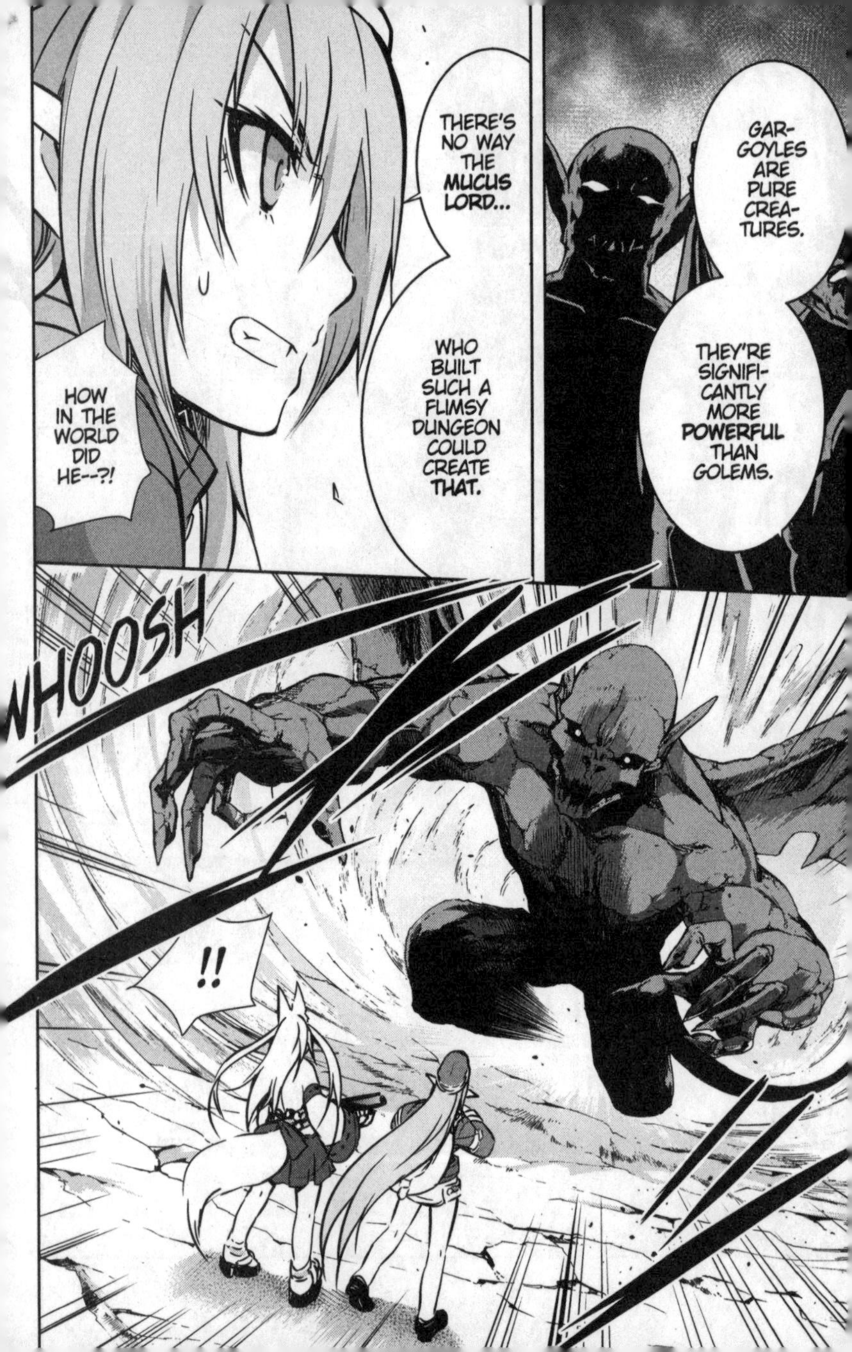
GAR-GOYLES ARE PURE CREA-TURES.
THEY'RE SIGNIFI-CANTLY MORE POWERFUL THAN GOLEMS.
THERE'S NO WAY THE MUCUS LORD...
WHO BUILT SUCH A FLIMSY DUNGEON COULD CREATE THAT.
HOW IN THE WORLD DID HE--?!
WHOOSH
!!

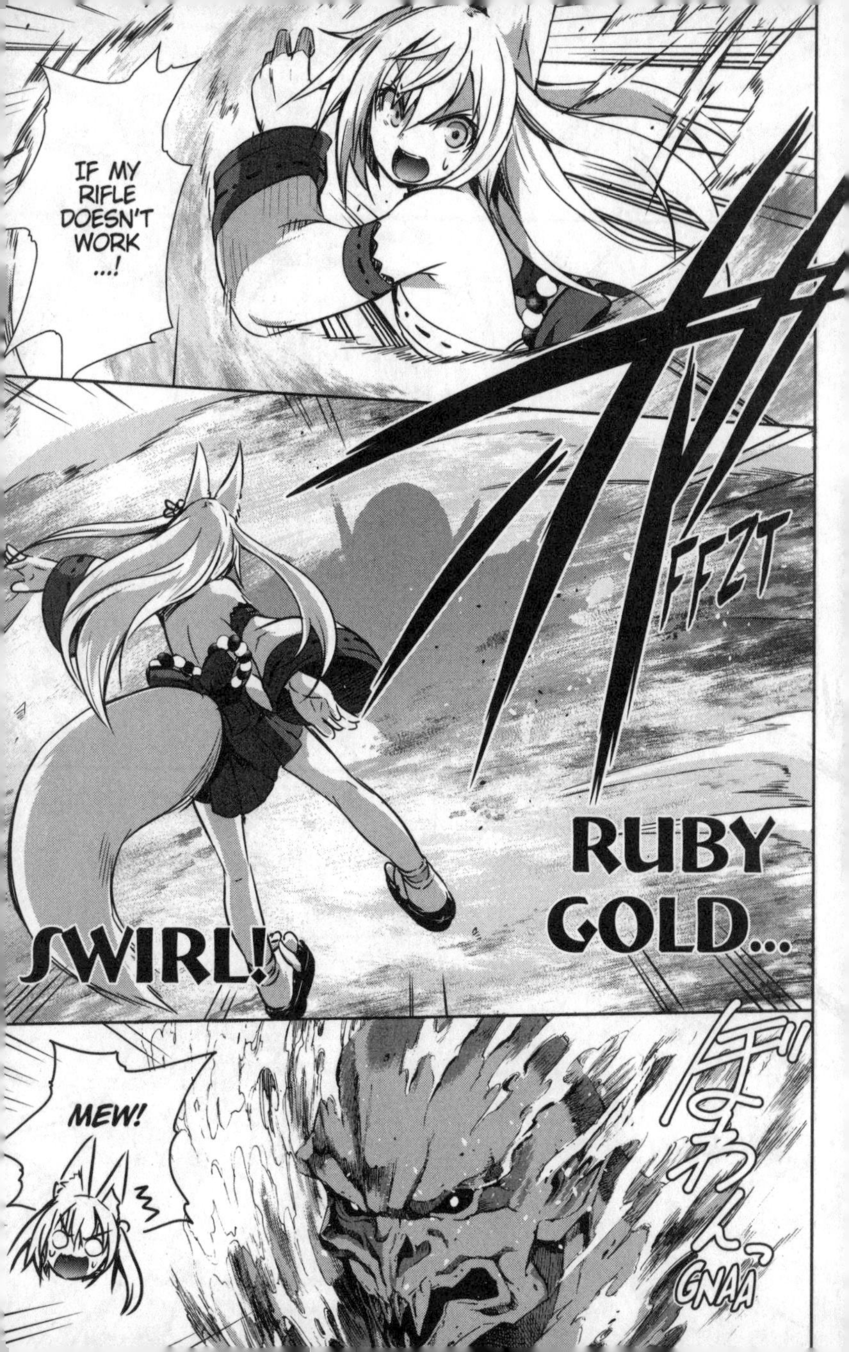
IF MY RIFLE DOESN'T WORK ...!
FFZT
RUBY GOLD...
SWIRL!
GNAA
MEW!

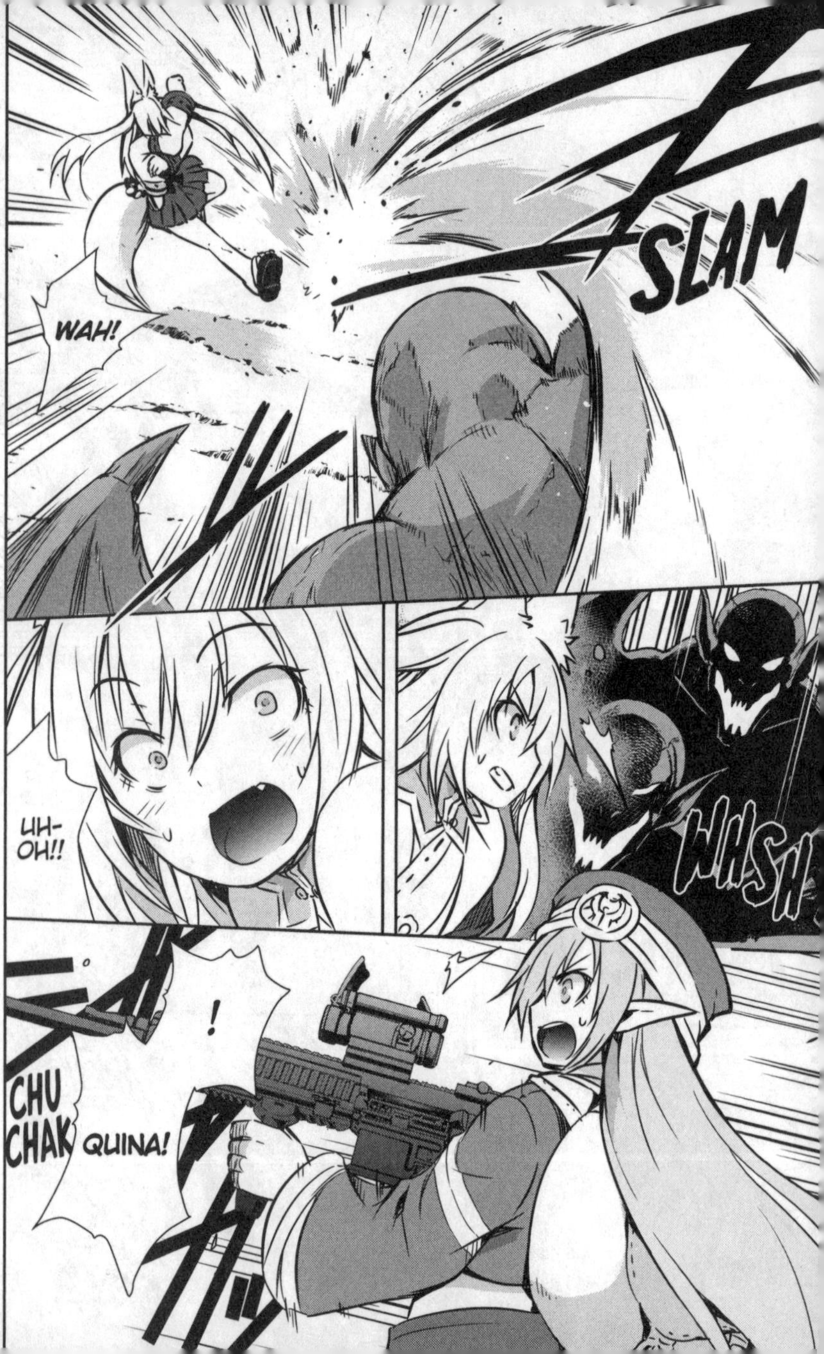
SLAM
WAH!
WHSH
UH-OH!!
!
QUINA!
CHU CHAK

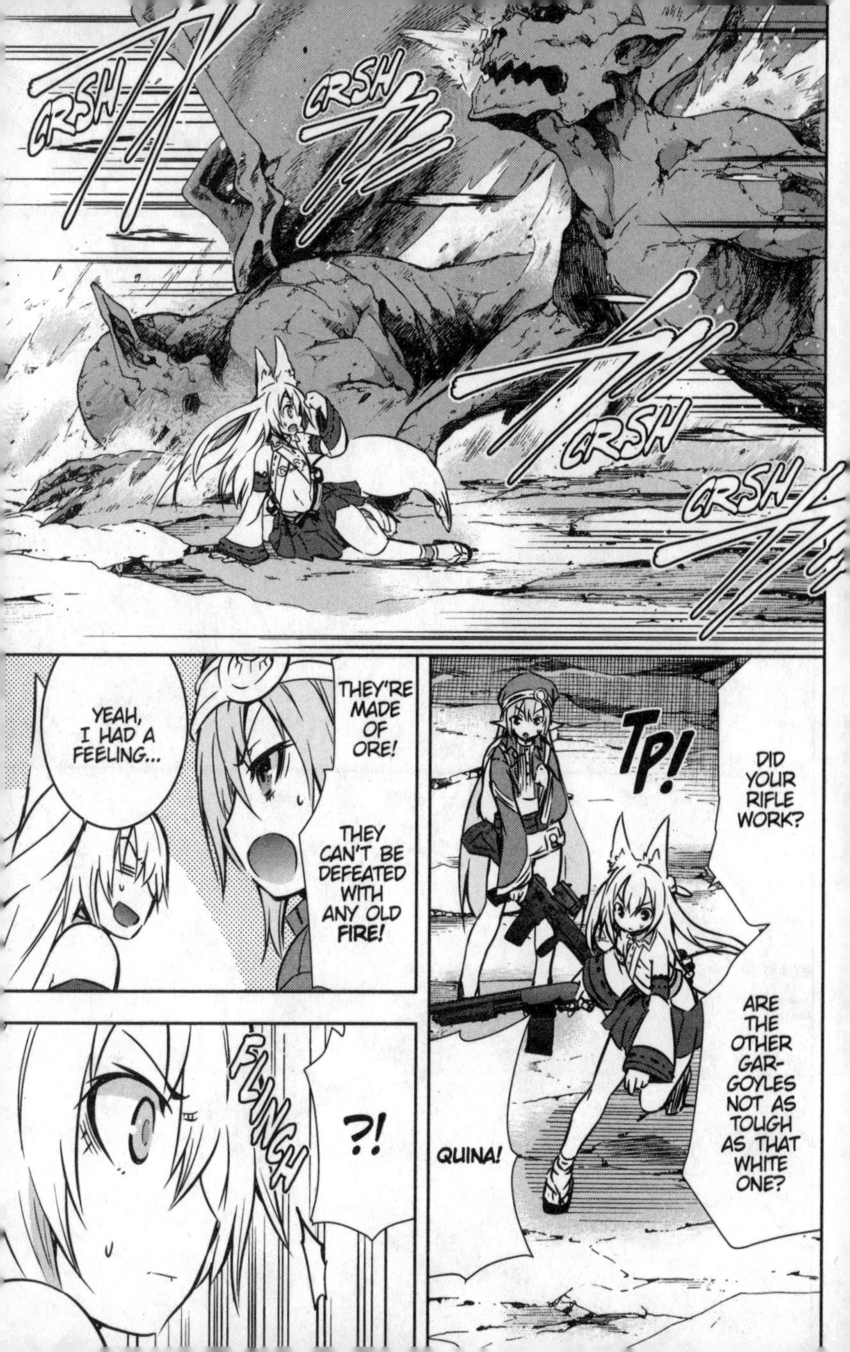

CRSH
CRSH
CRSH
CRSH
DID YOUR RIFLE WORK?
Tp!
ARE THE OTHER GAR-GOYLES NOT AS TOUGH AS THAT WHITE ONE?
QUINA!
THEY'RE MADE OF ORE!
THEY CAN'T BE DEFEATED WITH ANY OLD FIRE!
YEAH, I HAD A FEELING...
FLINCH
?!

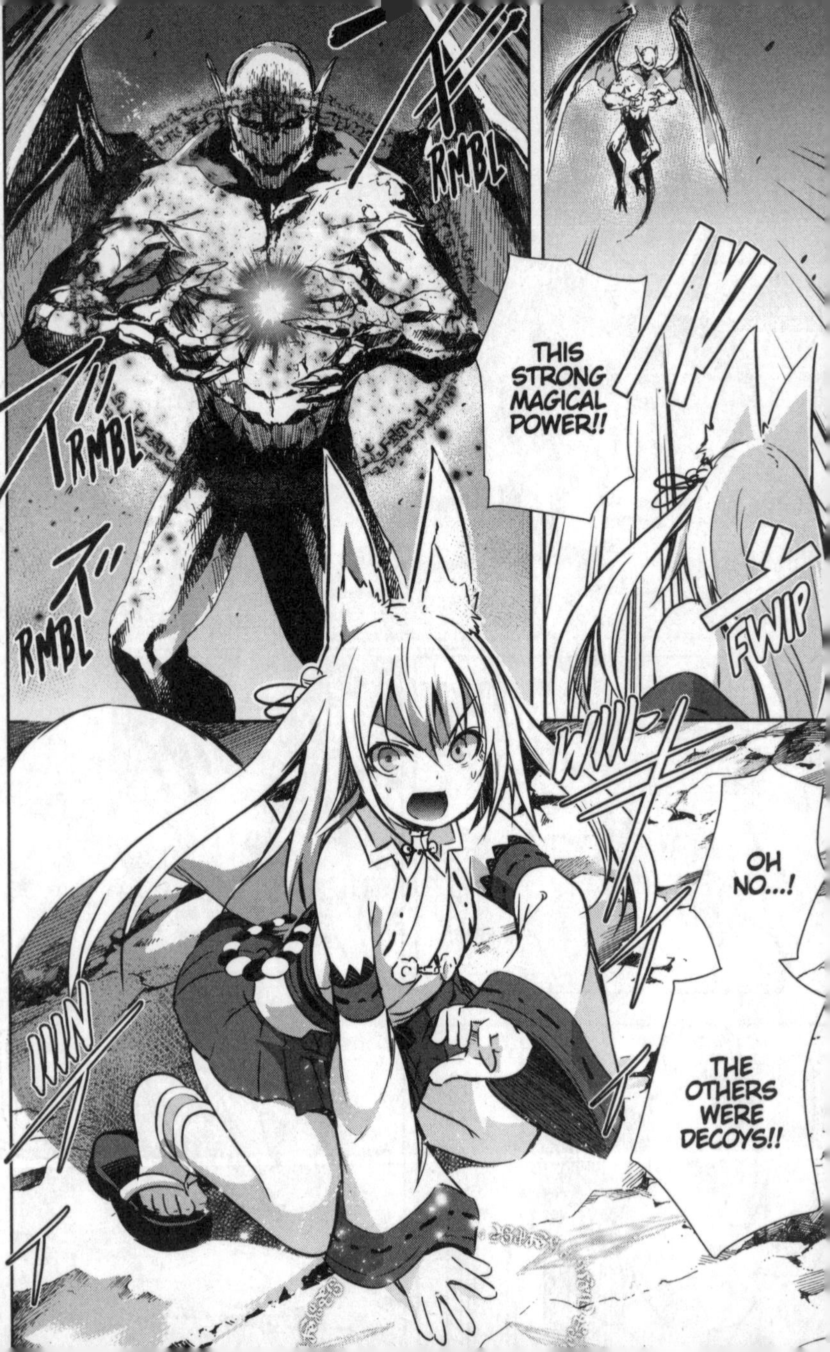
THIS STRONG MAGICAL POWER!!
FWIP
RMBL
RMBL
RMBL
WIII-
OH NO...!
THE OTHERS WERE DECOYS!!
IIIN

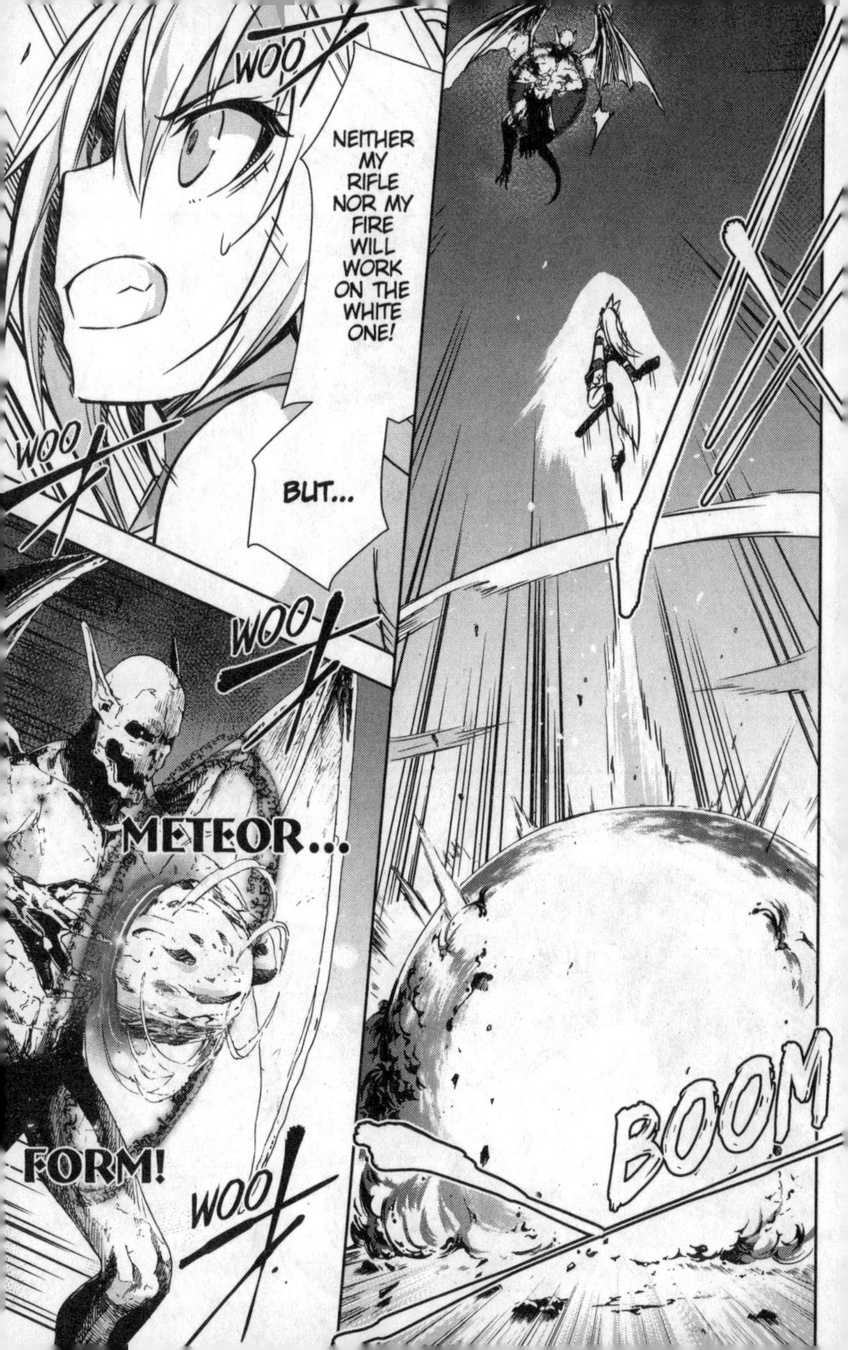
BOOM
WOO
NEITHER MY RIFLE NOR MY FIRE WILL WORK ON THE WHITE ONE!
BUT...
WOO
WOO
METEOR...
FORM!
WOO

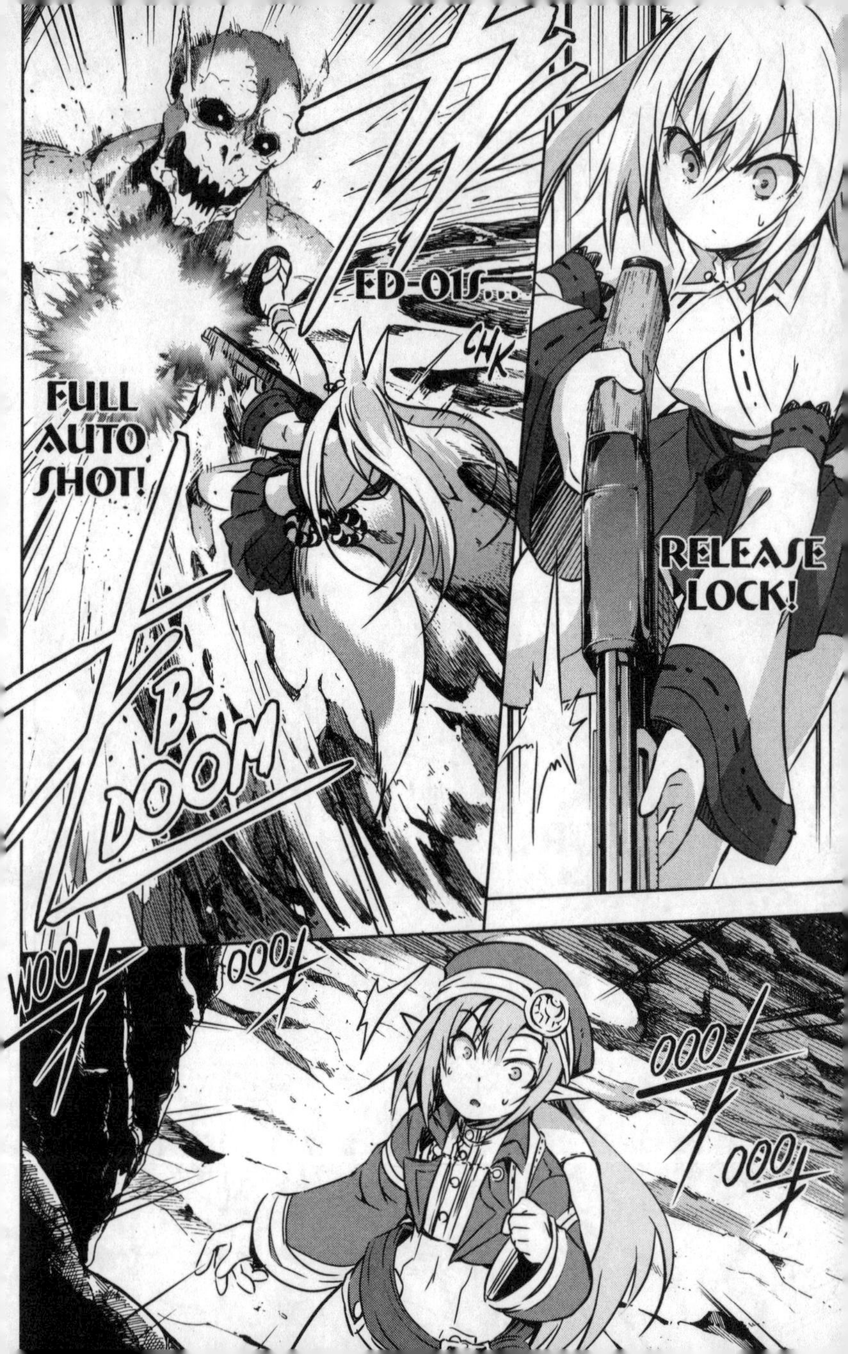
RELEASE LOCK!
ED-01S...
CHK
FULL AUTO SHOT!
B-DOOM
WOO
OOO
OOO
OOO

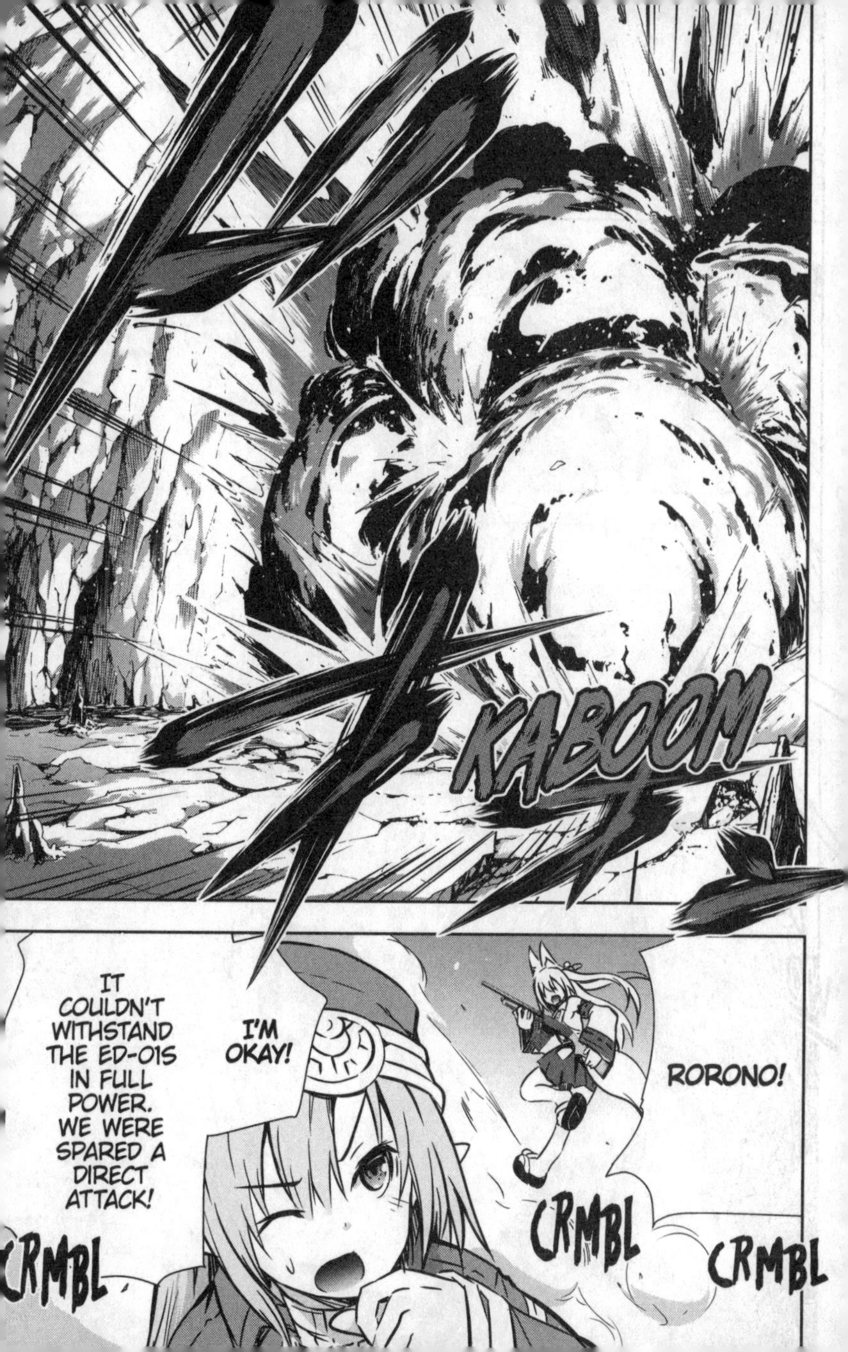
KABOOM
RORONO!
I'M OKAY!
IT COULDN'T WITHSTAND THE ED-01S IN FULL POWER. WE WERE SPARED A DIRECT ATTACK!
CRMBL
CRMBL
CRMBL

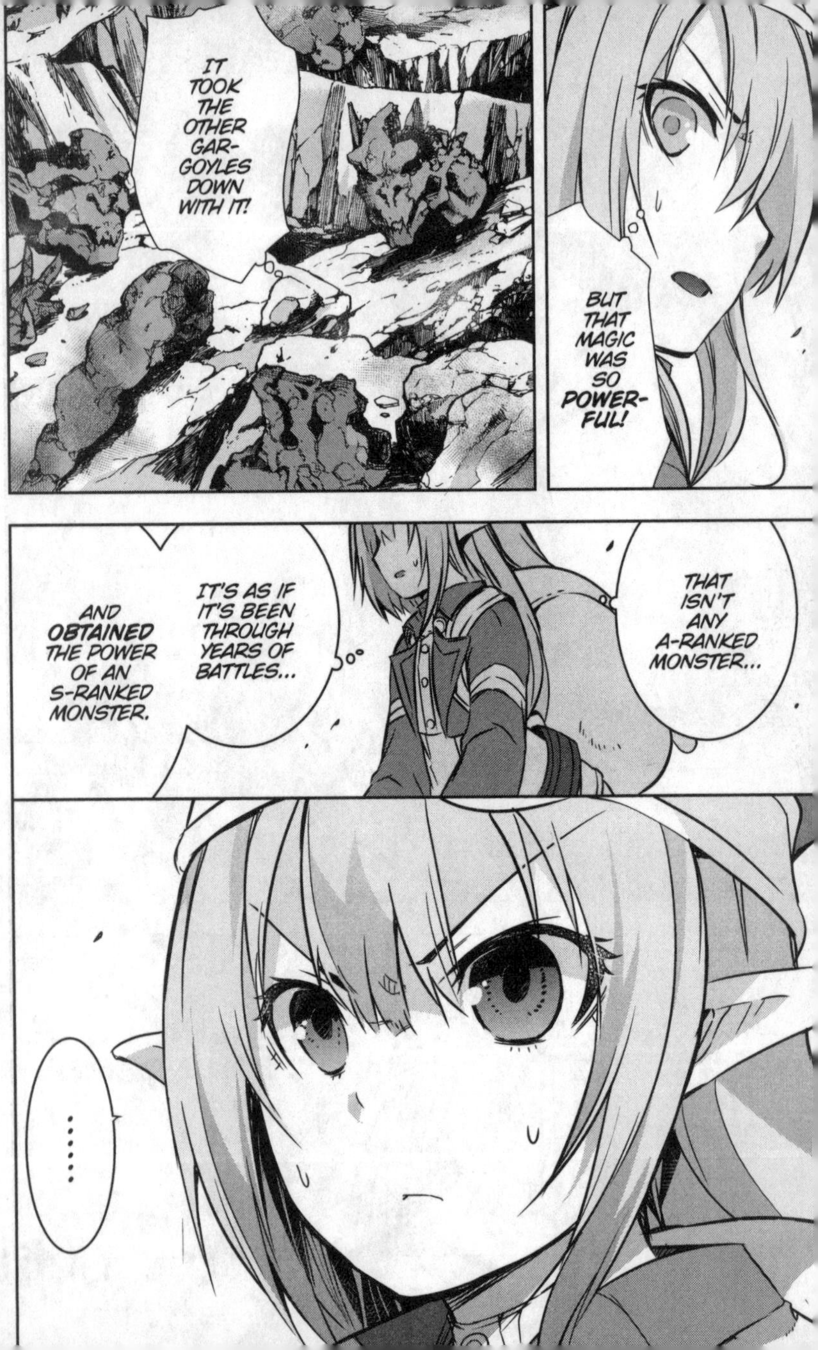
BUT THAT MAGIC WAS SO POWERFUL!
IT TOOK THE OTHER GARGOYLES DOWN WITH IT!
THAT ISN'T ANY A-RANKED MONSTER...
IT'S AS IF IT'S BEEN THROUGH YEARS OF BATTLES...
AND OBTAINED THE POWER OF AN S-RANKED MONSTER.
......

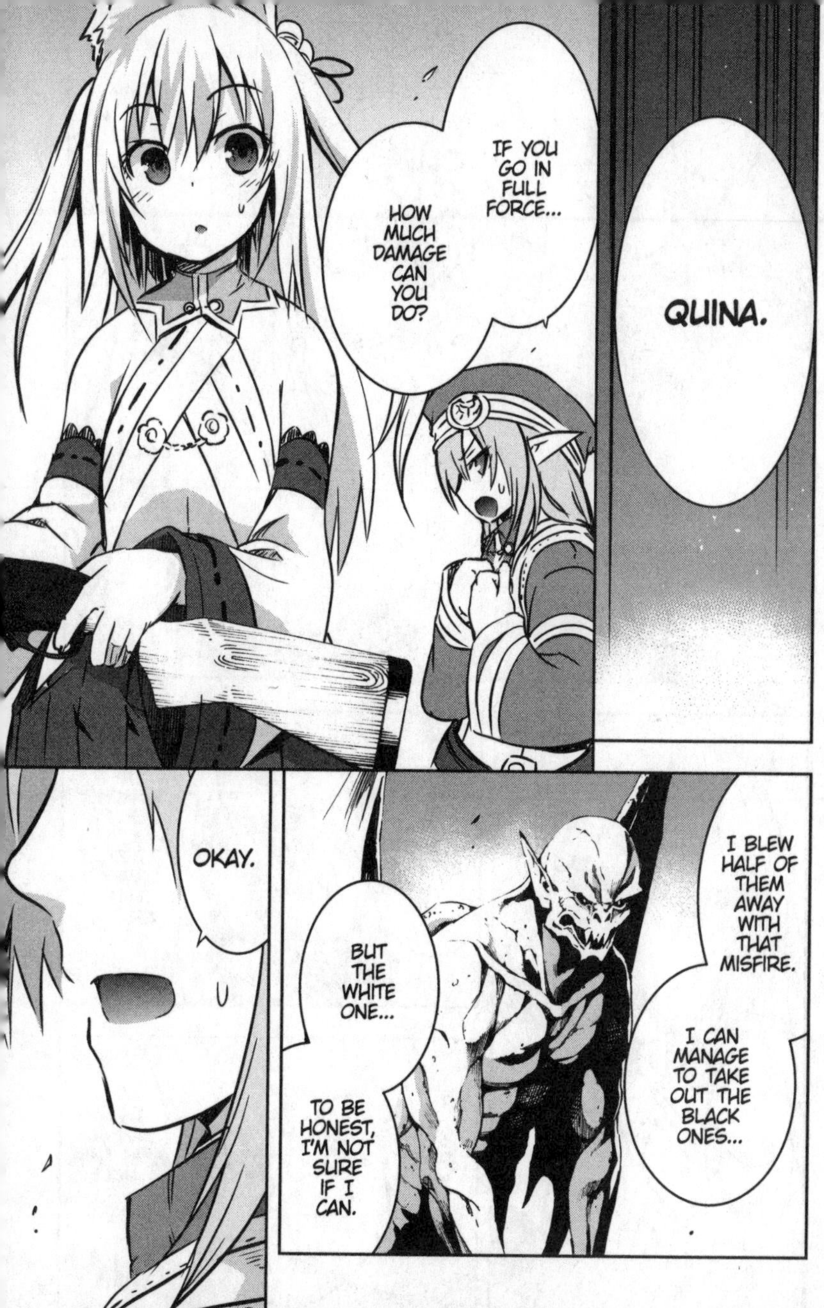
QUINA.
IF YOU GO IN FULL FORCE... HOW MUCH DAMAGE CAN YOU DO?
I BLEW HALF OF THEM AWAY WITH THAT MISFIRE.
I CAN MANAGE TO TAKE OUT THE BLACK ONES...
BUT THE WHITE ONE...
TO BE HONEST, I'M NOT SURE IF I CAN.
OKAY.

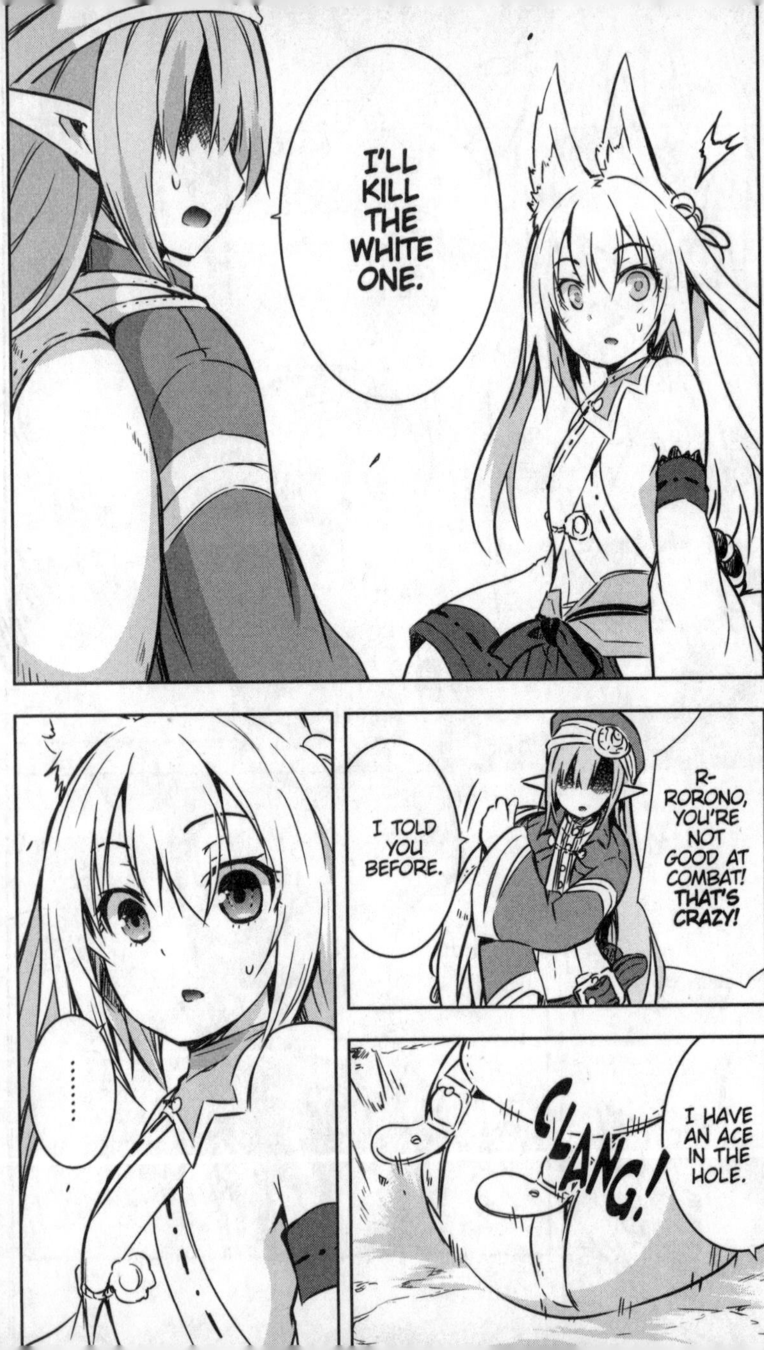
I'LL KILL THE WHITE ONE.
R-RORONO, YOU'RE NOT GOOD AT COMBAT! THAT'S CRAZY!
I TOLD YOU BEFORE.
I HAVE AN ACE IN THE HOLE.
CLANG!
......

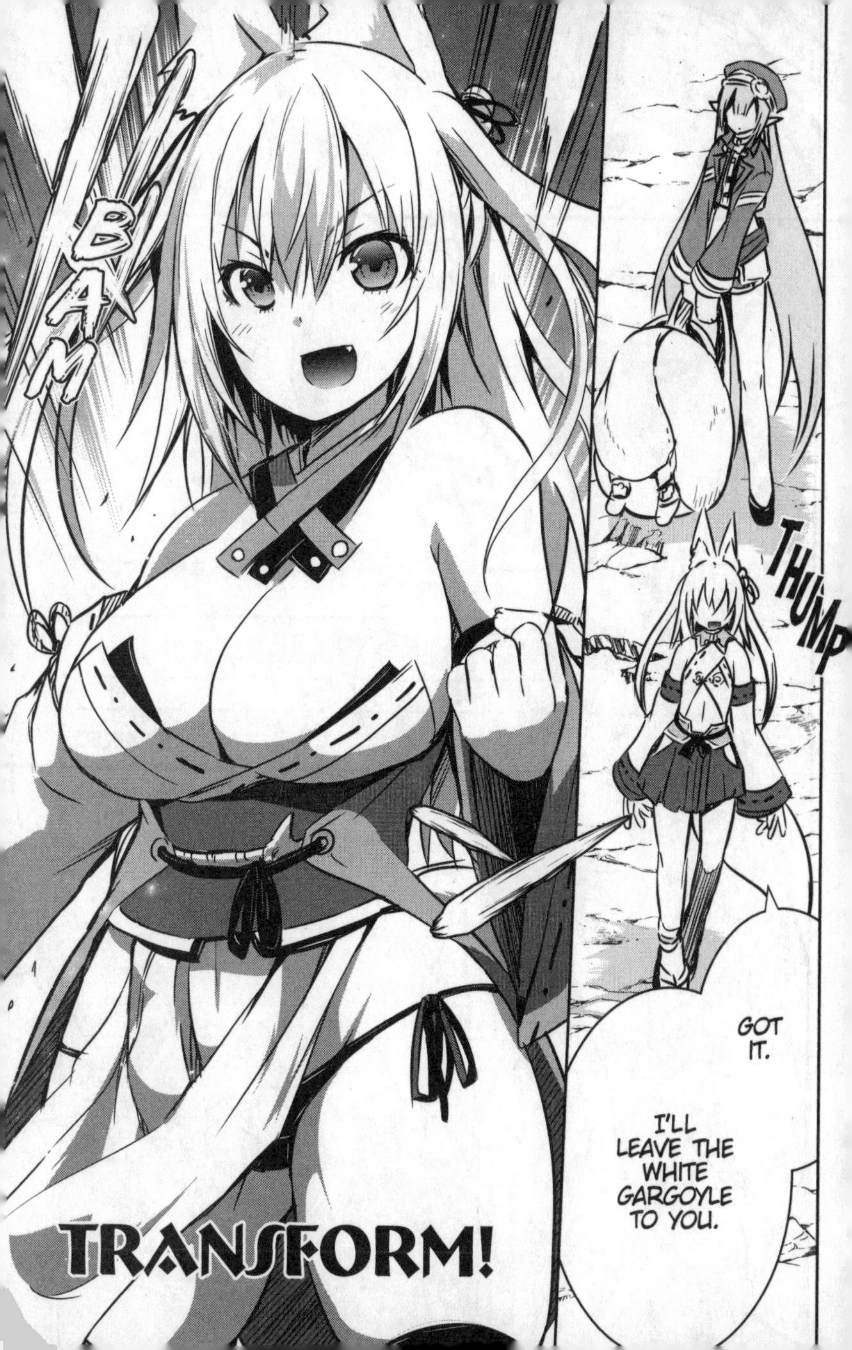
THUMP
GOT IT.
I'LL LEAVE THE WHITE GARGOYLE TO YOU.
BAM
TRANSFORM!

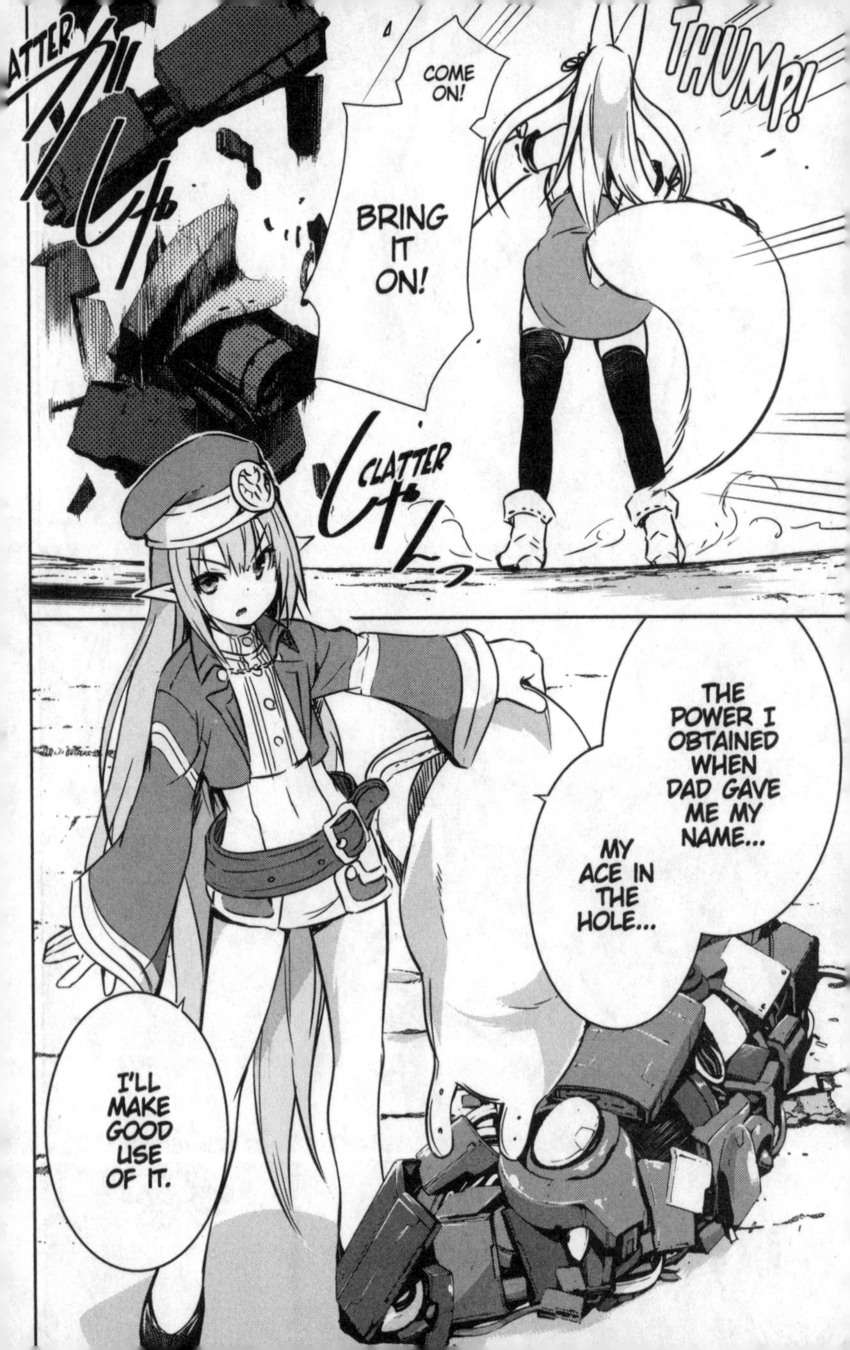
THUMP!
COME ON!
BRING IT ON!
ATTER
CLATTER
THE POWER I OBTAINED WHEN DAD GAVE ME MY NAME...
MY ACE IN THE HOLE...
I'LL MAKE GOOD USE OF IT.

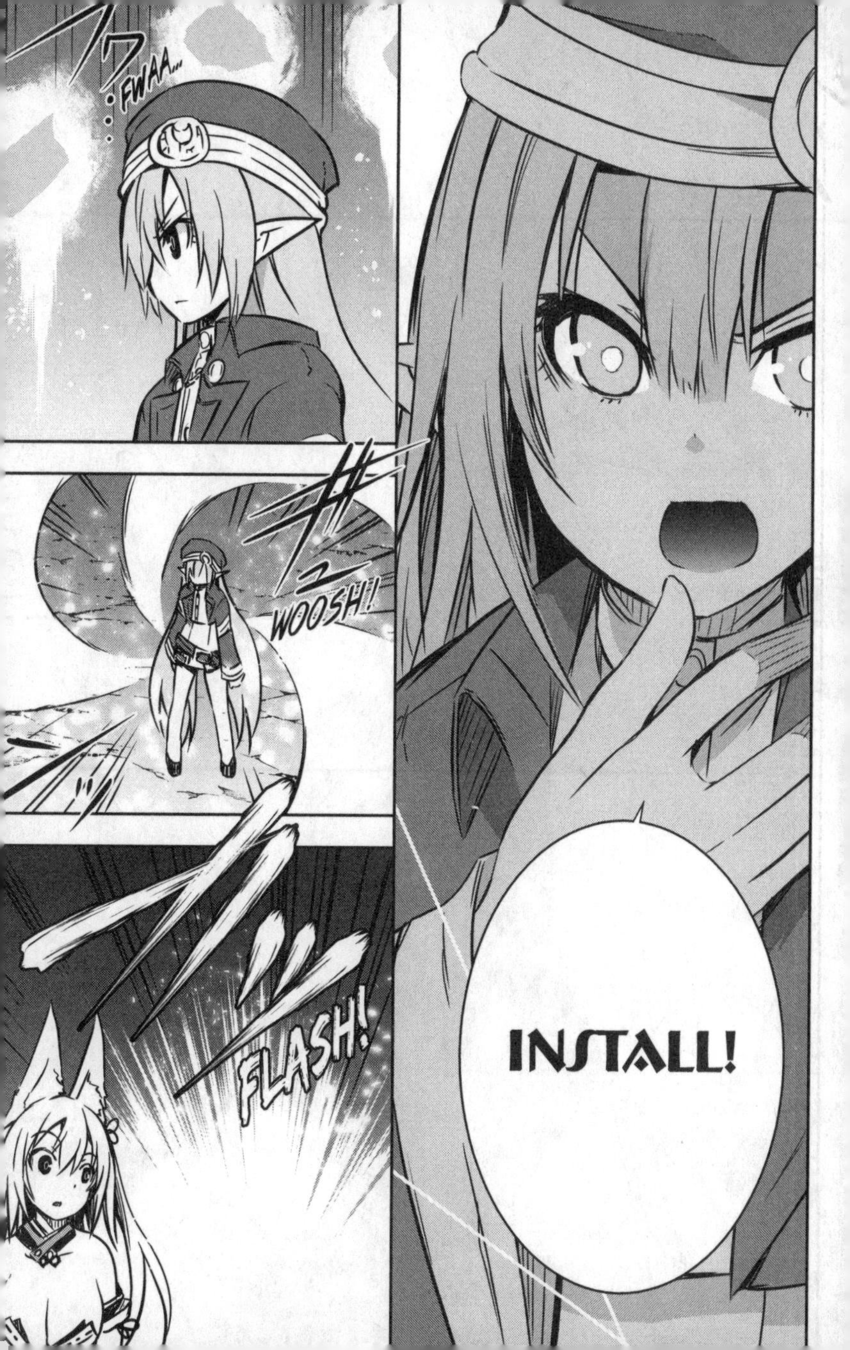
INSTALL!
FWAA...
WOOSH!
FLASH!

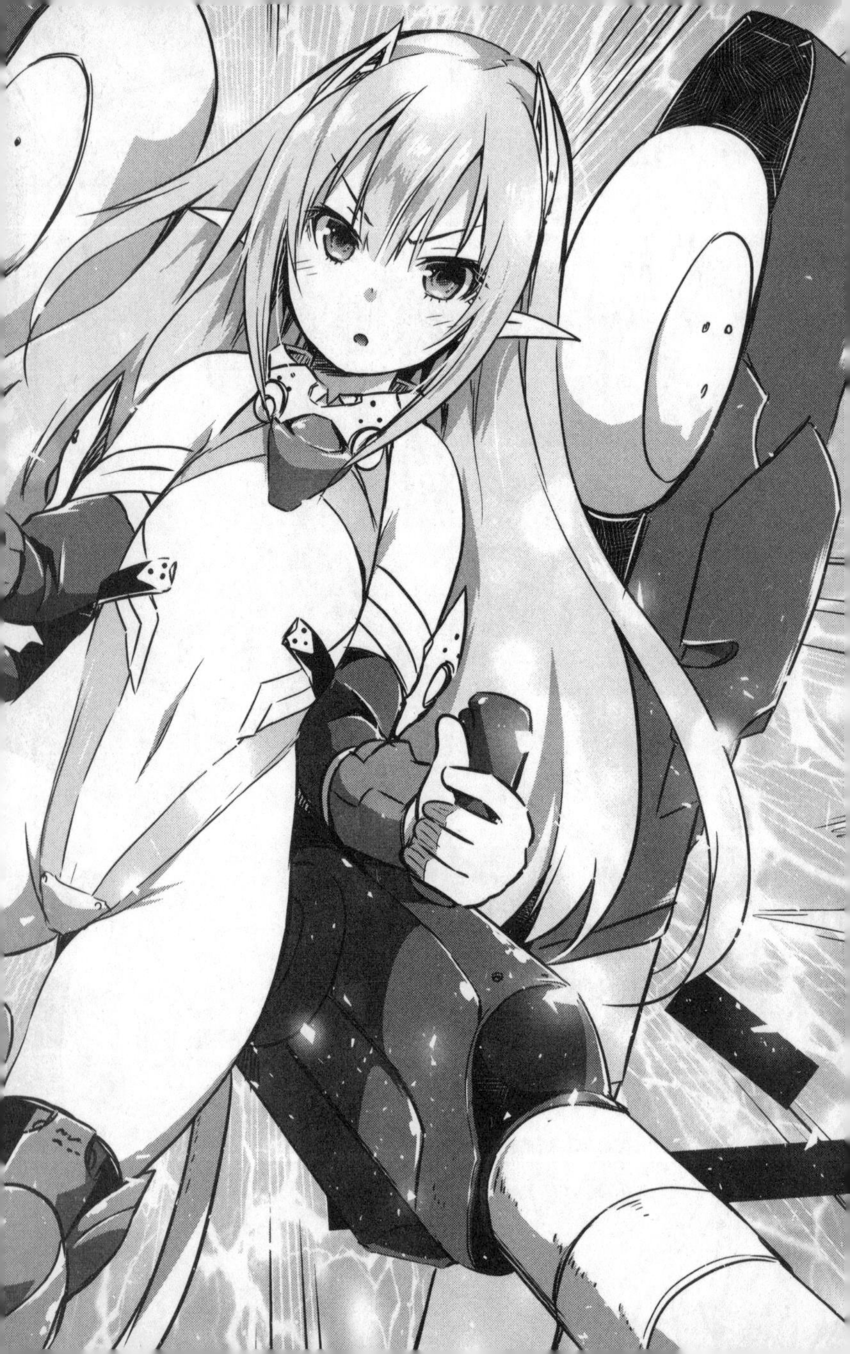

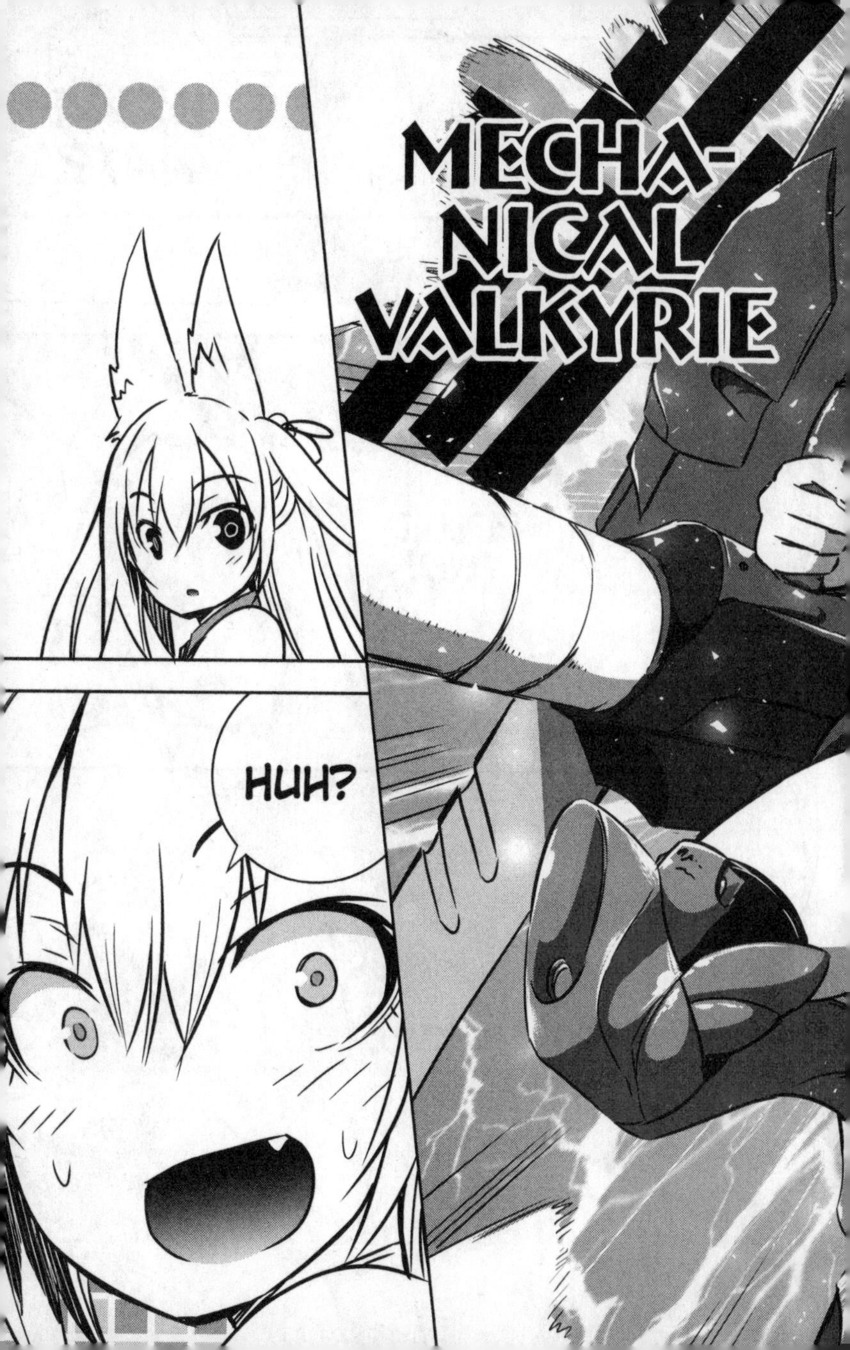
MECHA-
NICAL
VALKYRIE
HUH?

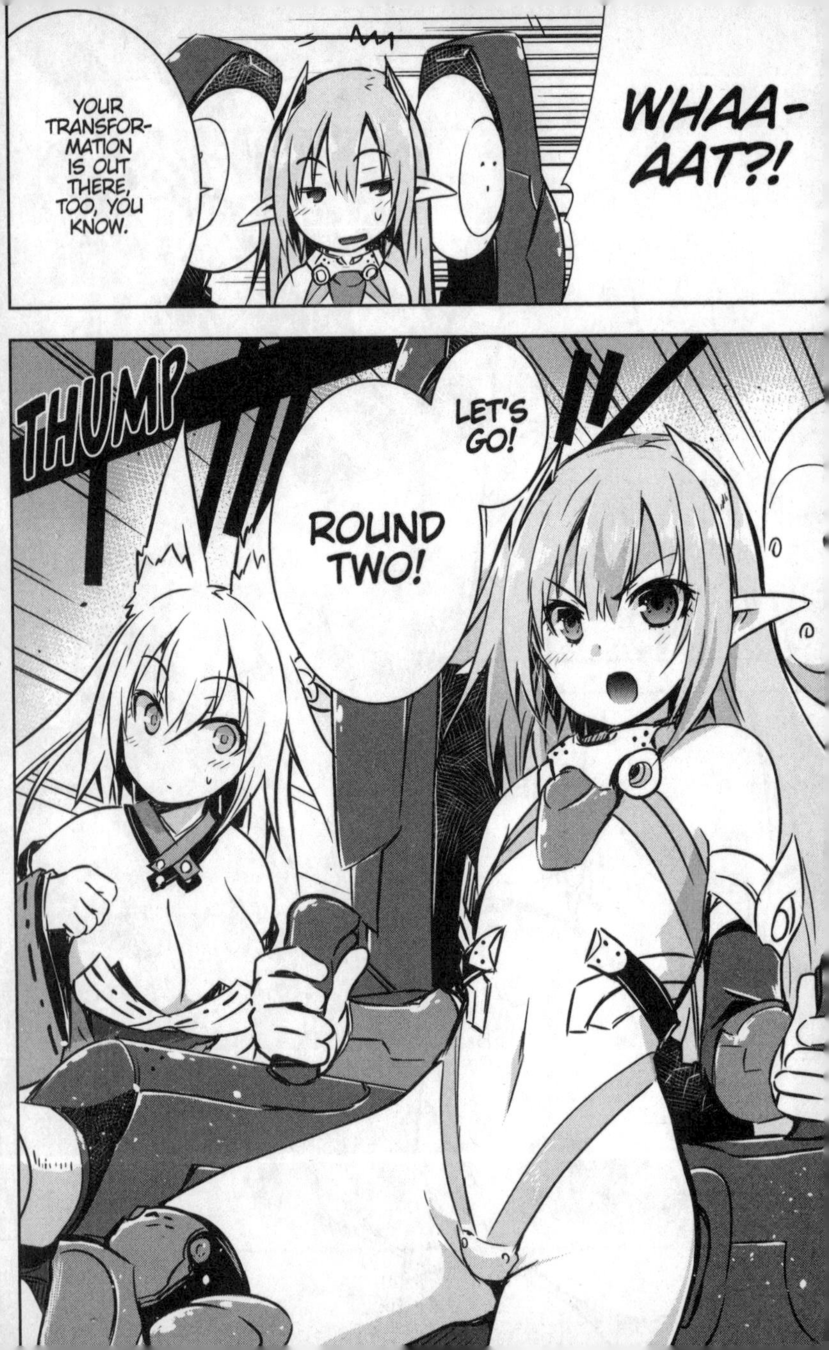
WHAAA-AAT?!
YOUR TRANSFORMATION IS OUT THERE, TOO, YOU KNOW.
LET'S GO!
ROUND TWO!
THUMP

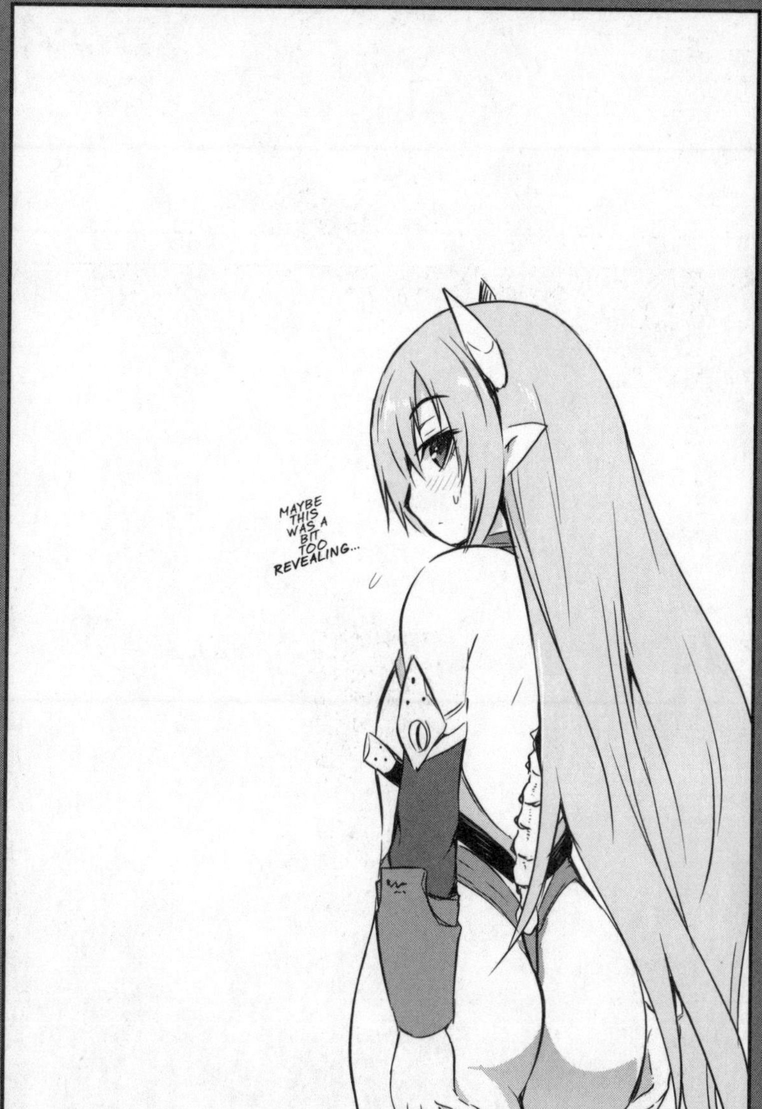
MAYBE THIS WAS A BIT TOO REVEALING...

DUNGEON BUILDER:
THE DEMON KING'S LABYRINTH IS A MODERN CITY!

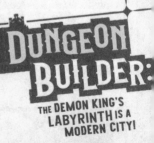

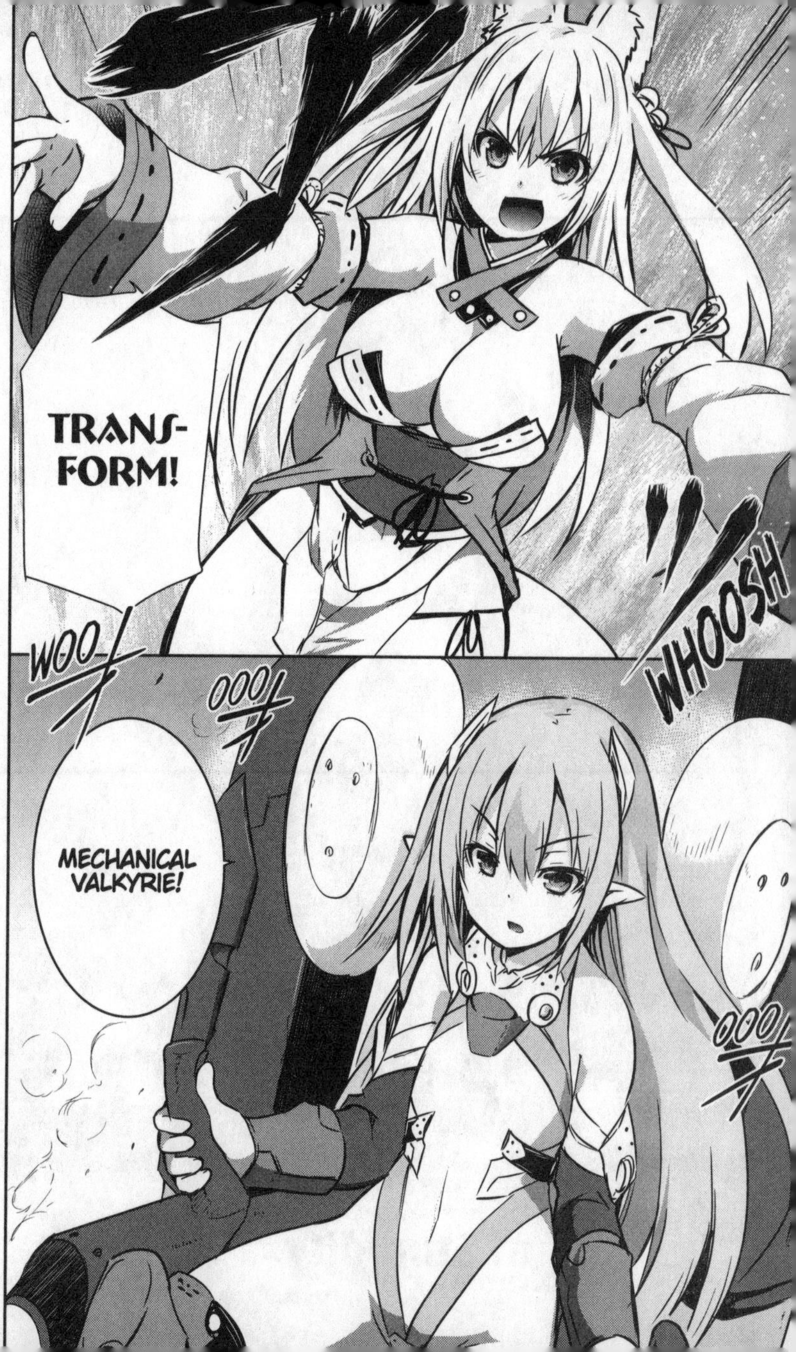
TRANS-FORM!
WHOOSH
WOO
OOO
MECHANICAL VALKYRIE!
OOO

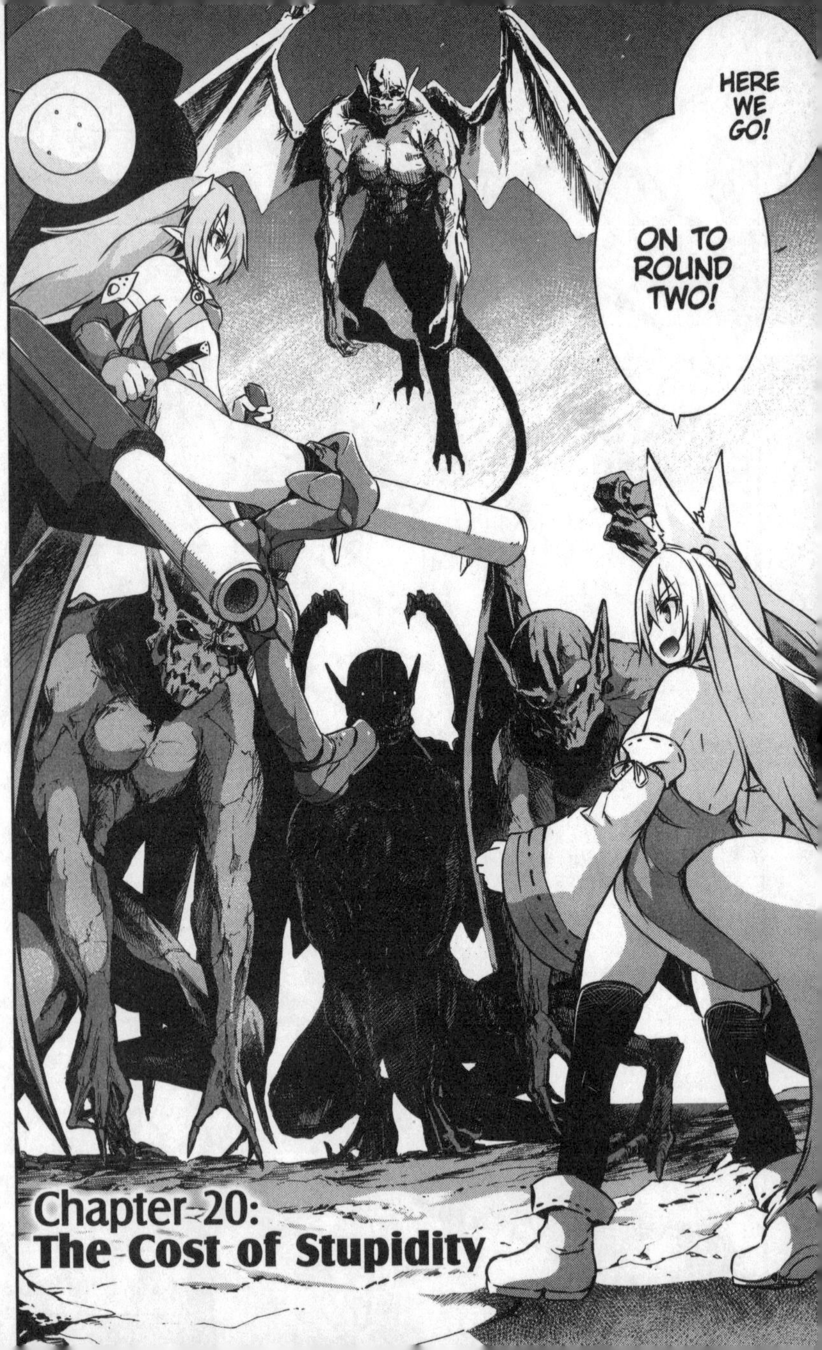
HERE WE GO!
ON TO ROUND TWO!
Chapter 20:
The Cost of Stupidity

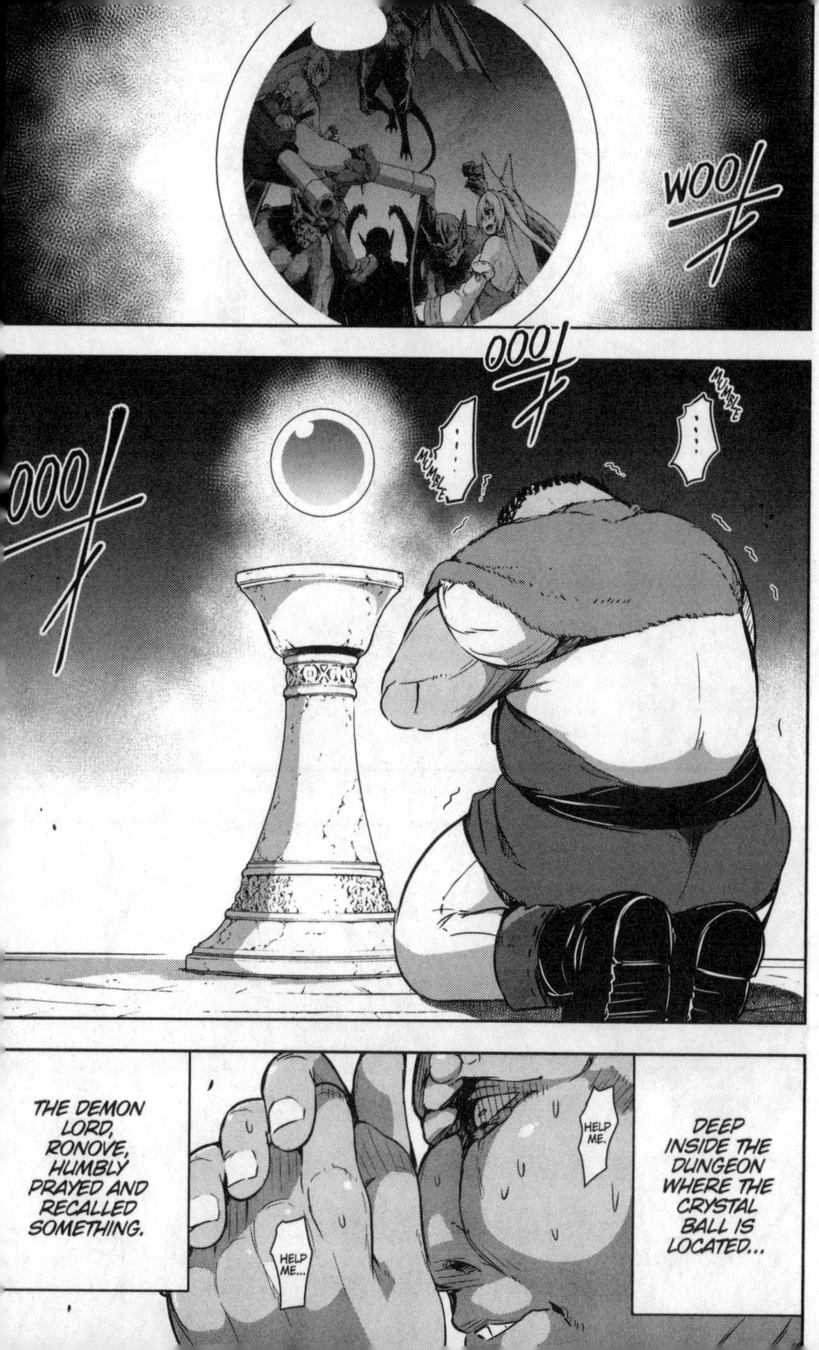
WOO
OOO
MUMBLE
......
MUMBLE
......
OOO
DEEP INSIDE THE DUNGEON WHERE THE CRYSTAL BALL IS LOCATED...
HELP ME.
HELP ME...
THE DEMON LORD, RONOVE, HUMBLY PRAYED AND RECALLED SOMETHING.

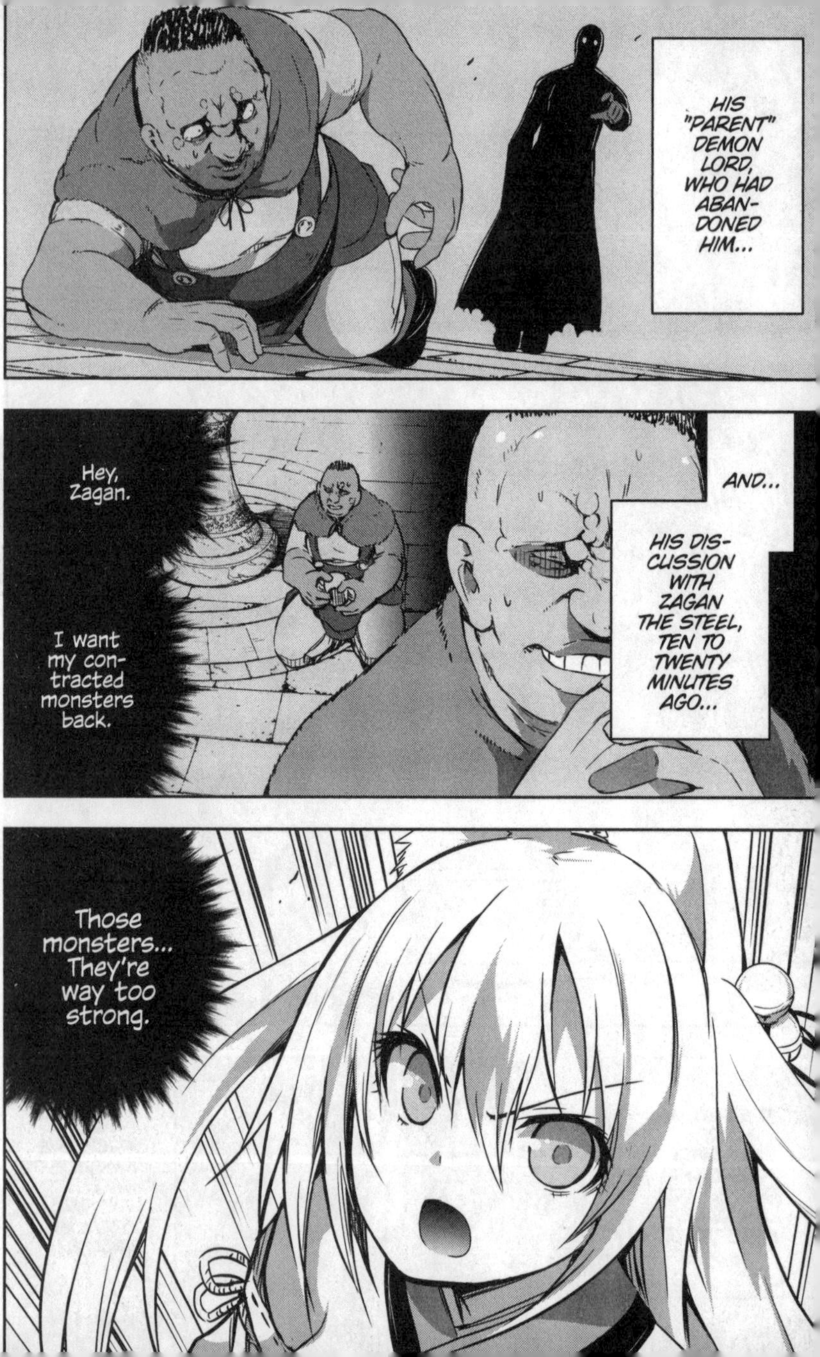
HIS "PARENT" DEMON LORD, WHO HAD ABAN-DONED HIM...
AND...
HIS DIS-CUSSION WITH ZAGAN THE STEEL, TEN TO TWENTY MINUTES AGO...
Hey, Zagan.
I want my con-tracted monsters back.
Those monsters... They're way too strong.

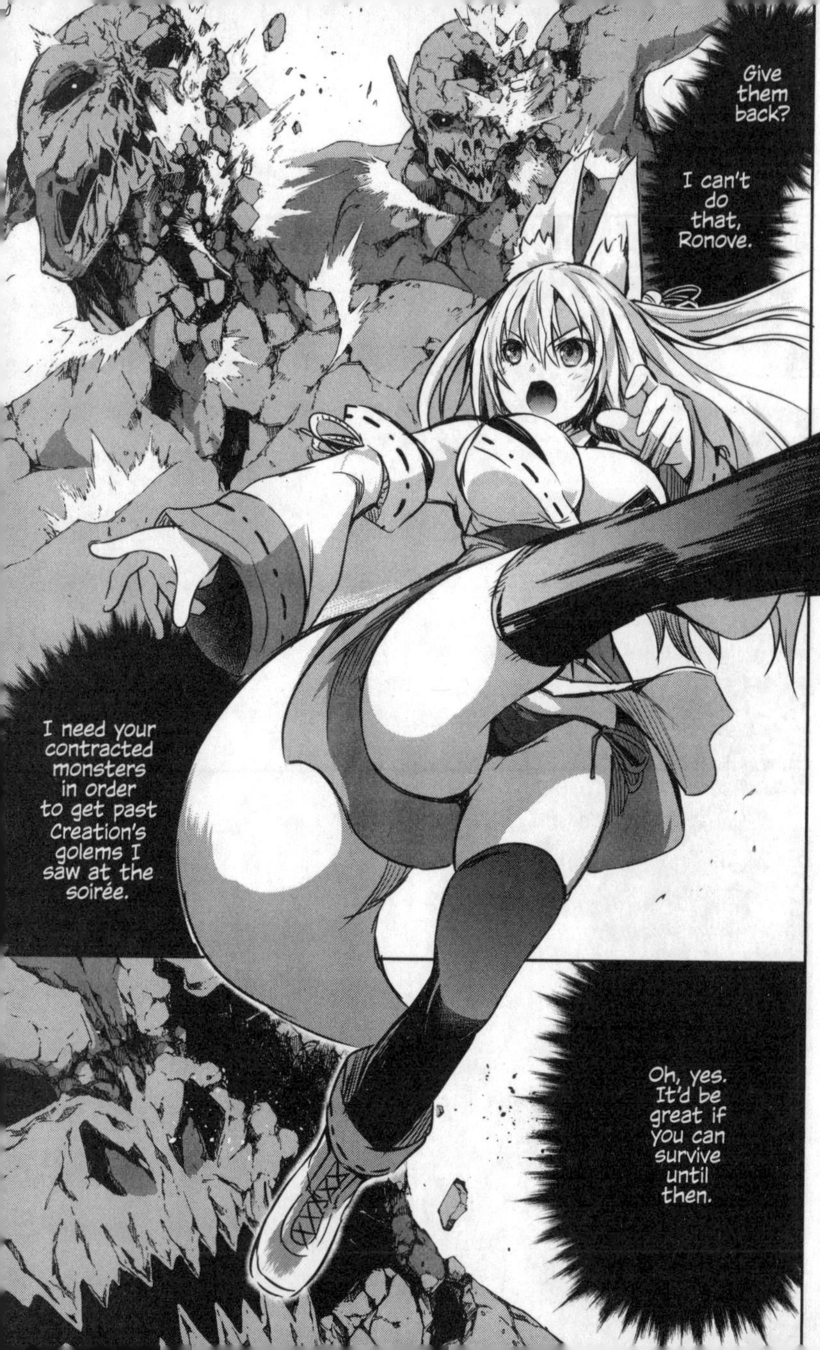
Give them back?
I can't do that, Ronove.
I need your contracted monsters in order to get past Creation's golems I saw at the soirée.
Oh, yes. It'd be great if you can survive until then.

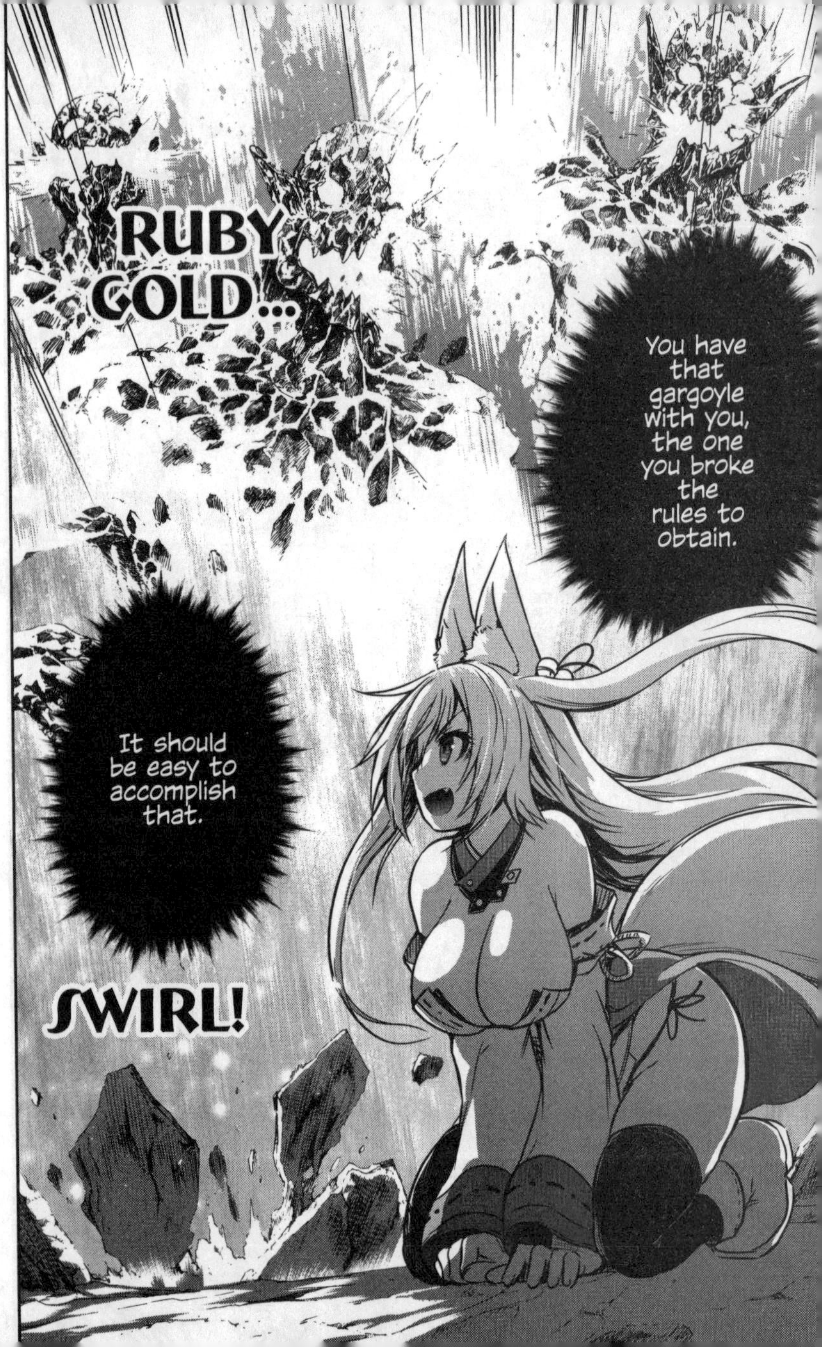
RUBY GOLD...
You have that gargoyle with you, the one you broke the rules to obtain.
It should be easy to accomplish that.
SWIRL!

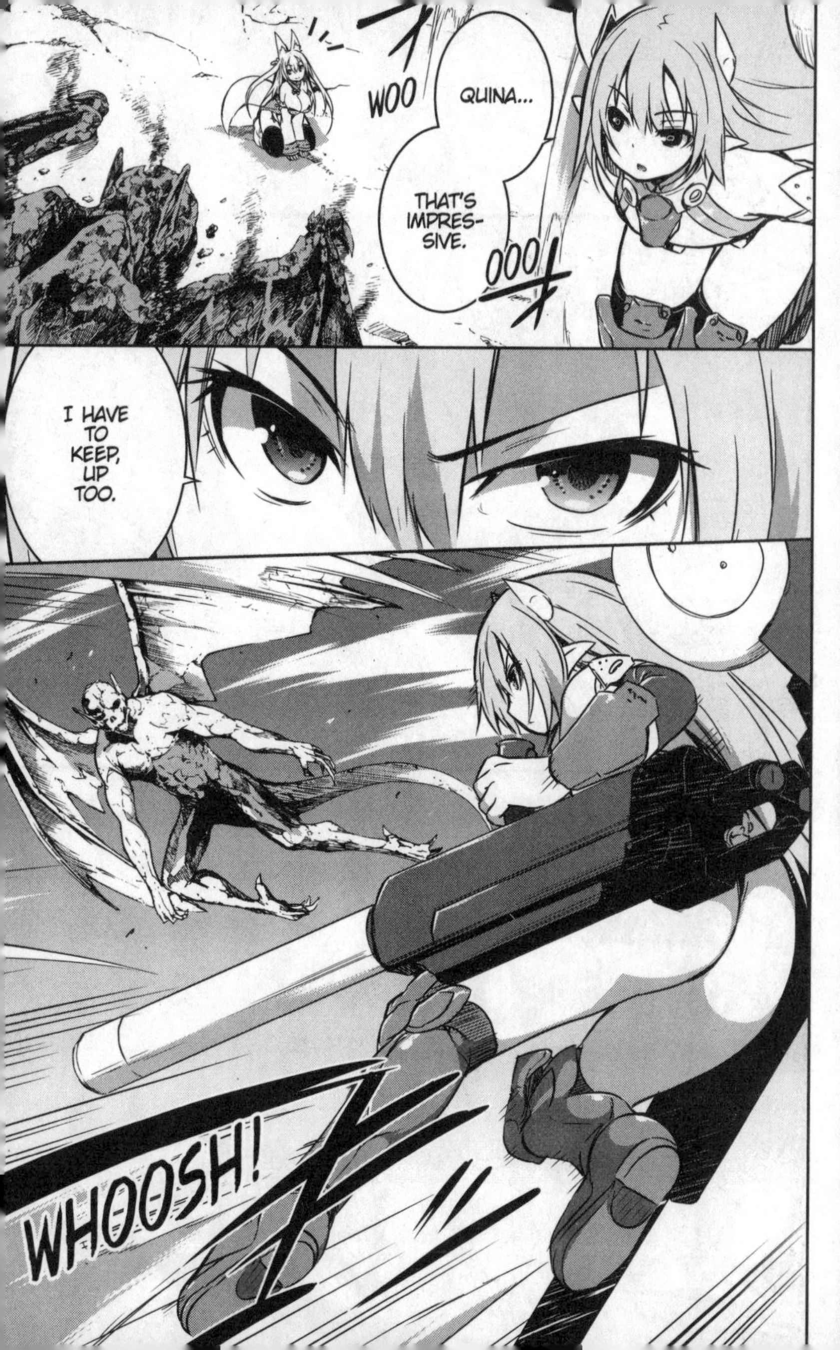
WOO
QUINA...
THAT'S IMPRESSIVE.
OOO
I HAVE TO KEEP, UP TOO.
WHOOSH!

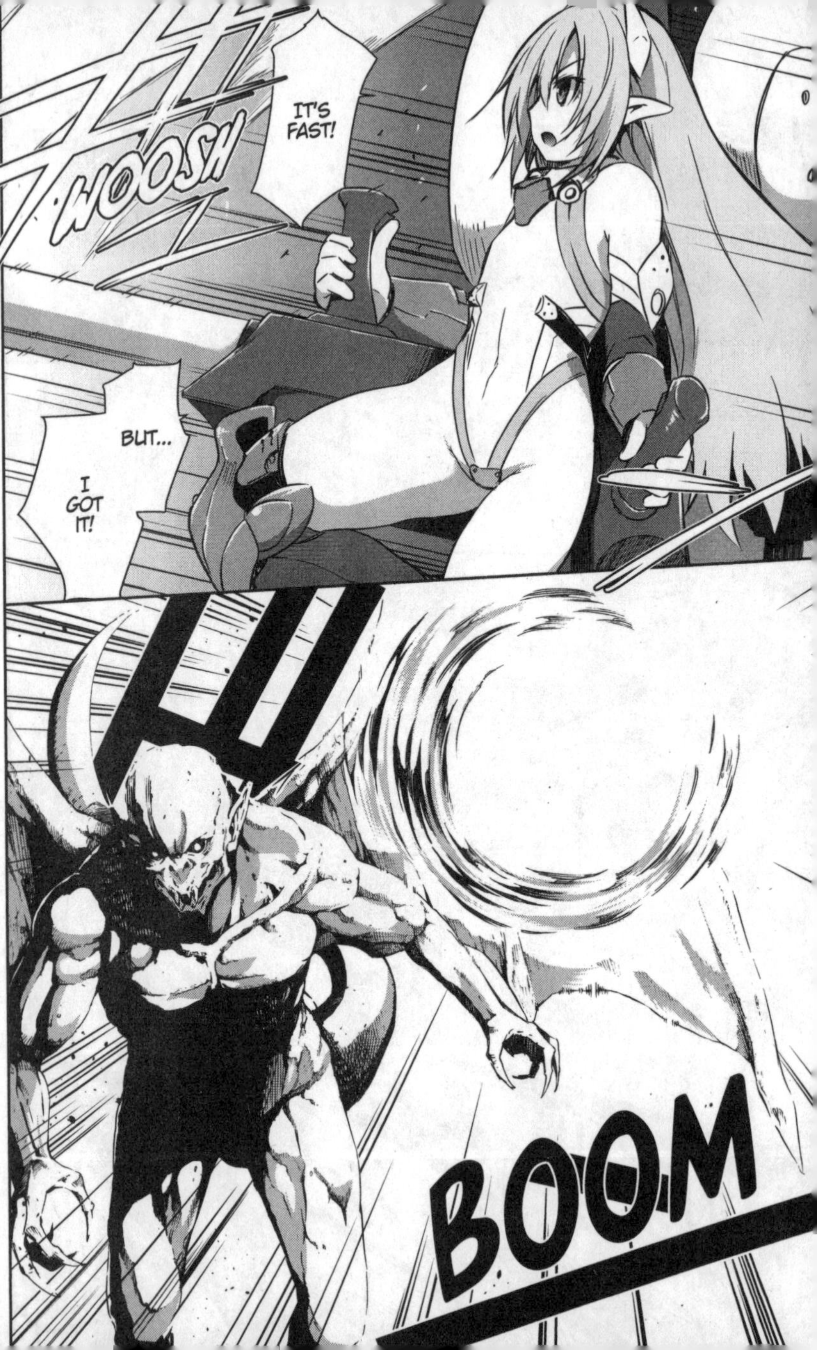
IT'S FAST!
WOOSH
BUT...
I GOT IT!
BOOM

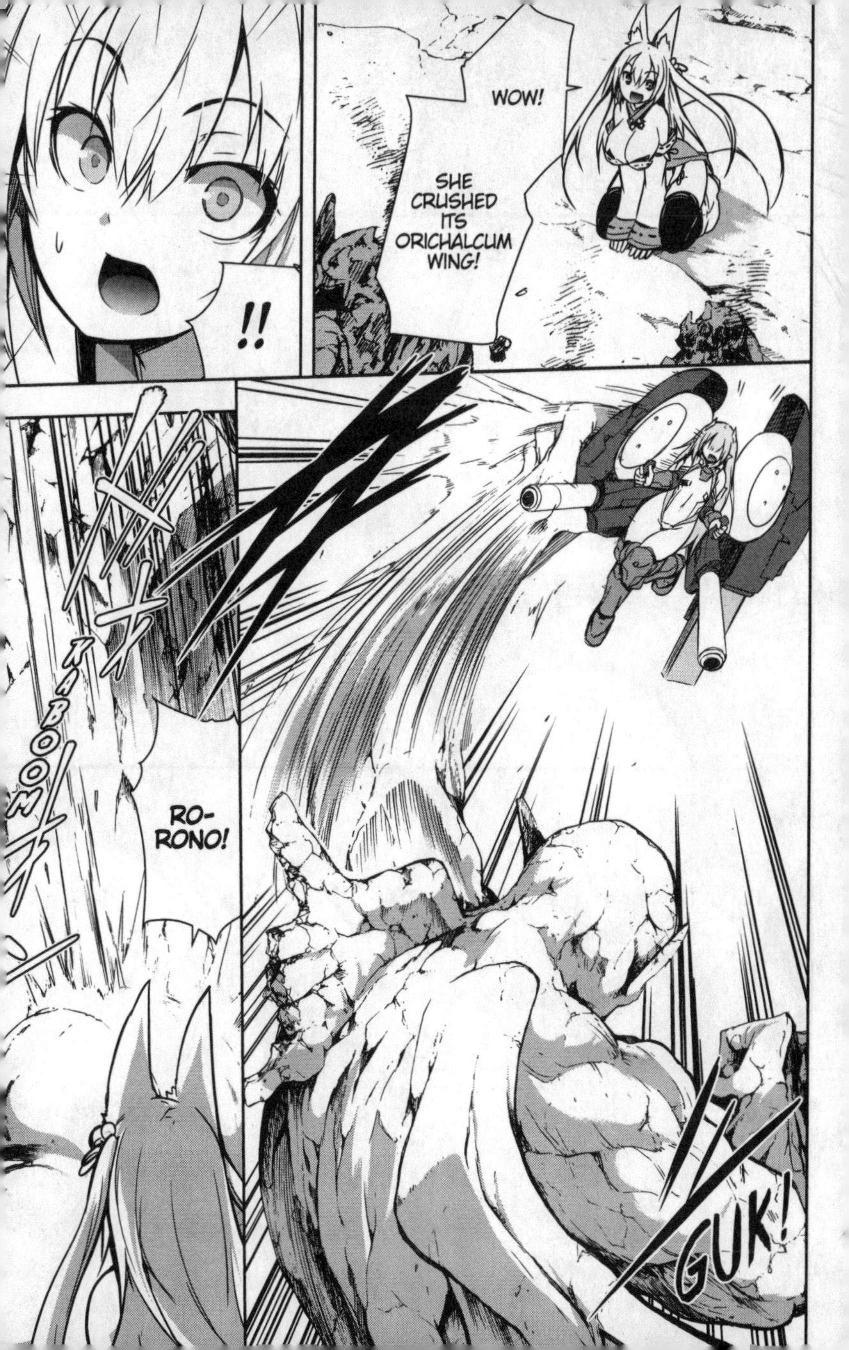
WOW!
SHE CRUSHED ITS ORICHALCUM WING!
!!
GUK!
KABOOM
RO-RONO!

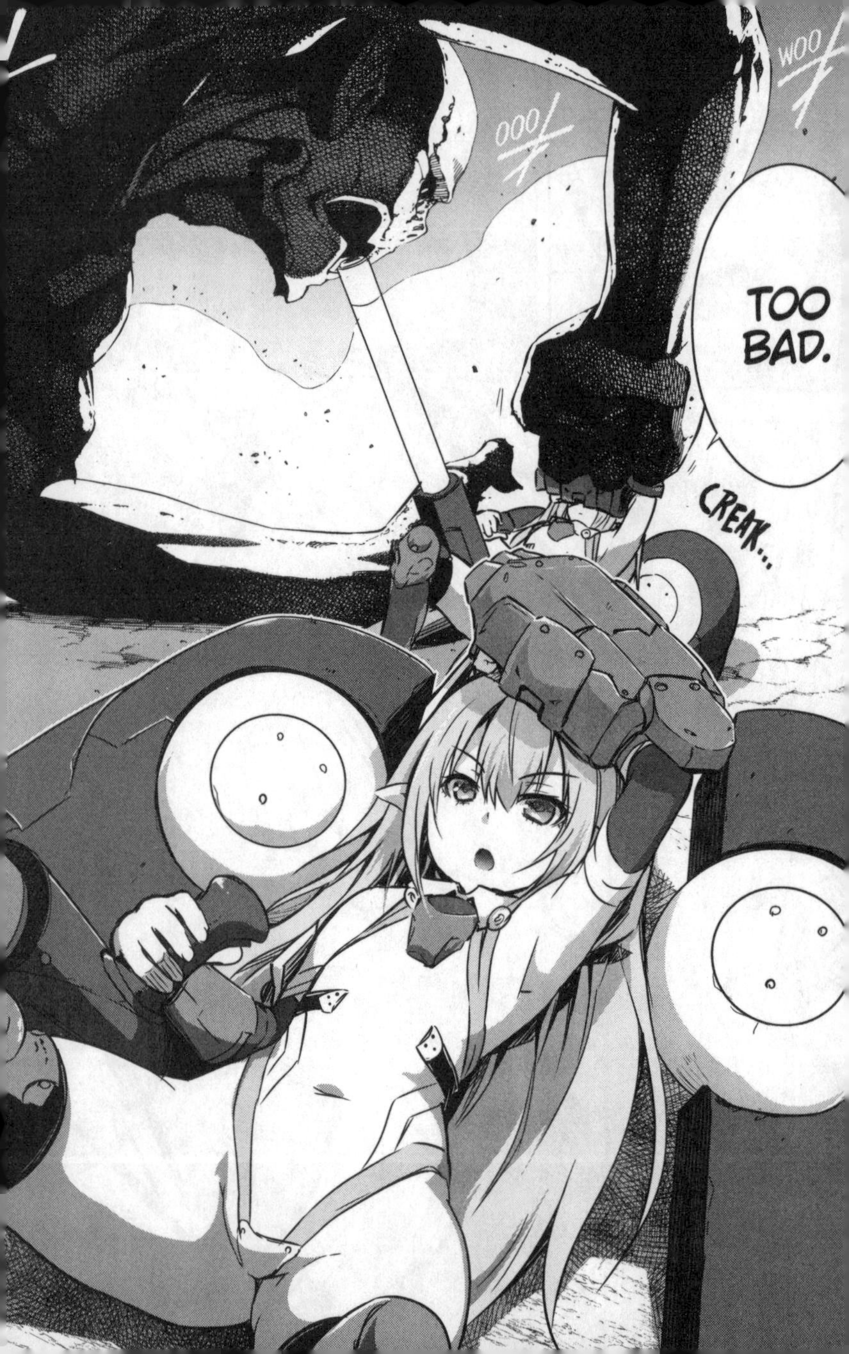
WOO
OOO
TOO BAD.
CREAK...

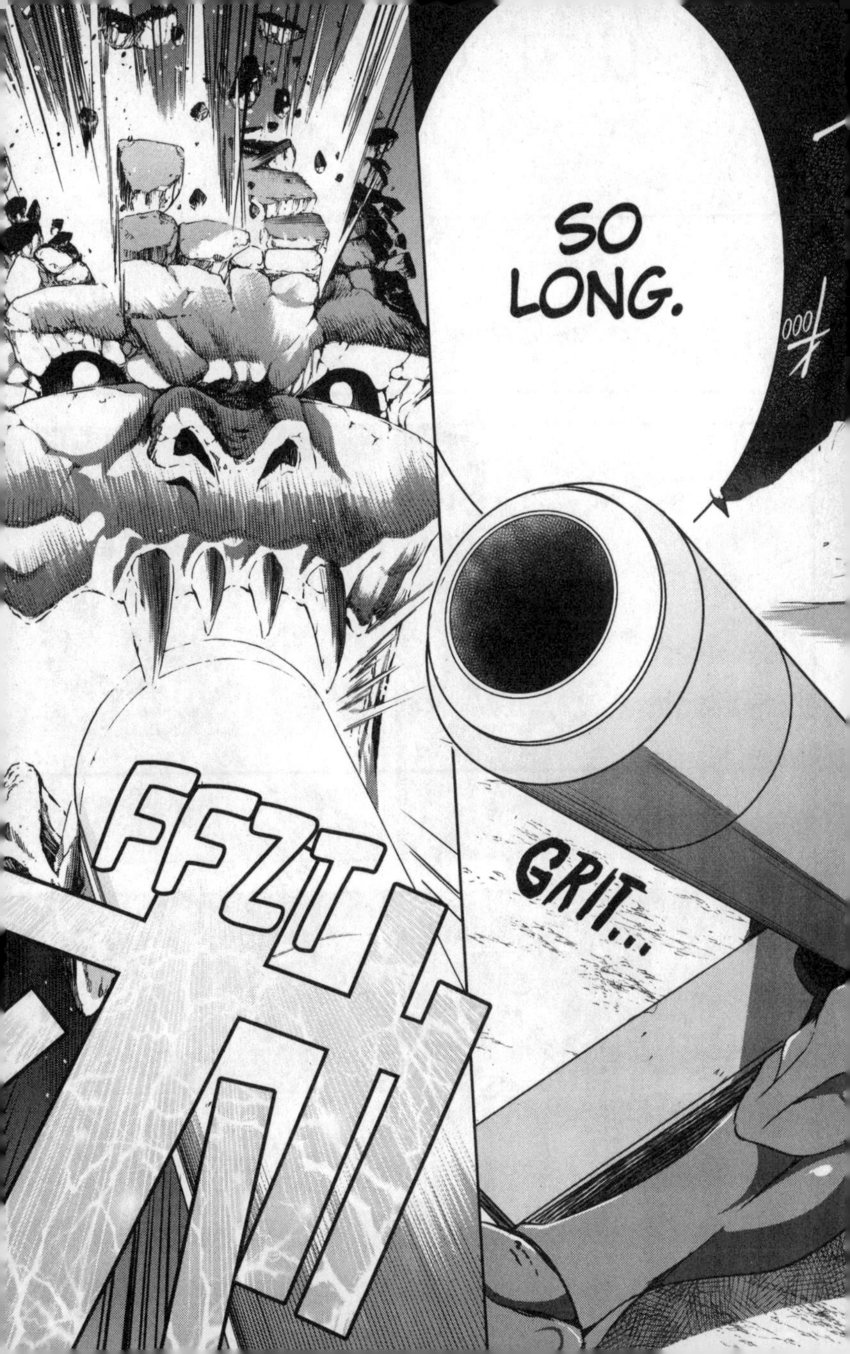
SO LONG.
GRIT...
FFZT!!

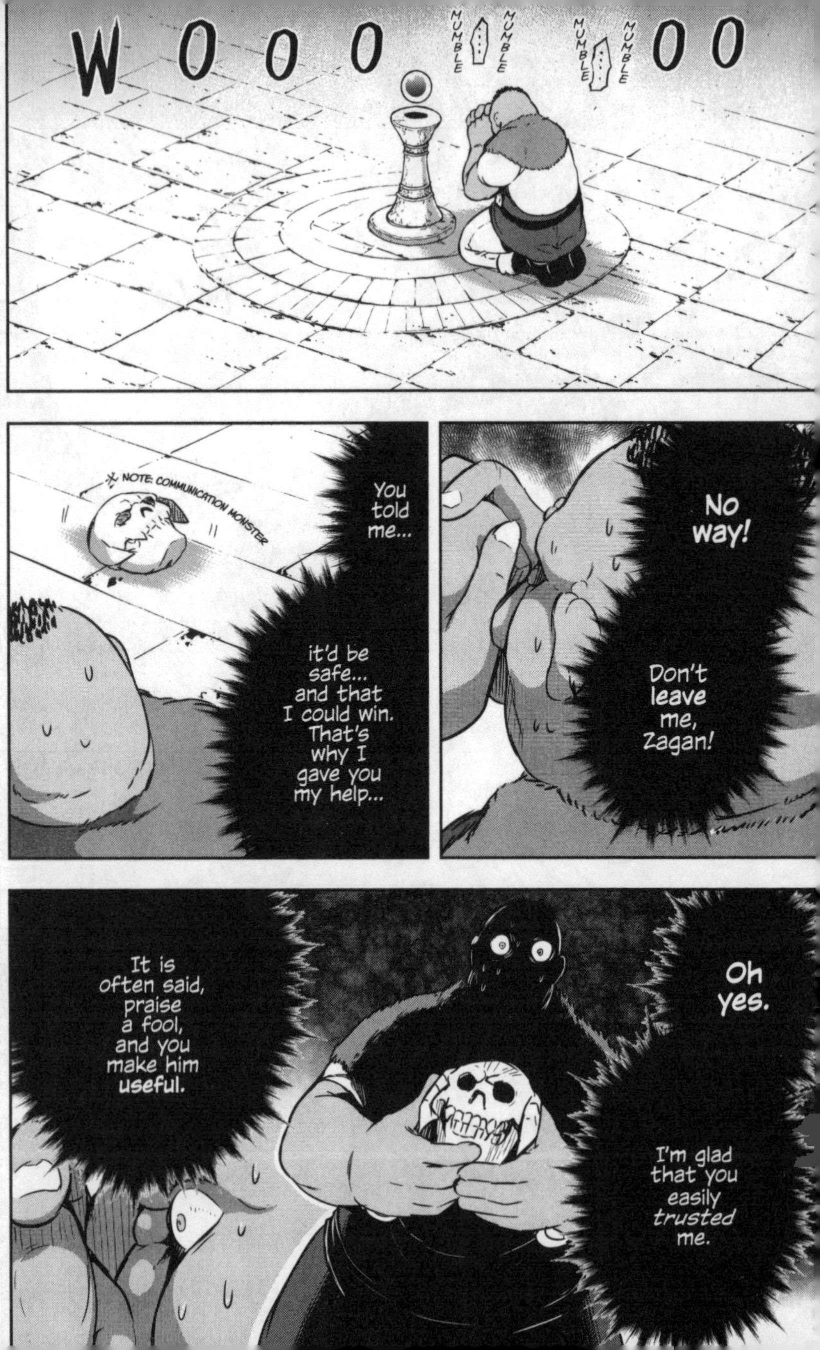
WOOO
MUMBLE MUMBLE
MUMBLE MUMBLE
OO
No way!
Don't leave me, Zagan!
NOTE: COMMUNICATION MONSTER
You told me...
it'd be safe... and that I could win. That's why I gave you my help...
Oh yes.
It is often said, praise a fool, and you make him useful.
I'm glad that you easily *trusted* me.

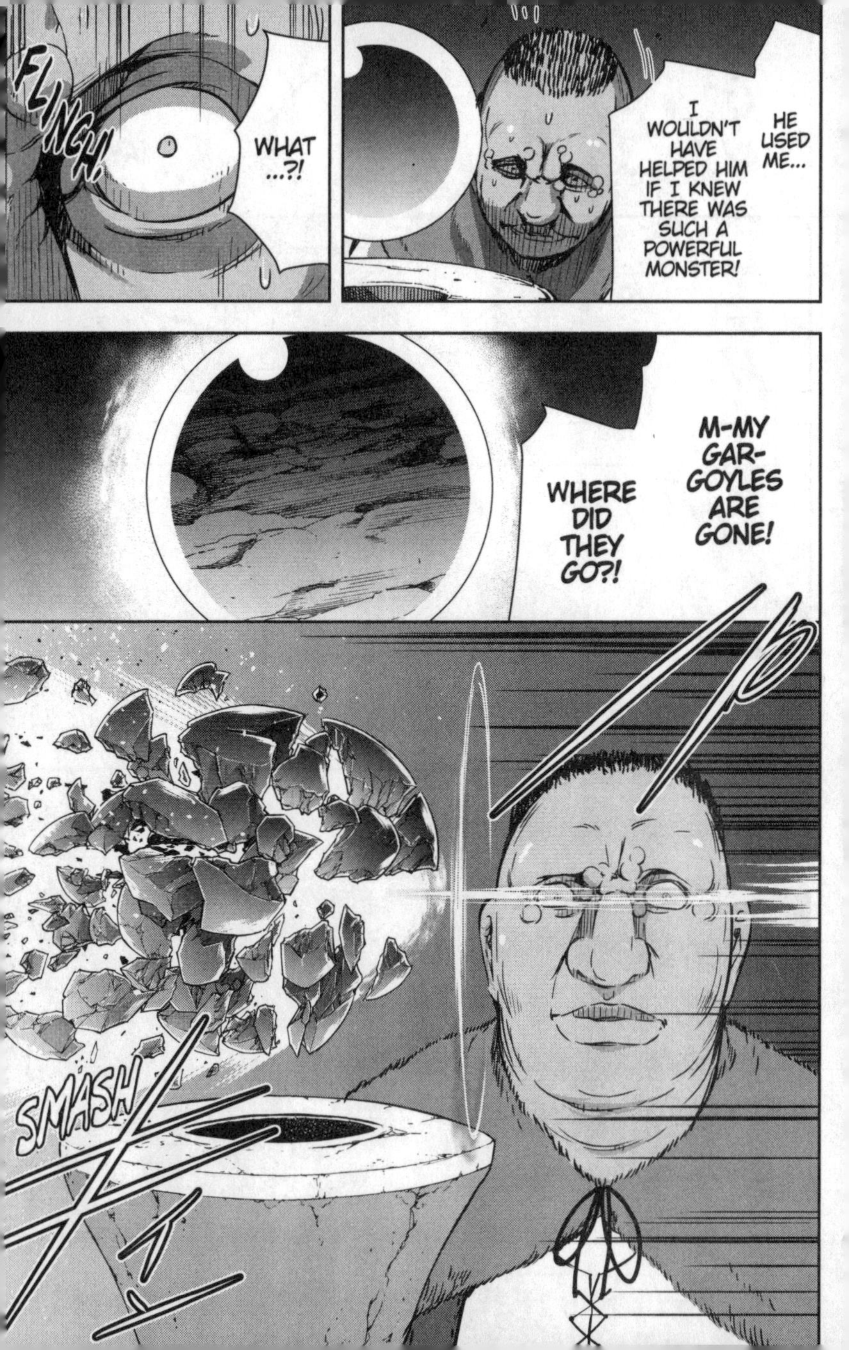
HE USED ME...
I WOULDN'T HAVE HELPED HIM IF I KNEW THERE WAS SUCH A POWERFUL MONSTER!
FLINCH!
WHAT ...?!
M-MY GAR-GOYLES ARE GONE!
WHERE DID THEY GO?!
SMASH

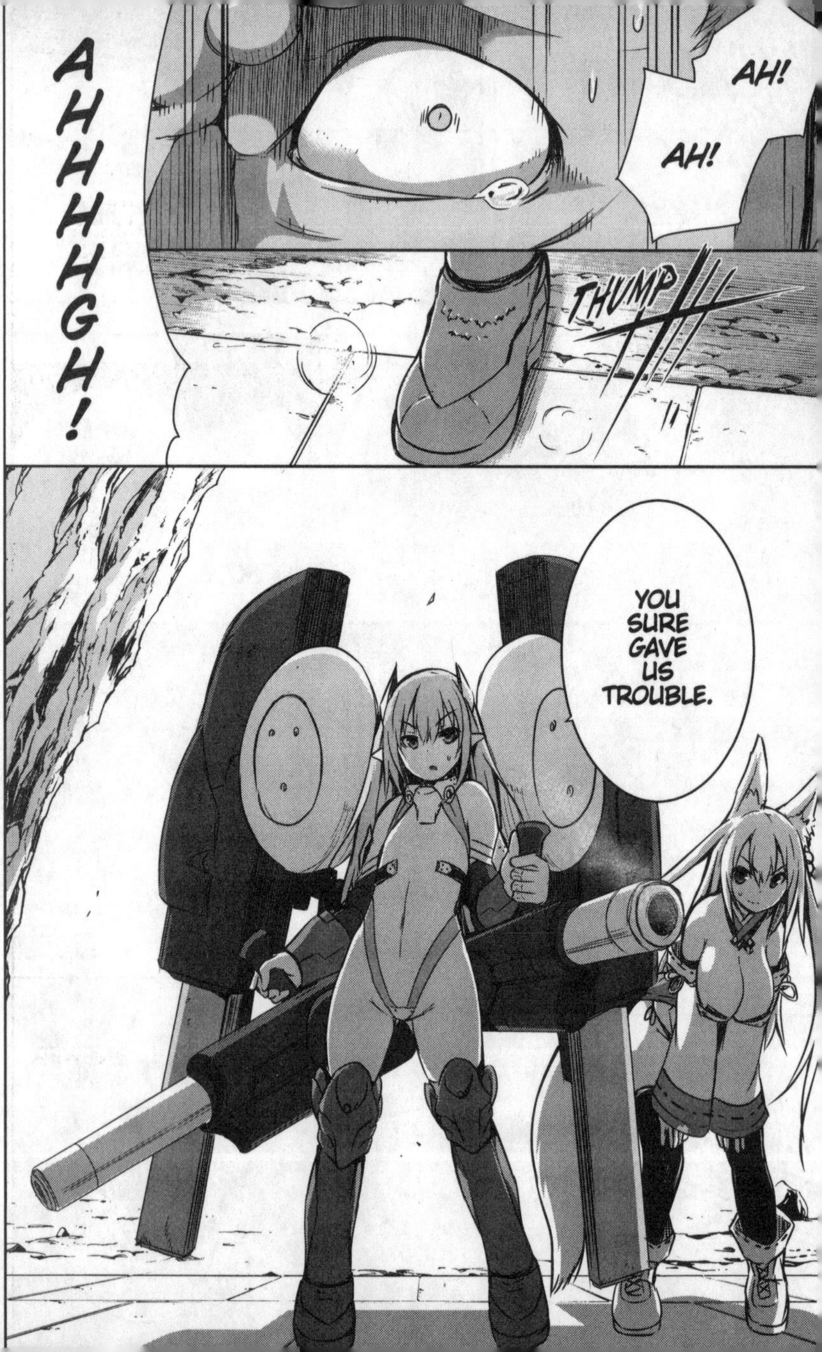
AH!
AH!
AHHHHGH!
THUMP
YOU SURE GAVE US TROUBLE.

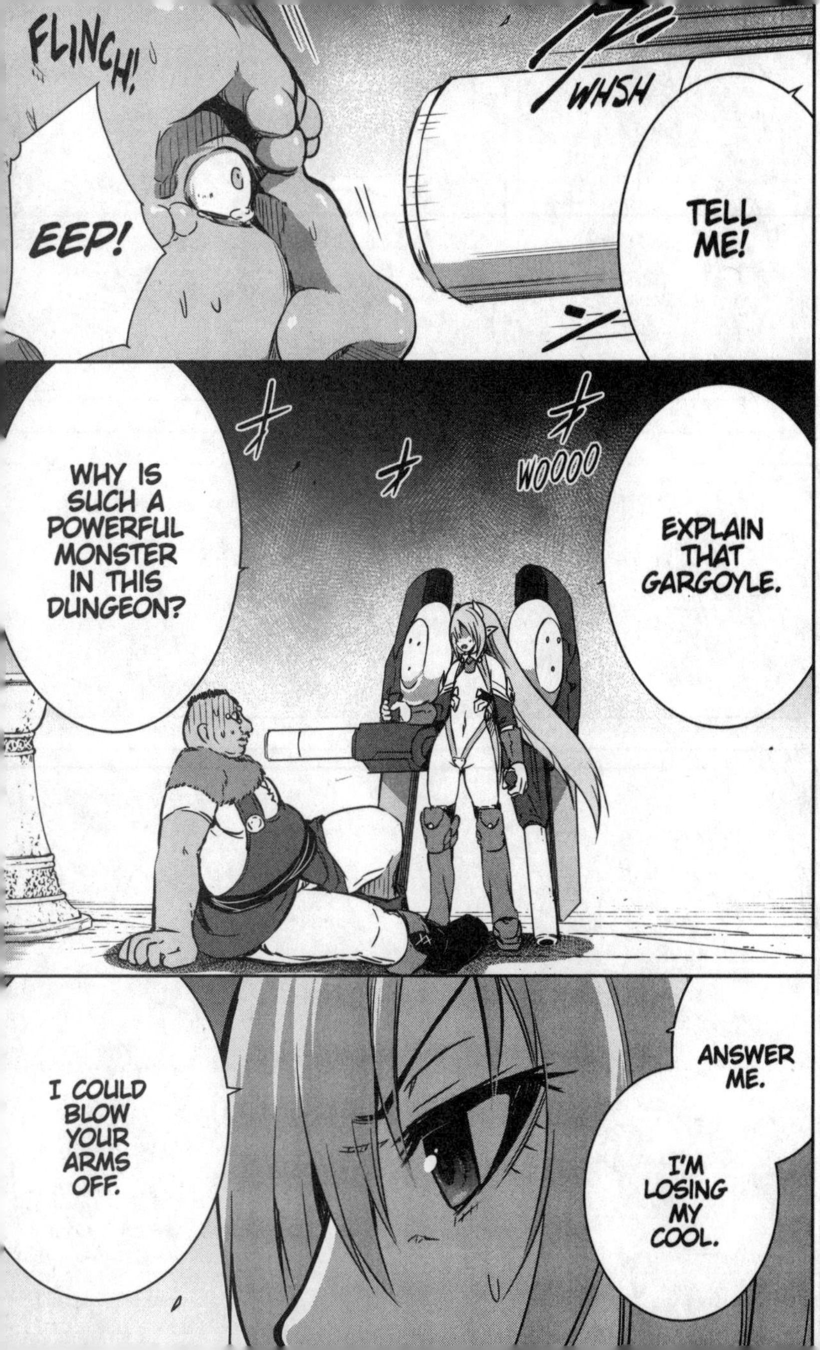
WHSH
TELL ME!
FLINCH!
EEP!
EXPLAIN THAT GARGOYLE.
WOOOO
WHY IS SUCH A POWERFUL MONSTER IN THIS DUNGEON?
ANSWER ME.
I'M LOSING MY COOL.
I COULD BLOW YOUR ARMS OFF.

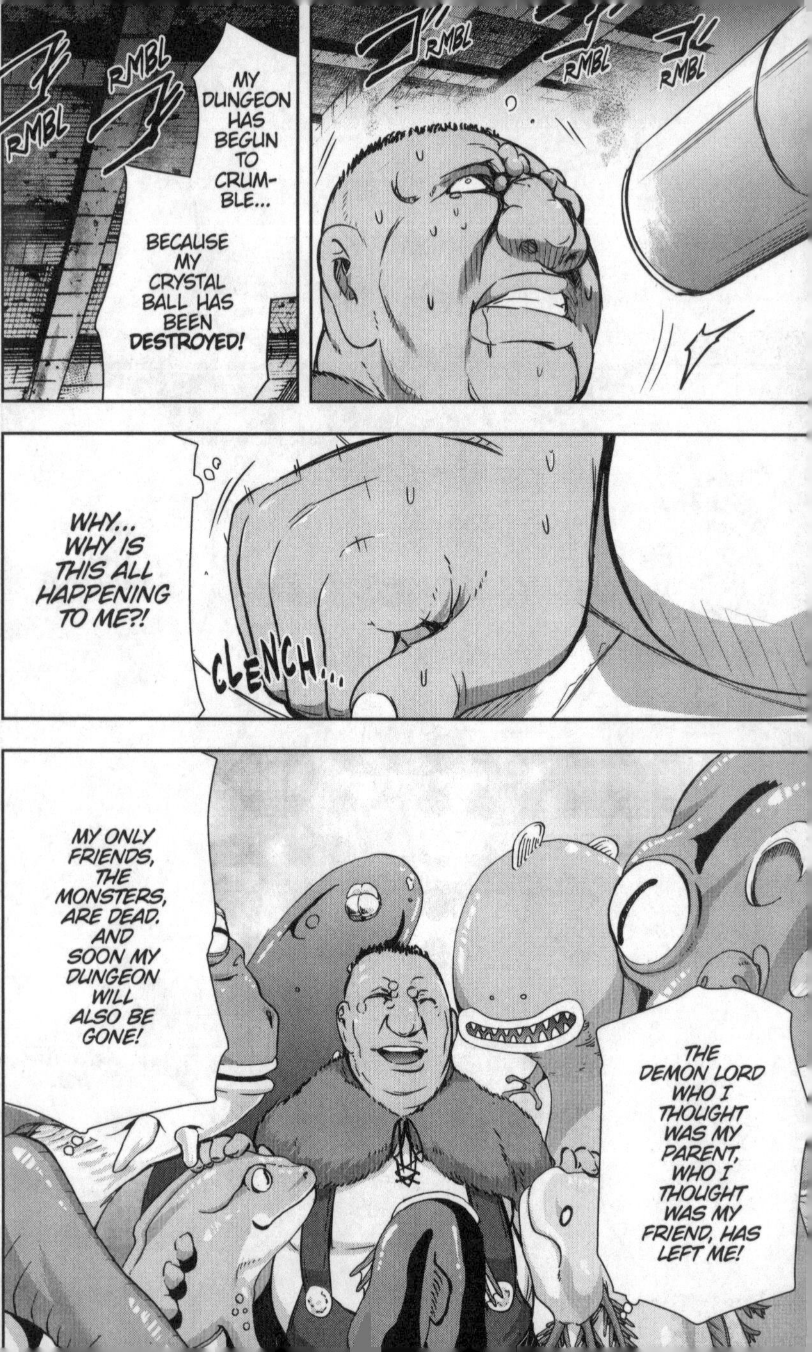
RMBL
RMBL
RMBL
RMBL
RMBL
MY DUNGEON HAS BEGUN TO CRUMBLE...
BECAUSE MY CRYSTAL BALL HAS BEEN DESTROYED!
WHY... WHY IS THIS ALL HAPPENING TO ME?!
CLENCH...
MY ONLY FRIENDS, THE MONSTERS, ARE DEAD. AND SOON MY DUNGEON WILL ALSO BE GONE!
THE DEMON LORD WHO I THOUGHT WAS MY PARENT, WHO I THOUGHT WAS MY FRIEND, HAS LEFT ME!

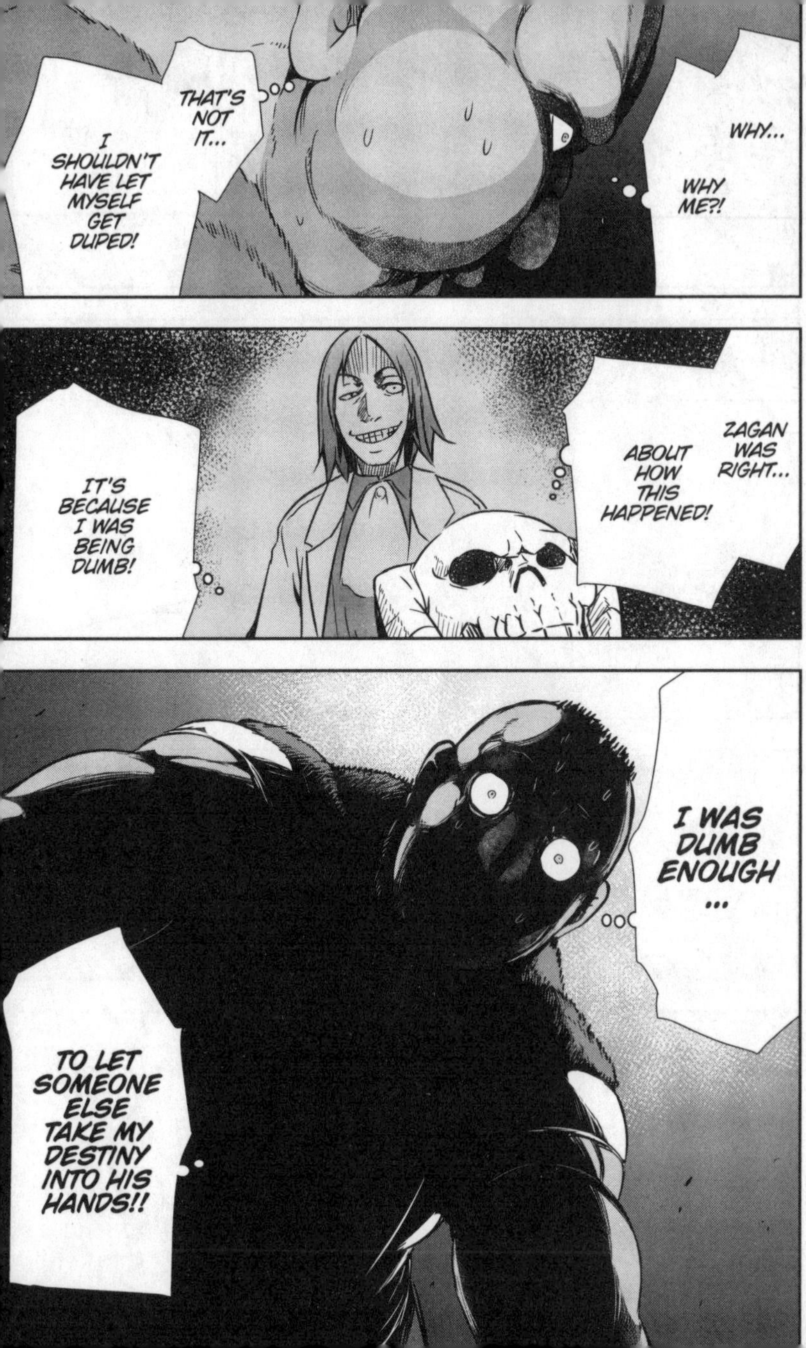
WHY...
WHY ME?!
THAT'S NOT IT...
I SHOULDN'T HAVE LET MYSELF GET DUPED!
ZAGAN WAS RIGHT...
ABOUT HOW THIS HAPPENED!
IT'S BECAUSE I WAS BEING DUMB!
I WAS DUMB ENOUGH ...
TO LET SOMEONE ELSE TAKE MY DESTINY INTO HIS HANDS!!

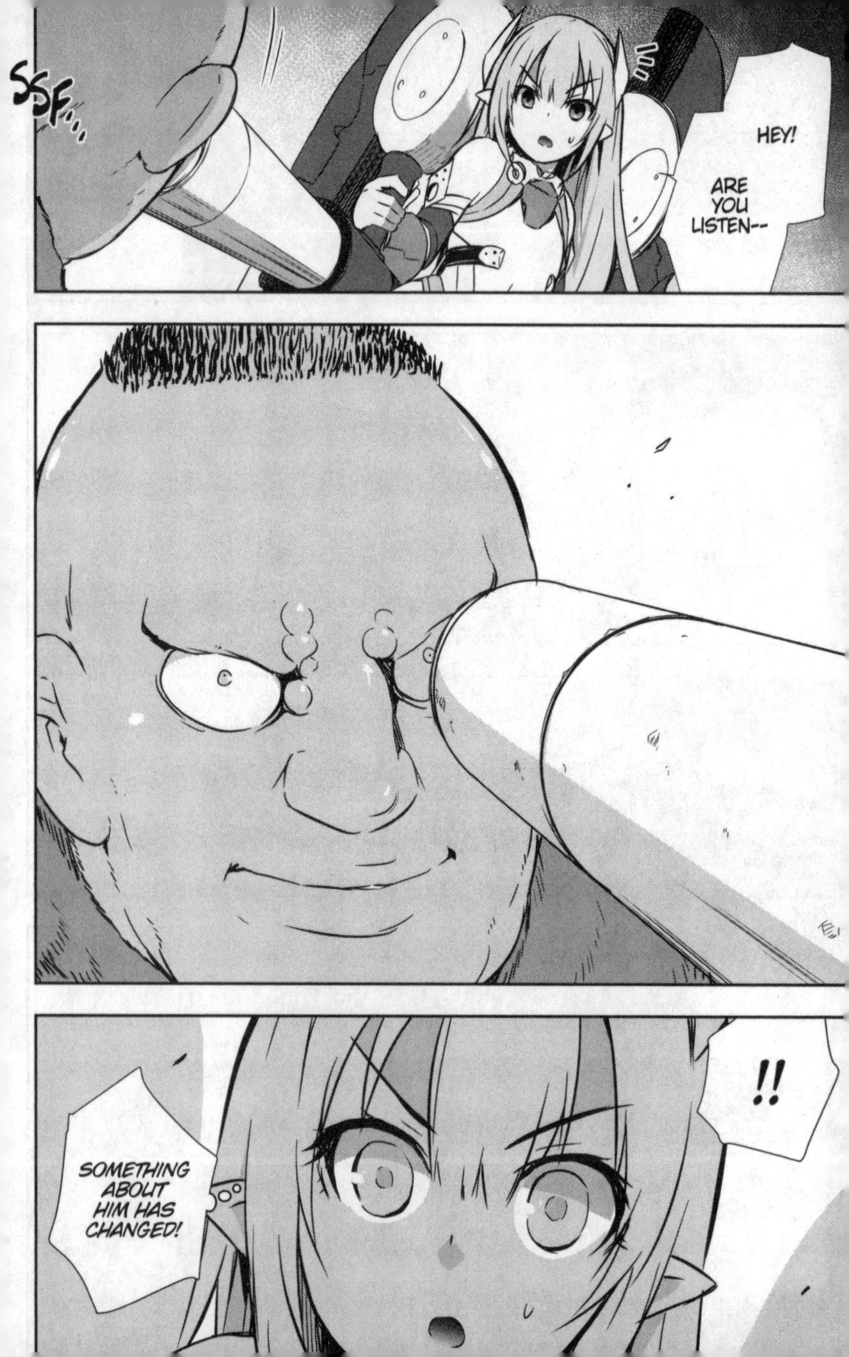
HEY!
ARE YOU LISTEN--
SSF...
!!
SOMETHING ABOUT HIM HAS CHANGED!

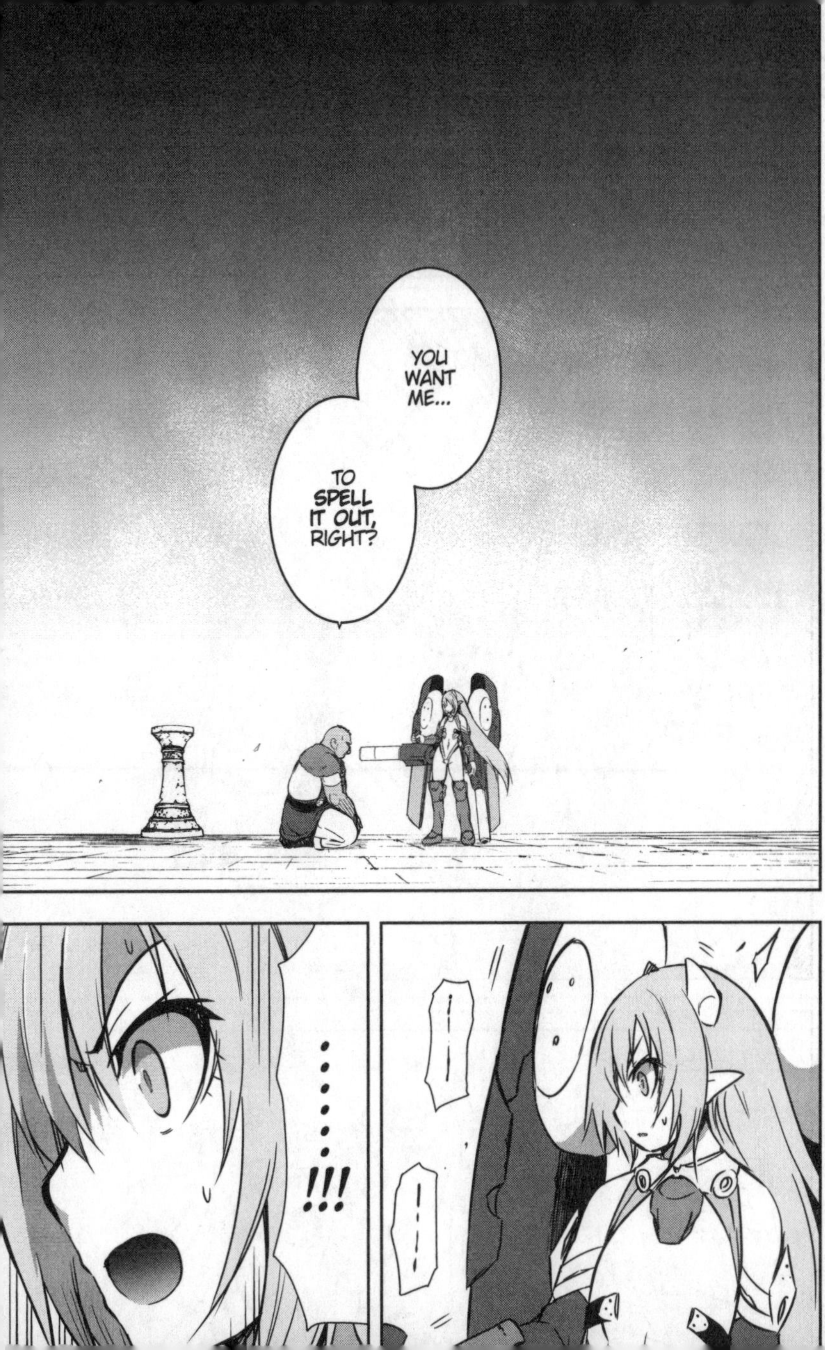
YOU WANT ME...
TO SPELL IT OUT, RIGHT?
!—
!—
......!!!

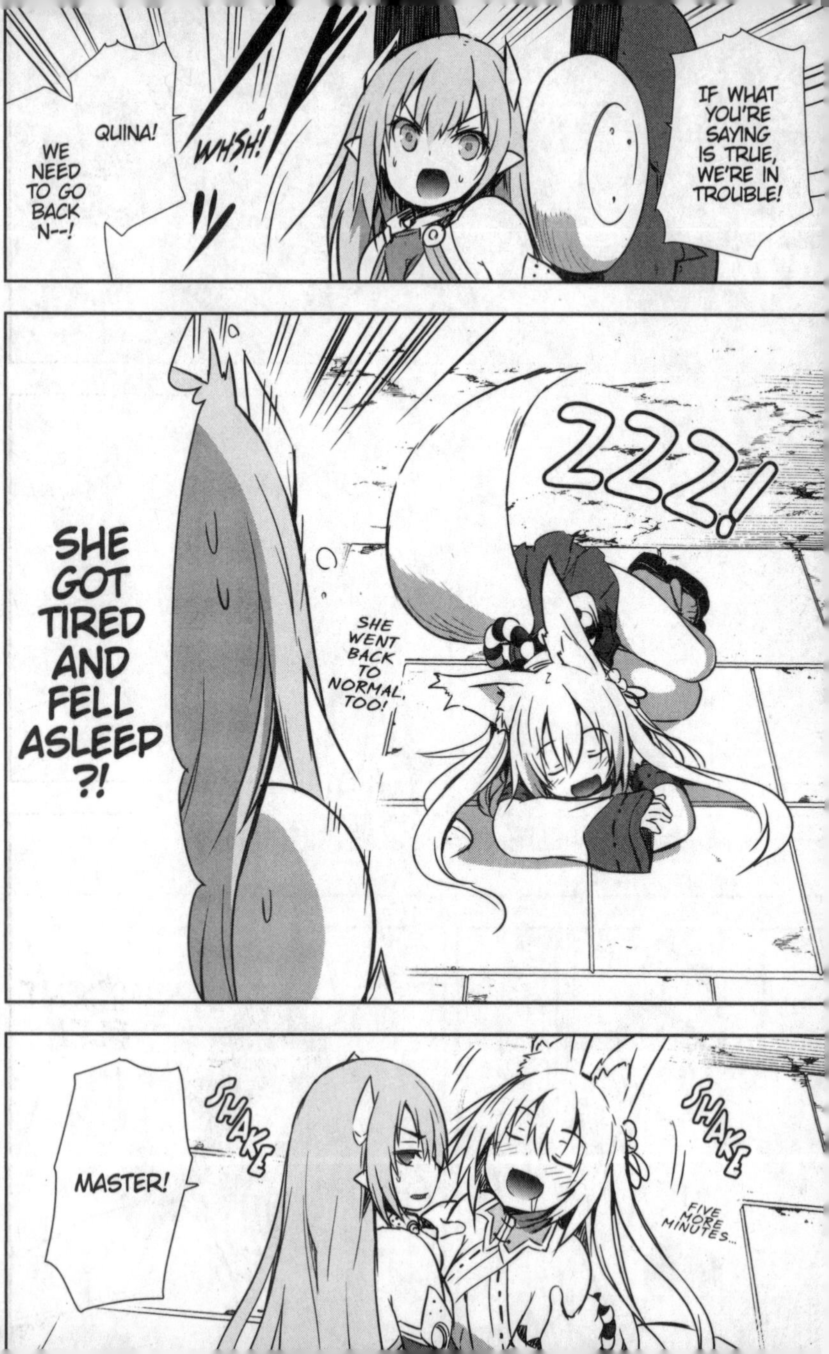
IF WHAT YOU'RE SAYING IS TRUE, WE'RE IN TROUBLE!
WHSH!
QUINA!
WE NEED TO GO BACK N--!
ZZZ!
SHE WENT BACK TO NORMAL, TOO!
SHE GOT TIRED AND FELL ASLEEP?!
SHAKE
FIVE MORE MINUTES...
SHAKE
MASTER!

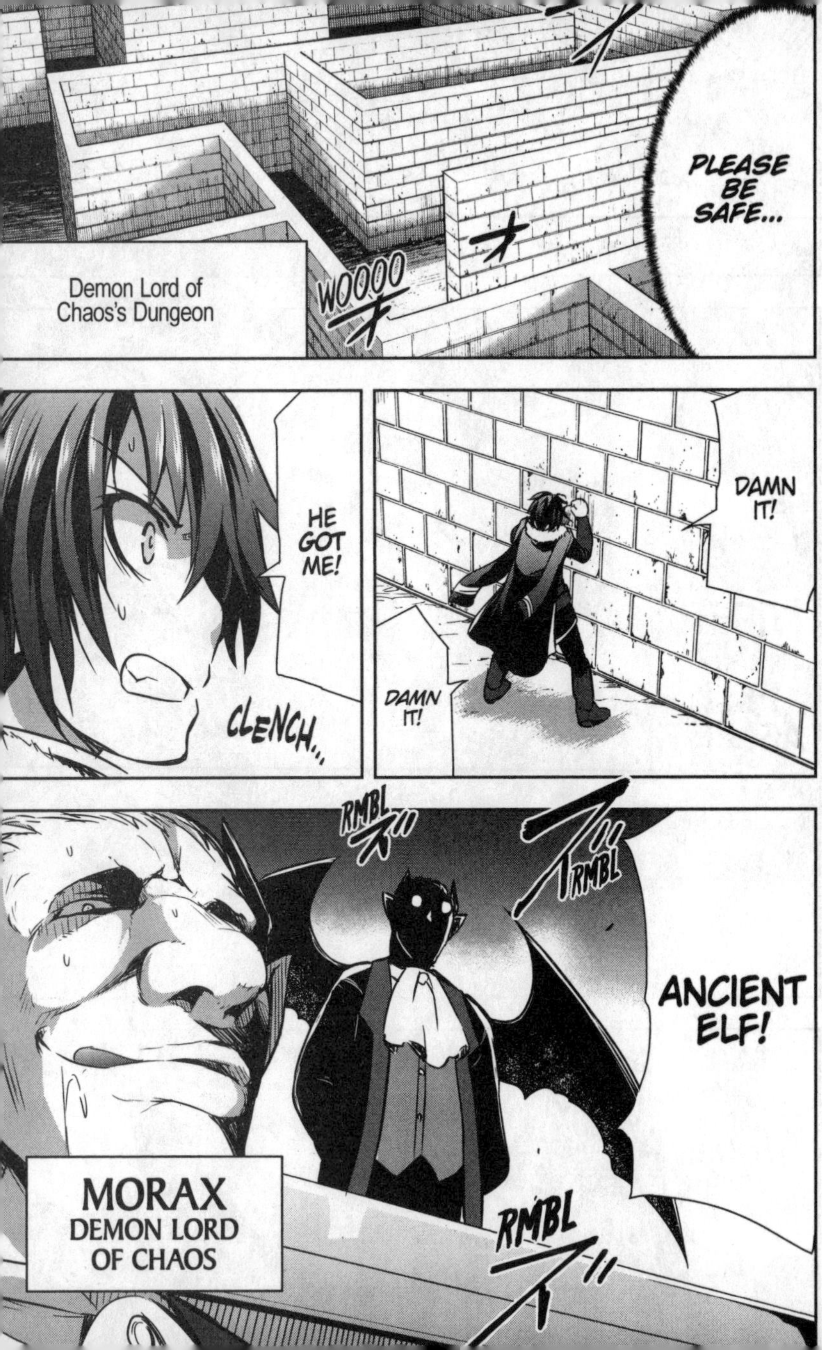
PLEASE BE SAFE...
WOOOO
Demon Lord of Chaos's Dungeon
DAMN IT!
DAMN IT!
HE GOT ME!
CLENCH...
RMBL
RMBL
ANCIENT ELF!
MORAX DEMON LORD OF CHAOS
RMBL

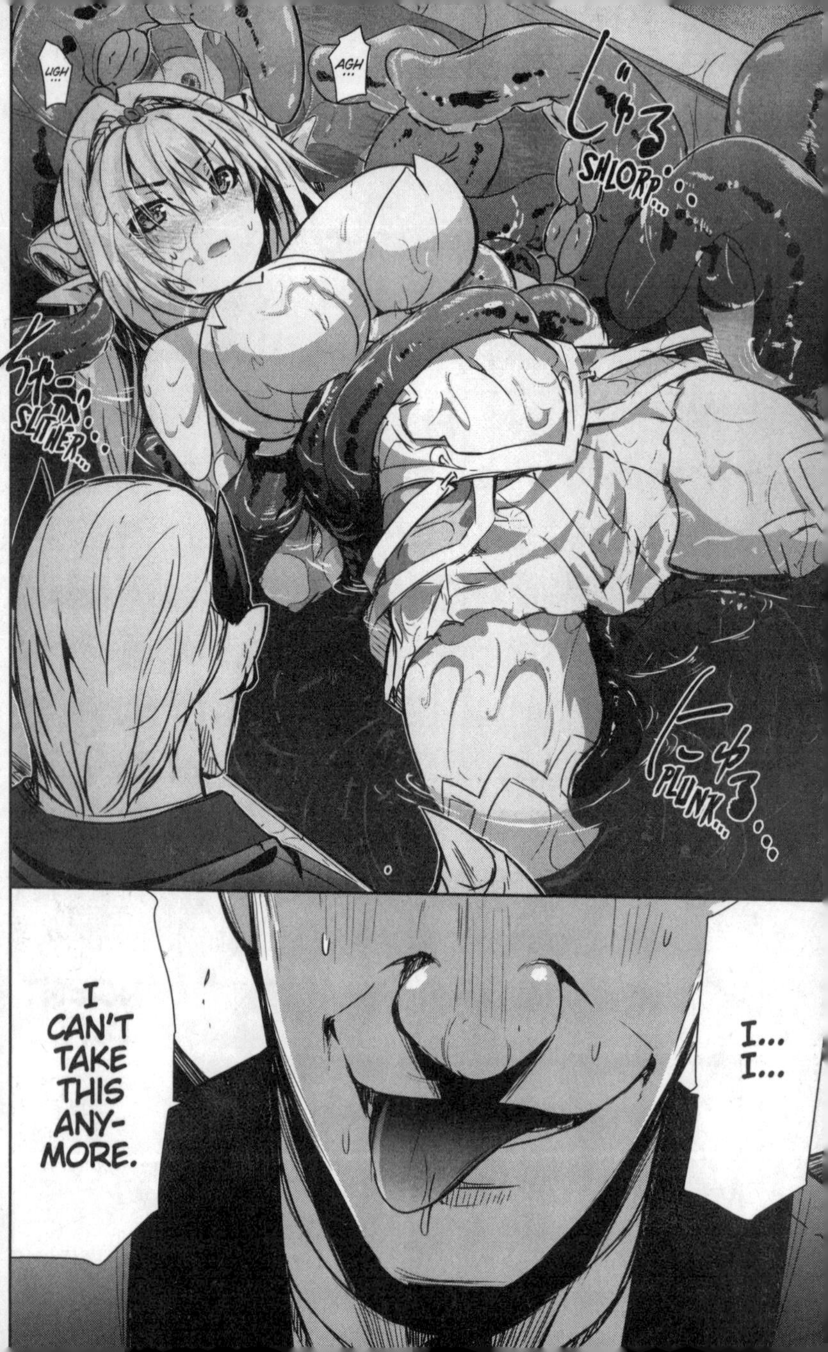
AGH ...
じゅる
SHLORP...
UGH ...
SLITHER...
PLUNK...
I... I...
I CAN'T TAKE THIS ANY-MORE.

Chapter 21: The One Who Fell into the Trap

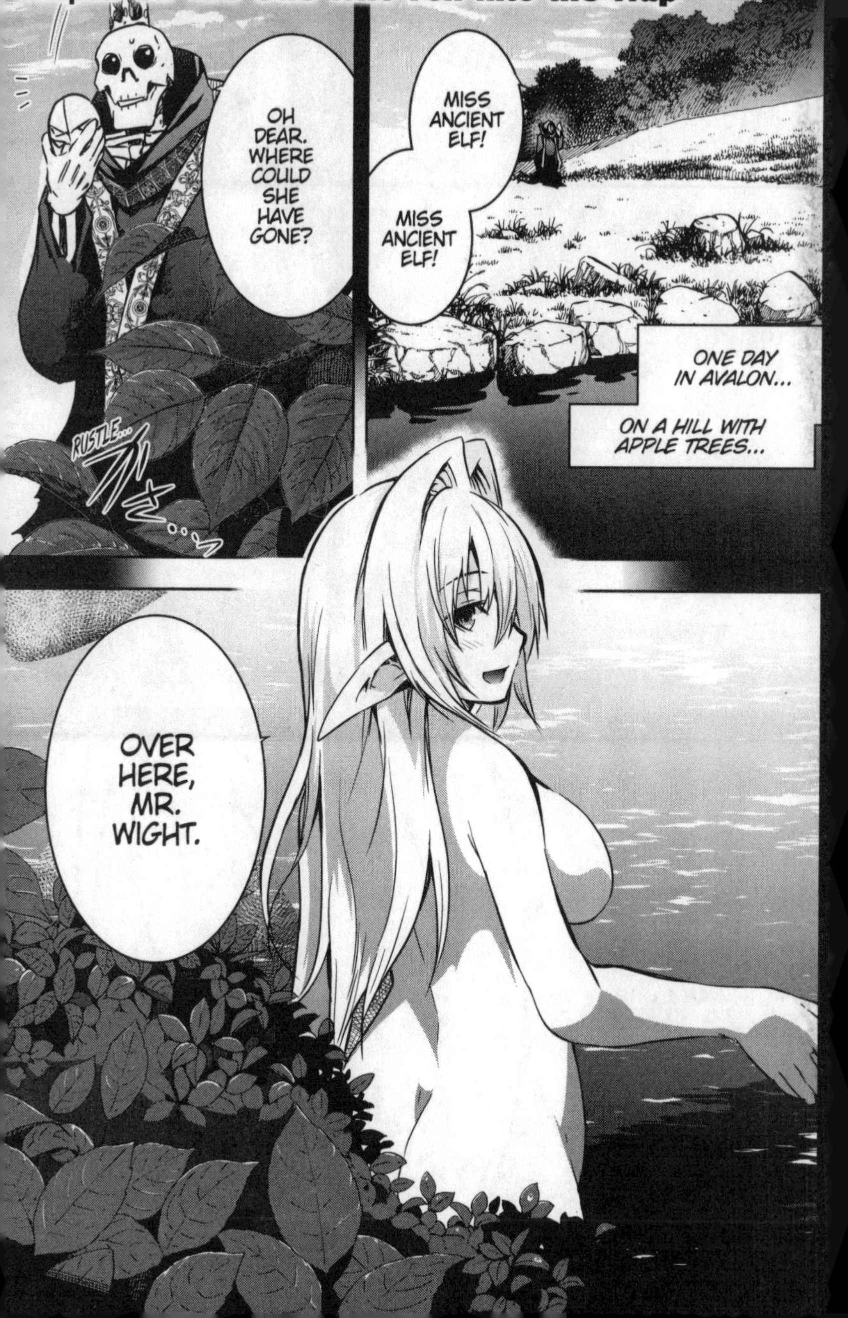
MISS ANCIENT ELF!
MISS ANCIENT ELF!
ONE DAY IN AVALON...
ON A HILL WITH APPLE TREES...
OH DEAR. WHERE COULD SHE HAVE GONE?
RUSTLE...
OVER HERE, MR. WIGHT.

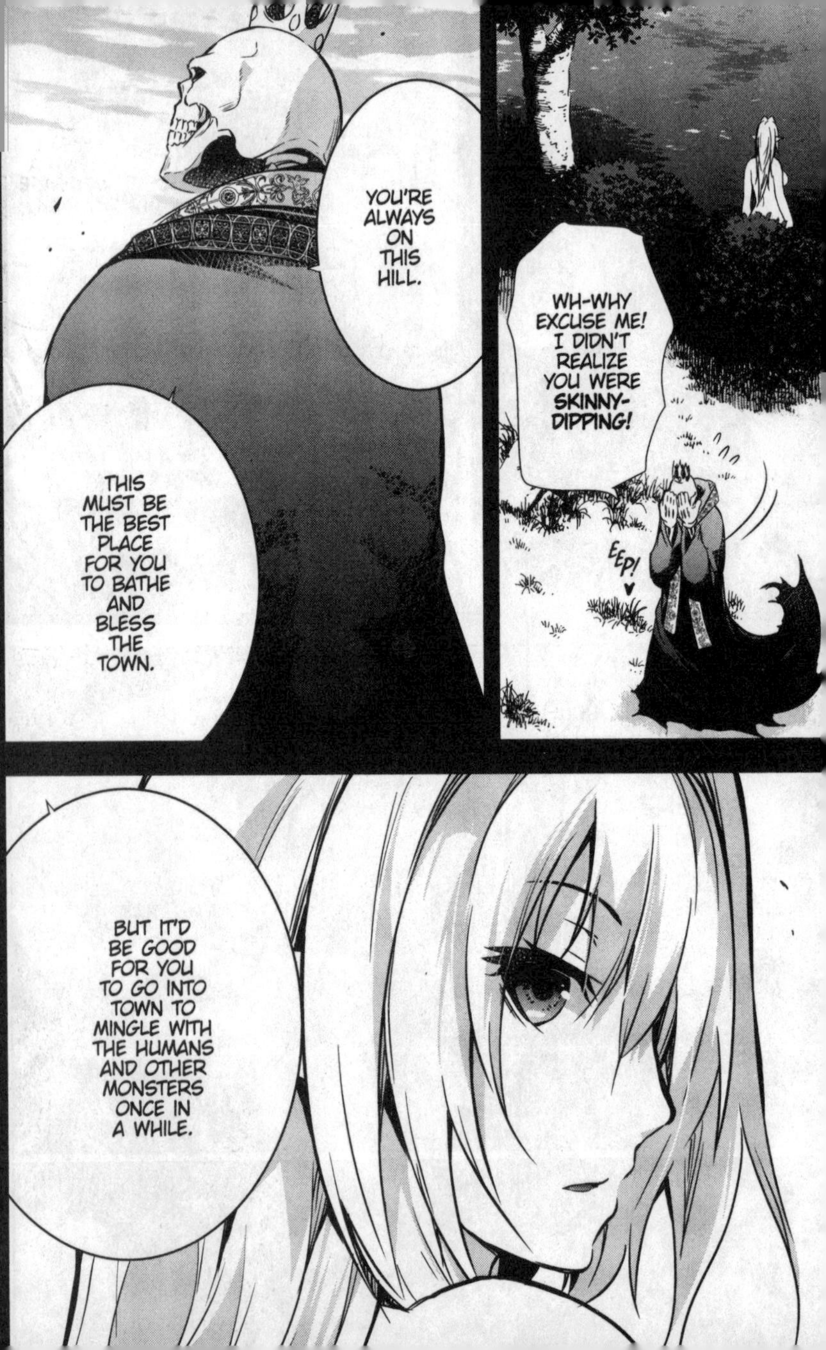
WH-WHY EXCUSE ME! I DIDN'T REALIZE YOU WERE SKINNY-DIPPING!
EEP!
YOU'RE ALWAYS ON THIS HILL.
THIS MUST BE THE BEST PLACE FOR YOU TO BATHE AND BLESS THE TOWN.
BUT IT'D BE GOOD FOR YOU TO GO INTO TOWN TO MINGLE WITH THE HUMANS AND OTHER MONSTERS ONCE IN A WHILE.

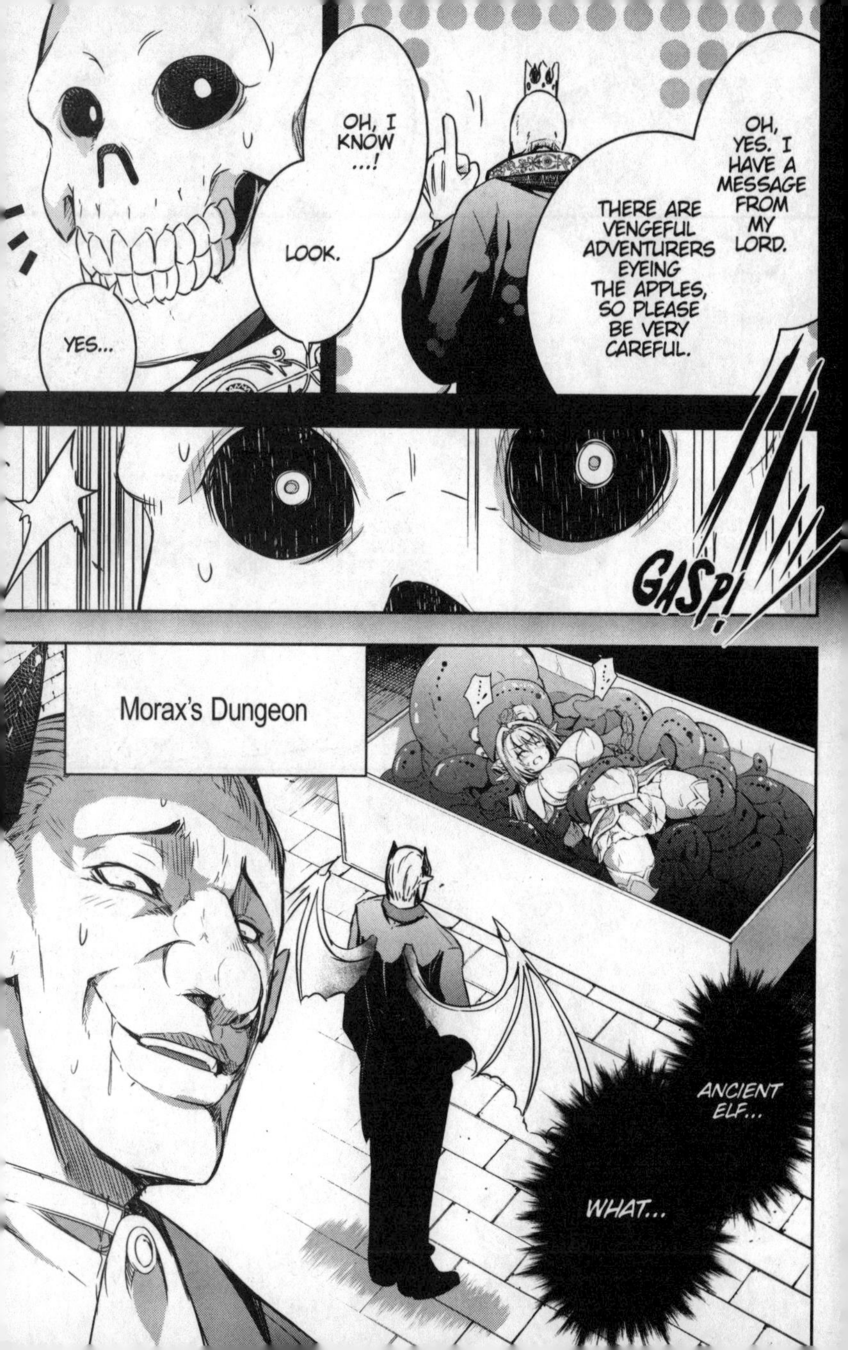
OH, YES. I HAVE A MESSAGE FROM MY LORD.
THERE ARE VENGEFUL ADVENTURERS EYEING THE APPLES, SO PLEASE BE VERY CAREFUL.
OH, I KNOW ...!
LOOK.
YES...
GASP!
Morax's Dungeon
ANCIENT ELF...
WHAT...

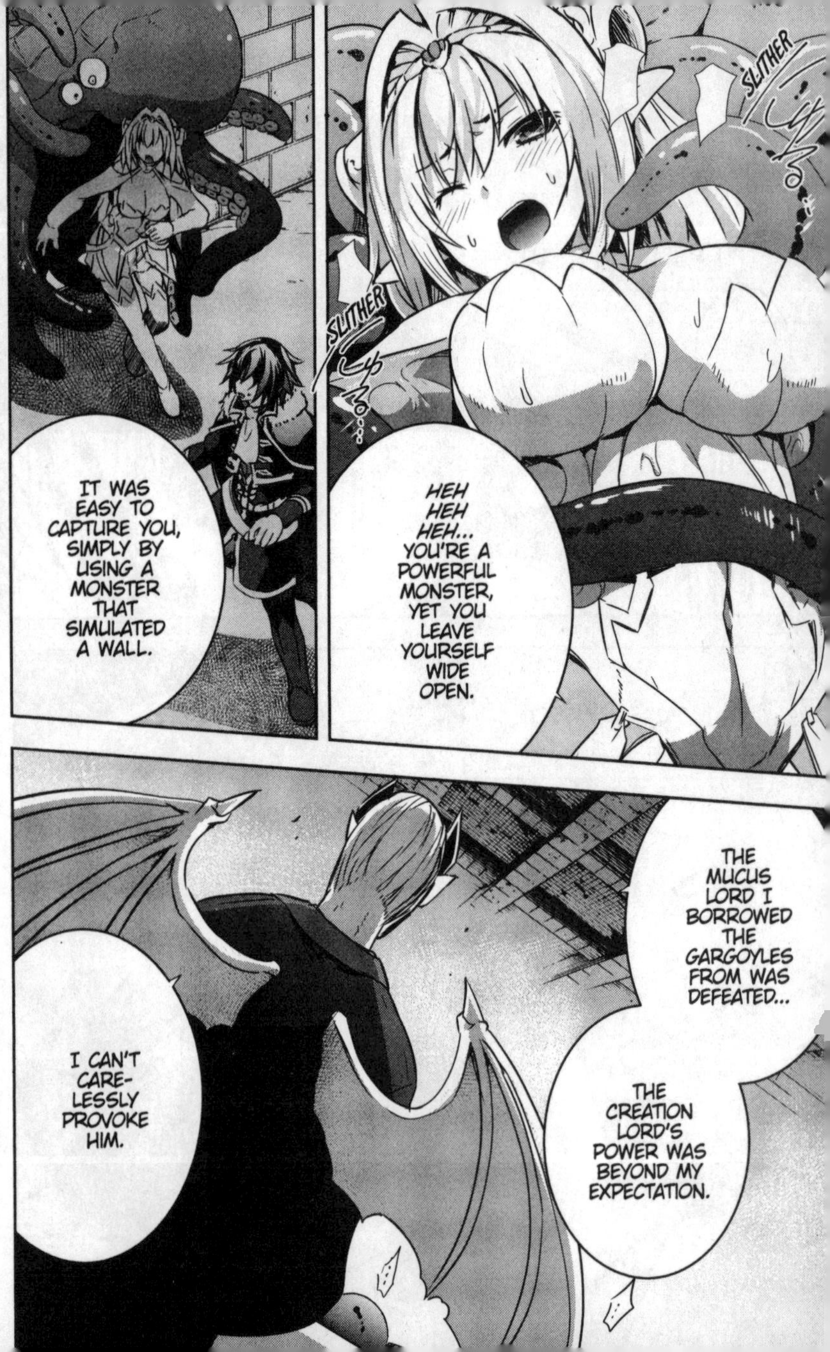
SLITHER
SLITHER
HEH HEH HEH... YOU'RE A POWERFUL MONSTER, YET YOU LEAVE YOURSELF WIDE OPEN.
IT WAS EASY TO CAPTURE YOU, SIMPLY BY USING A MONSTER THAT SIMULATED A WALL.
THE MUCUS LORD I BORROWED THE GARGOYLES FROM WAS DEFEATED...
THE CREATION LORD'S POWER WAS BEYOND MY EXPECTATION.
I CAN'T CARE-LESSLY PROVOKE HIM.

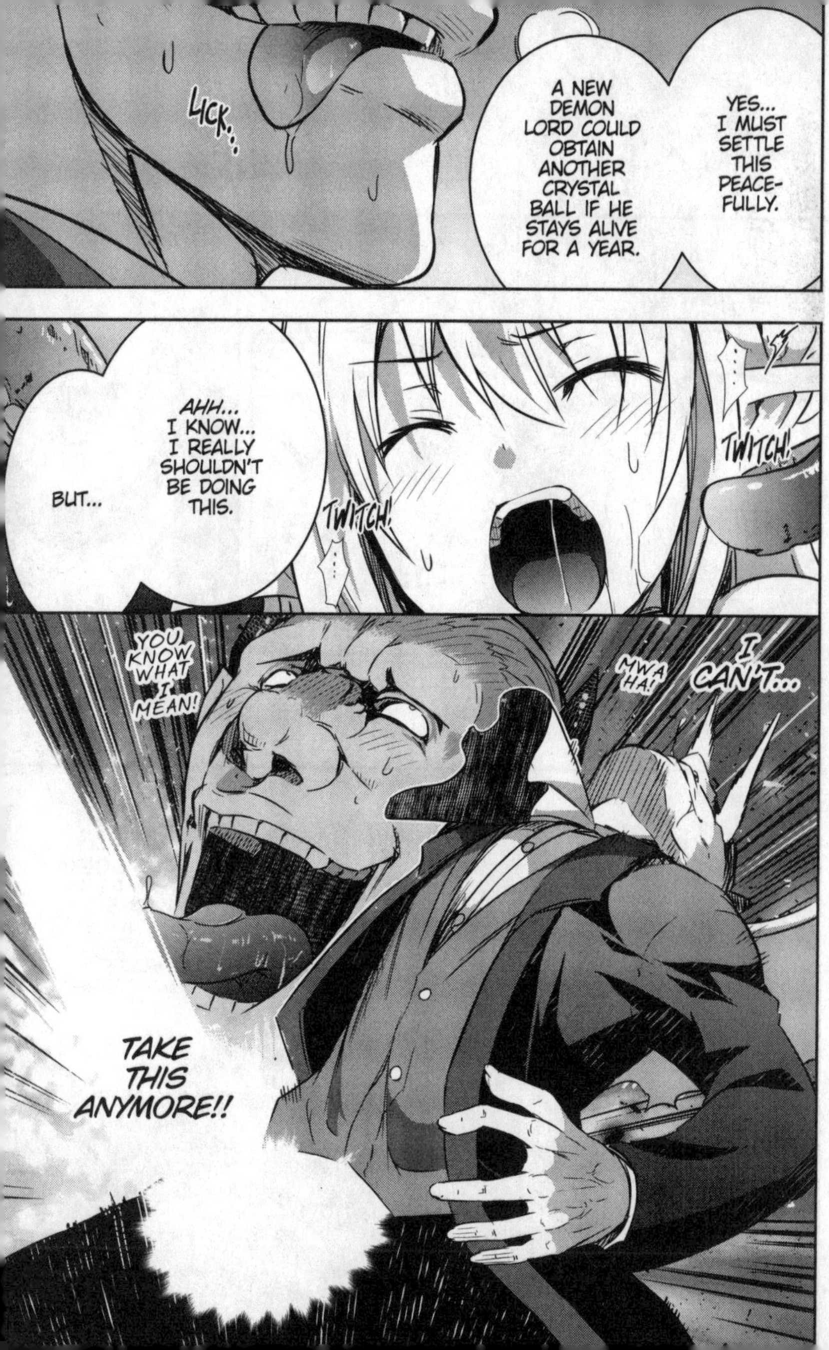
YES... I MUST SETTLE THIS PEACE-FULLY.
A NEW DEMON LORD COULD OBTAIN ANOTHER CRYSTAL BALL IF HE STAYS ALIVE FOR A YEAR.
LICK...
TWITCH!
TWITCH!
AHH... I KNOW... I REALLY SHOULDN'T BE DOING THIS.
BUT...
I CAN'T...
MWA HA!
YOU KNOW WHAT I MEAN!
TAKE THIS ANYMORE!!

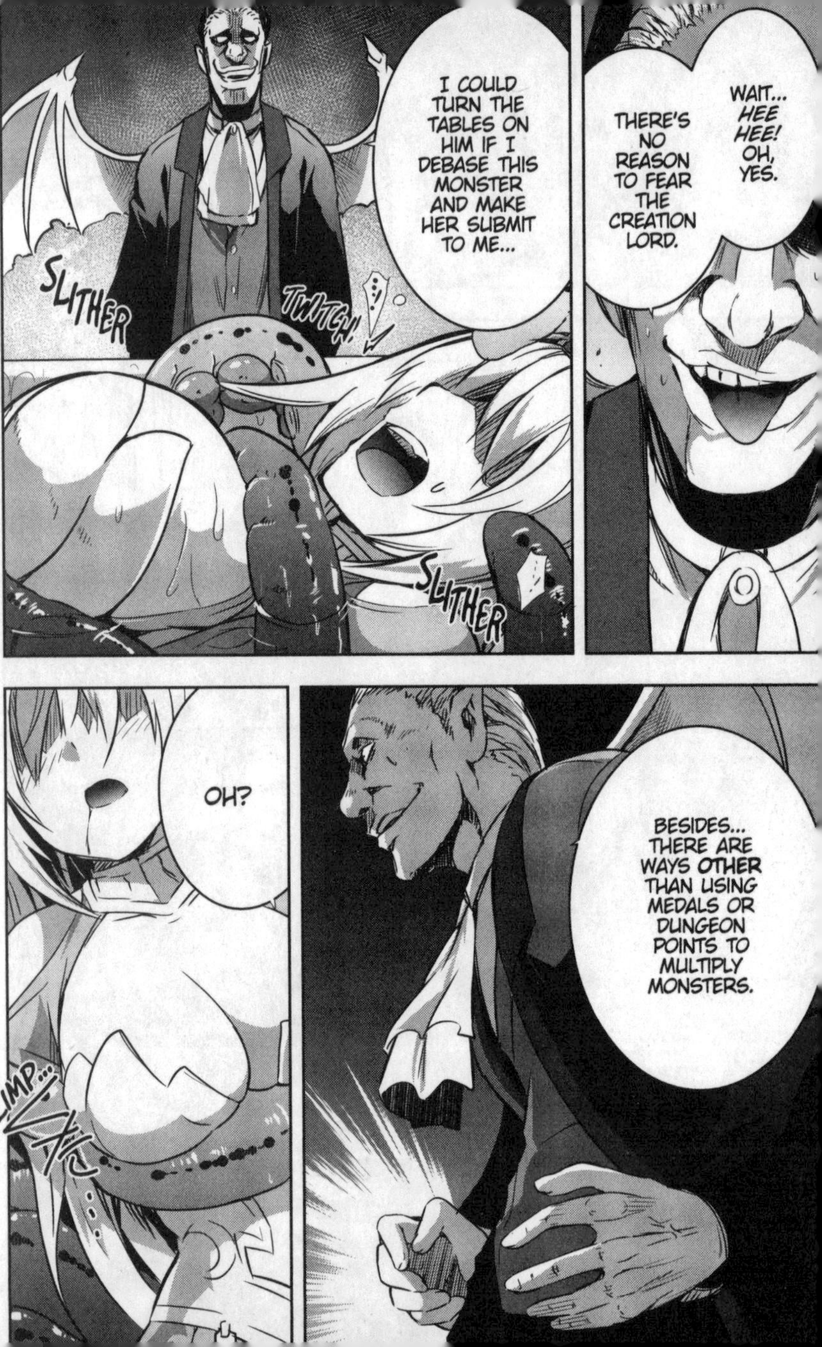
WAIT... HEE HEE! OH, YES.
THERE'S NO REASON TO FEAR THE CREATION LORD.
I COULD TURN THE TABLES ON HIM IF I DEBASE THIS MONSTER AND MAKE HER SUBMIT TO ME...
TWITCH!
SLITHER
SLITHER
BESIDES... THERE ARE WAYS OTHER THAN USING MEDALS OR DUNGEON POINTS TO MULTIPLY MONSTERS.
OH?
LIMP...

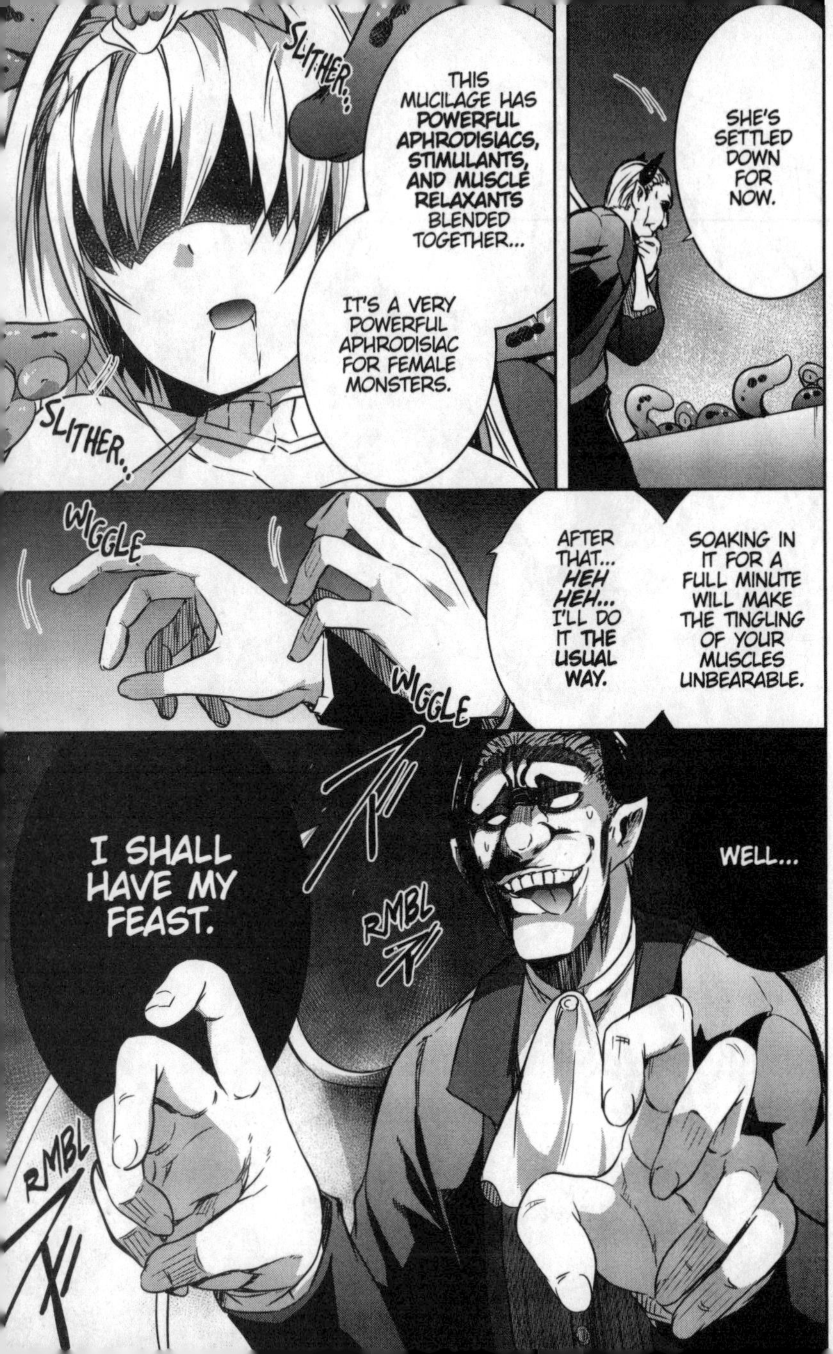
SHE'S SETTLED DOWN FOR NOW.
SLITHER...
THIS MUCILAGE HAS POWERFUL APHRODISIACS, STIMULANTS, AND MUSCLE RELAXANTS BLENDED TOGETHER...
IT'S A VERY POWERFUL APHRODISIAC FOR FEMALE MONSTERS.
SLITHER...
SOAKING IN IT FOR A FULL MINUTE WILL MAKE THE TINGLING OF YOUR MUSCLES UNBEARABLE.
AFTER THAT... HEH HEH... I'LL DO IT THE USUAL WAY.
WIGGLE
WIGGLE
WELL...
RMBL
I SHALL HAVE MY FEAST.
RMBL

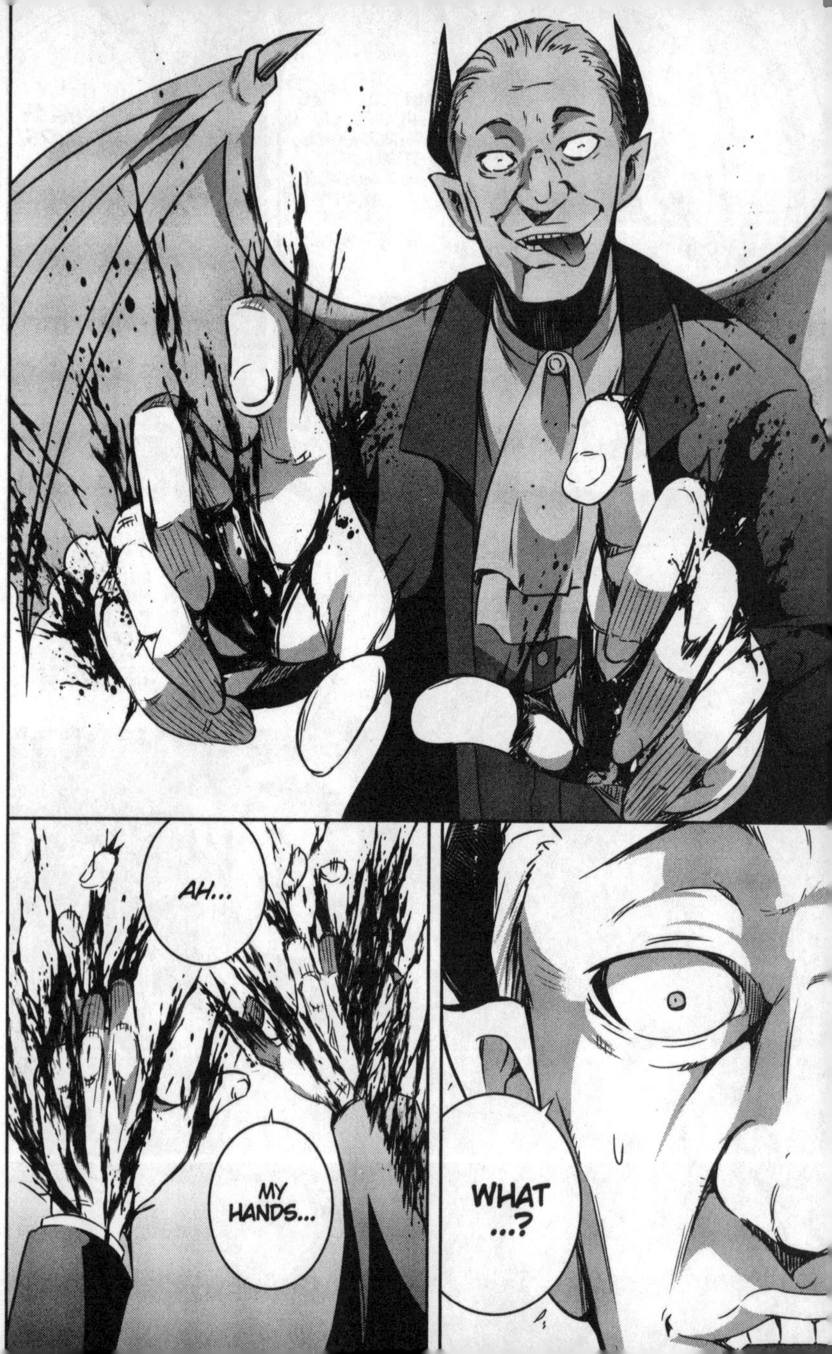
WHAT ...?
AH...
MY HANDS...

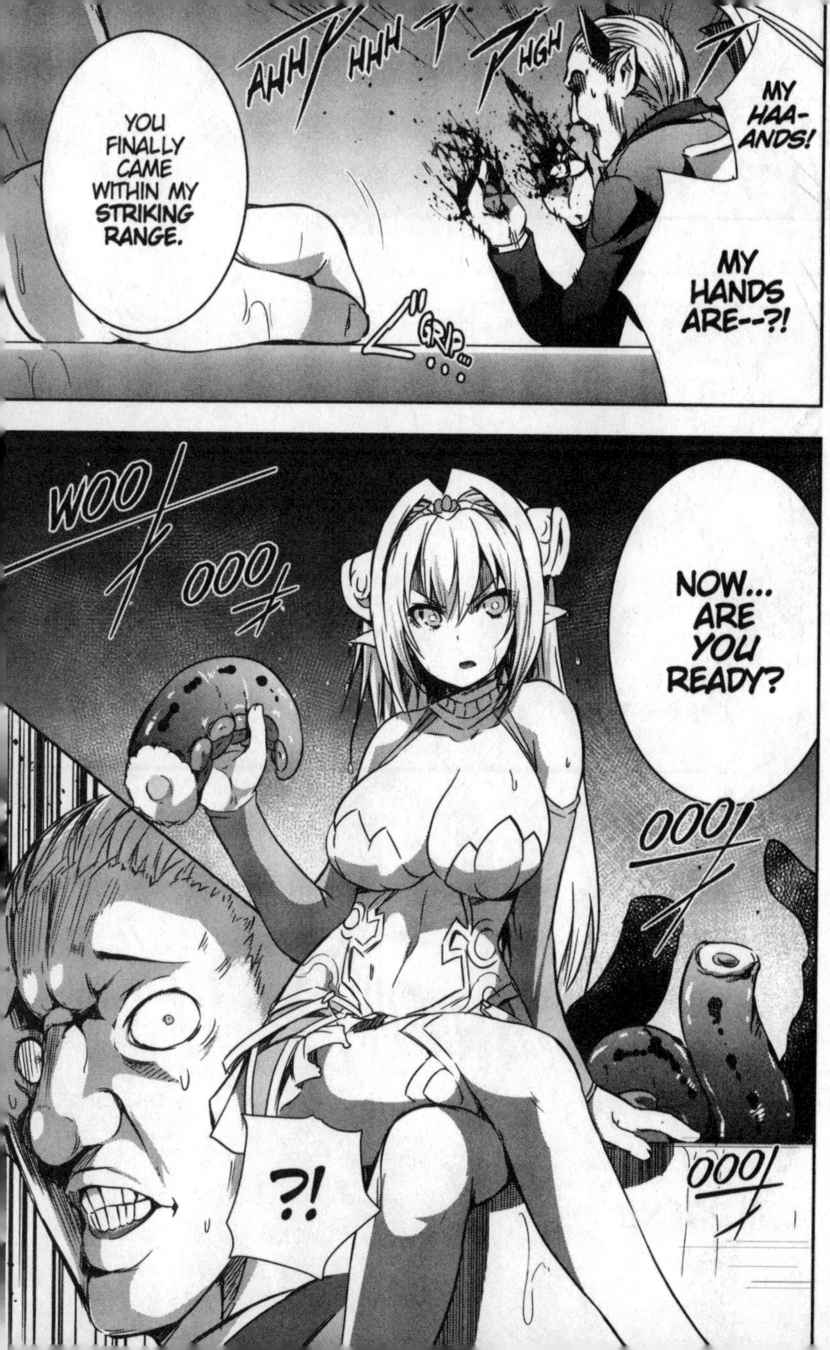
MY HAA-ANDS!
AHHHHHHGH
MY HANDS ARE--?!
YOU FINALLY CAME WITHIN MY STRIKING RANGE.
GRIP...
NOW... ARE YOU READY?
WOOOOO
OOO
OOO
?!

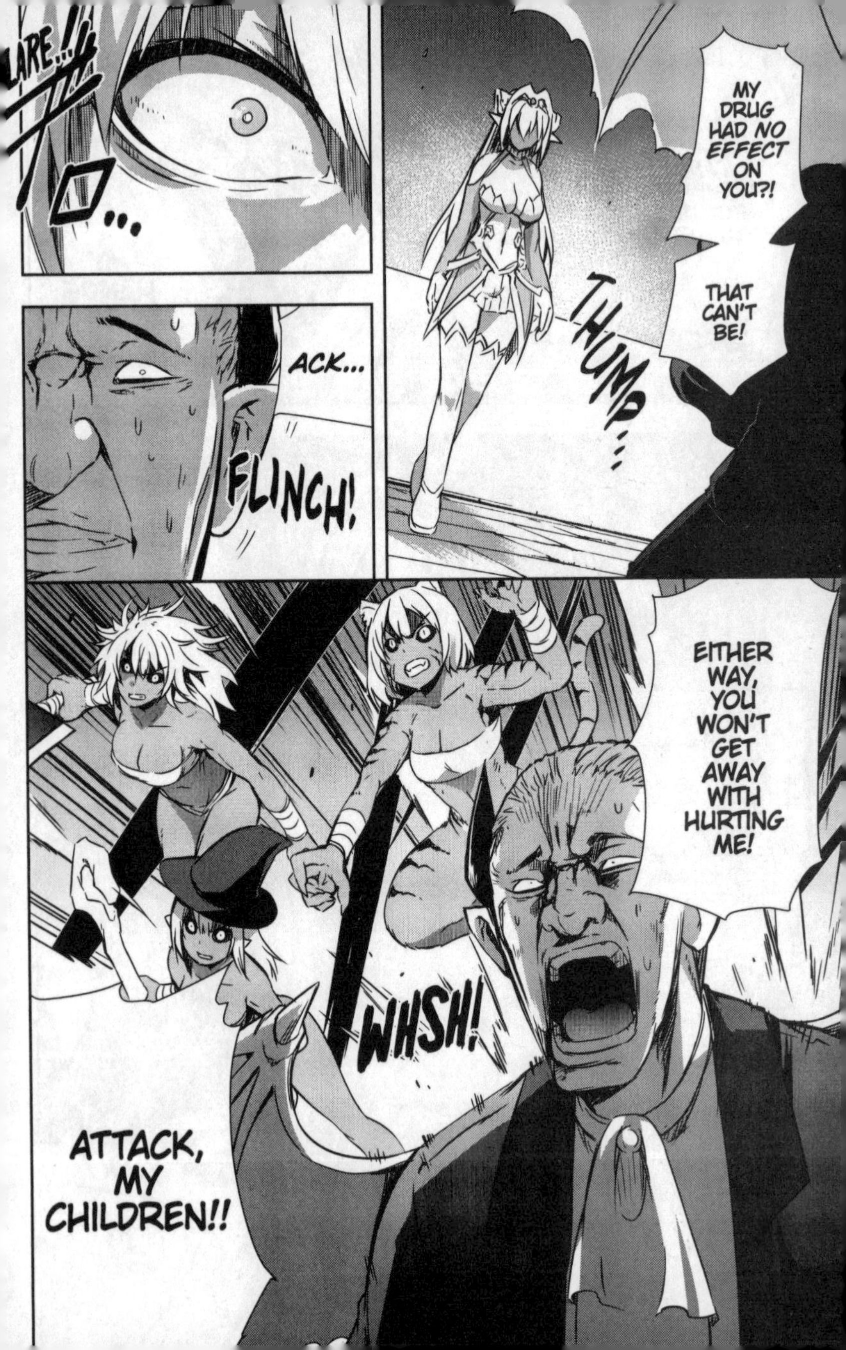
MY DRUG HAD NO EFFECT ON YOU?!
THAT CAN'T BE!
THUMP...
LARE...!!
ACK...
FLINCH!
EITHER WAY, YOU WON'T GET AWAY WITH HURTING ME!
WHSH!
ATTACK, MY CHILDREN!!

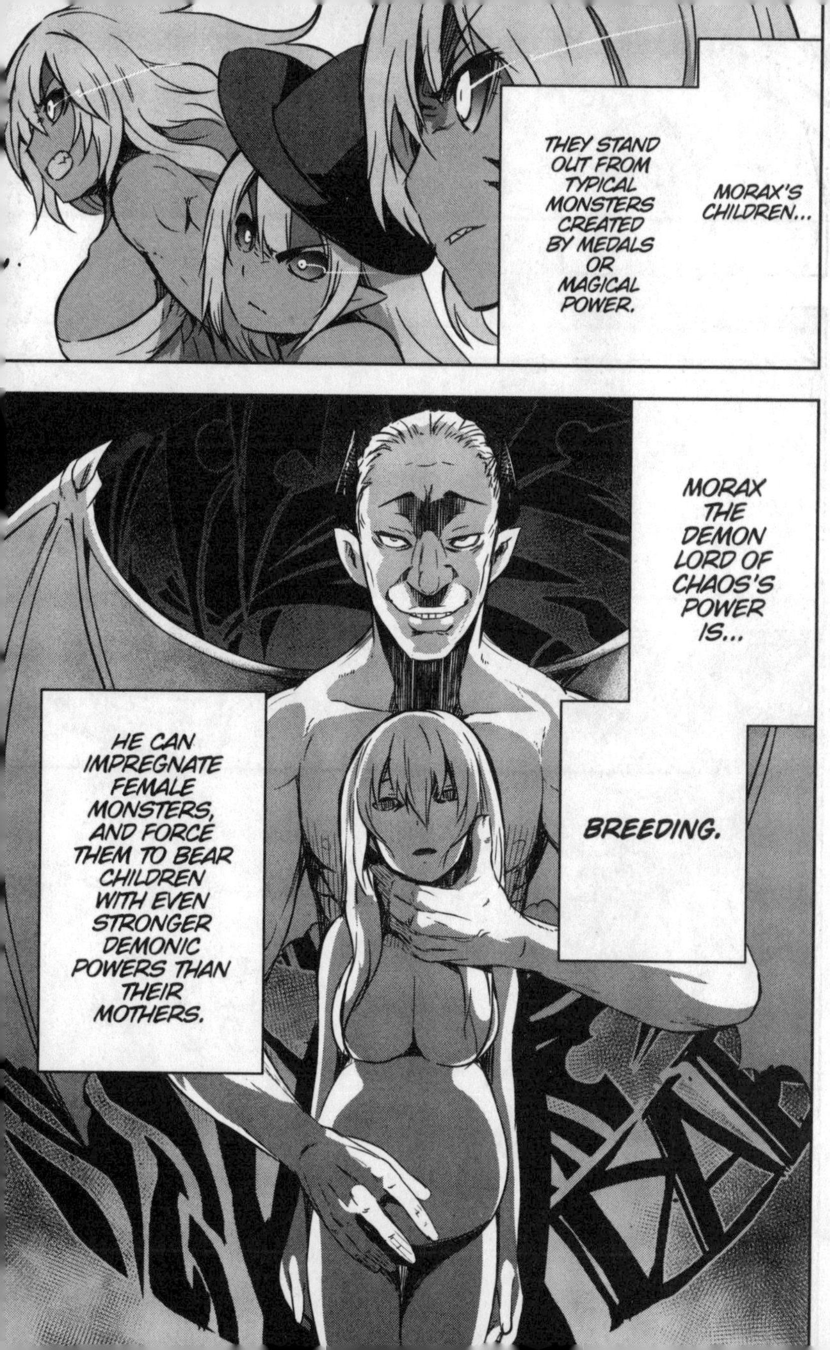
MORAX'S CHILDREN...
THEY STAND OUT FROM TYPICAL MONSTERS CREATED BY MEDALS OR MAGICAL POWER.
MORAX THE DEMON LORD OF CHAOS'S POWER IS...
BREEDING.
HE CAN IMPREGNATE FEMALE MONSTERS, AND FORCE THEM TO BEAR CHILDREN WITH EVEN STRONGER DEMONIC POWERS THAN THEIR MOTHERS.

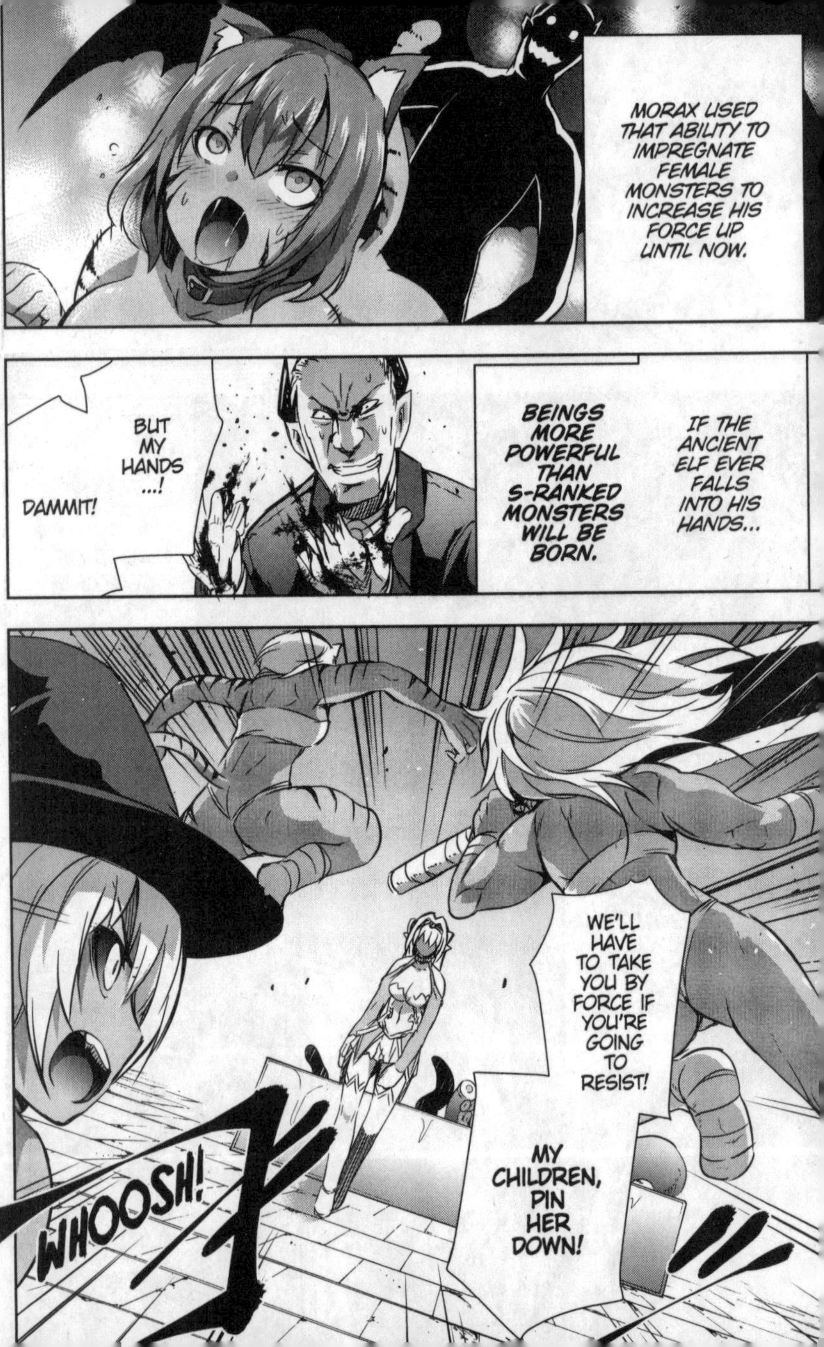
MORAX USED THAT ABILITY TO IMPREGNATE FEMALE MONSTERS TO INCREASE HIS FORCE UP UNTIL NOW.
IF THE ANCIENT ELF EVER FALLS INTO HIS HANDS...
BEINGS MORE POWERFUL THAN S-RANKED MONSTERS WILL BE BORN.
BUT MY HANDS ...!
DAMMIT!
WE'LL HAVE TO TAKE YOU BY FORCE IF YOU'RE GOING TO RESIST!
MY CHILDREN, PIN HER DOWN!
WHOOSH!

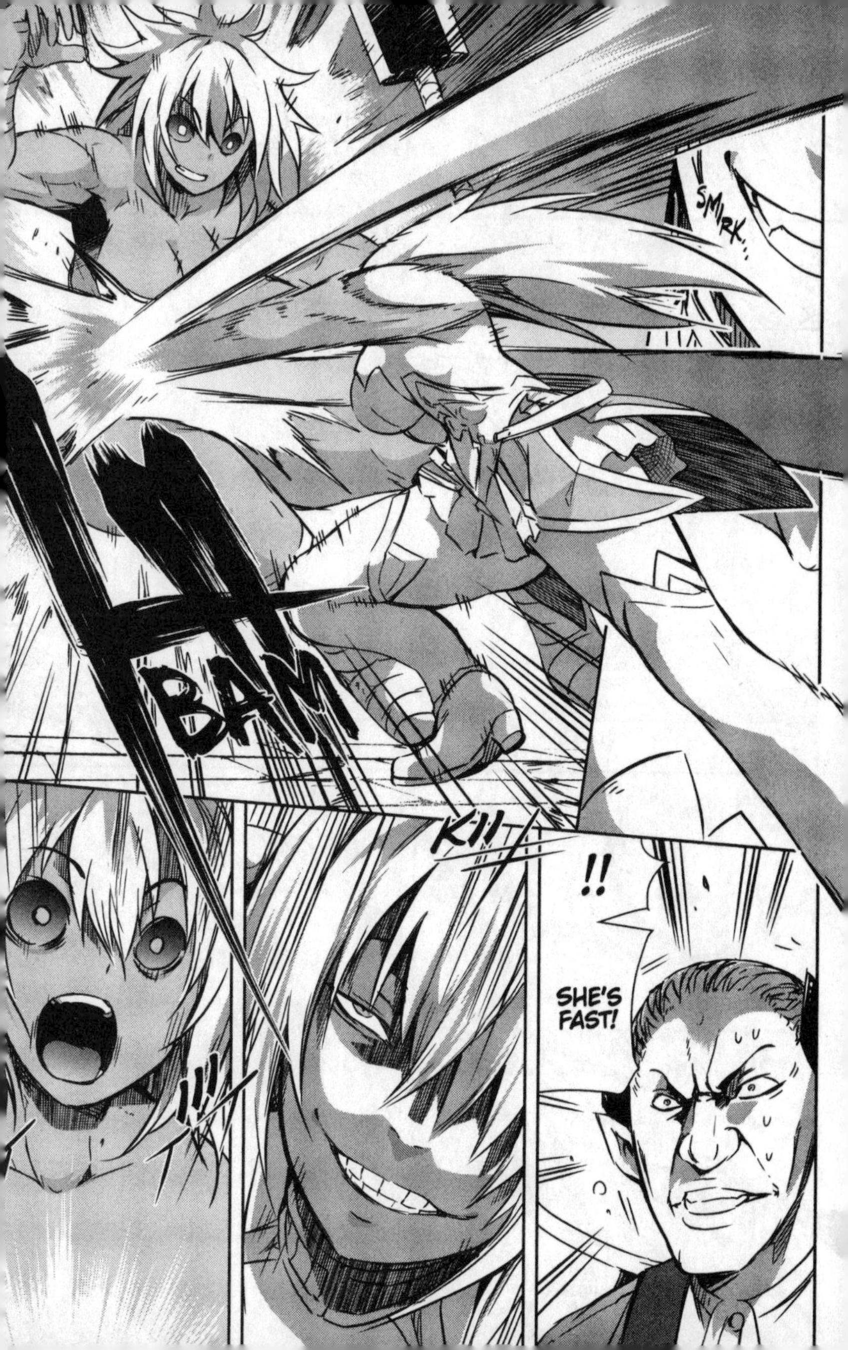
SMIRK...
BAM
KIII
!!
!!!
SHE'S FAST!

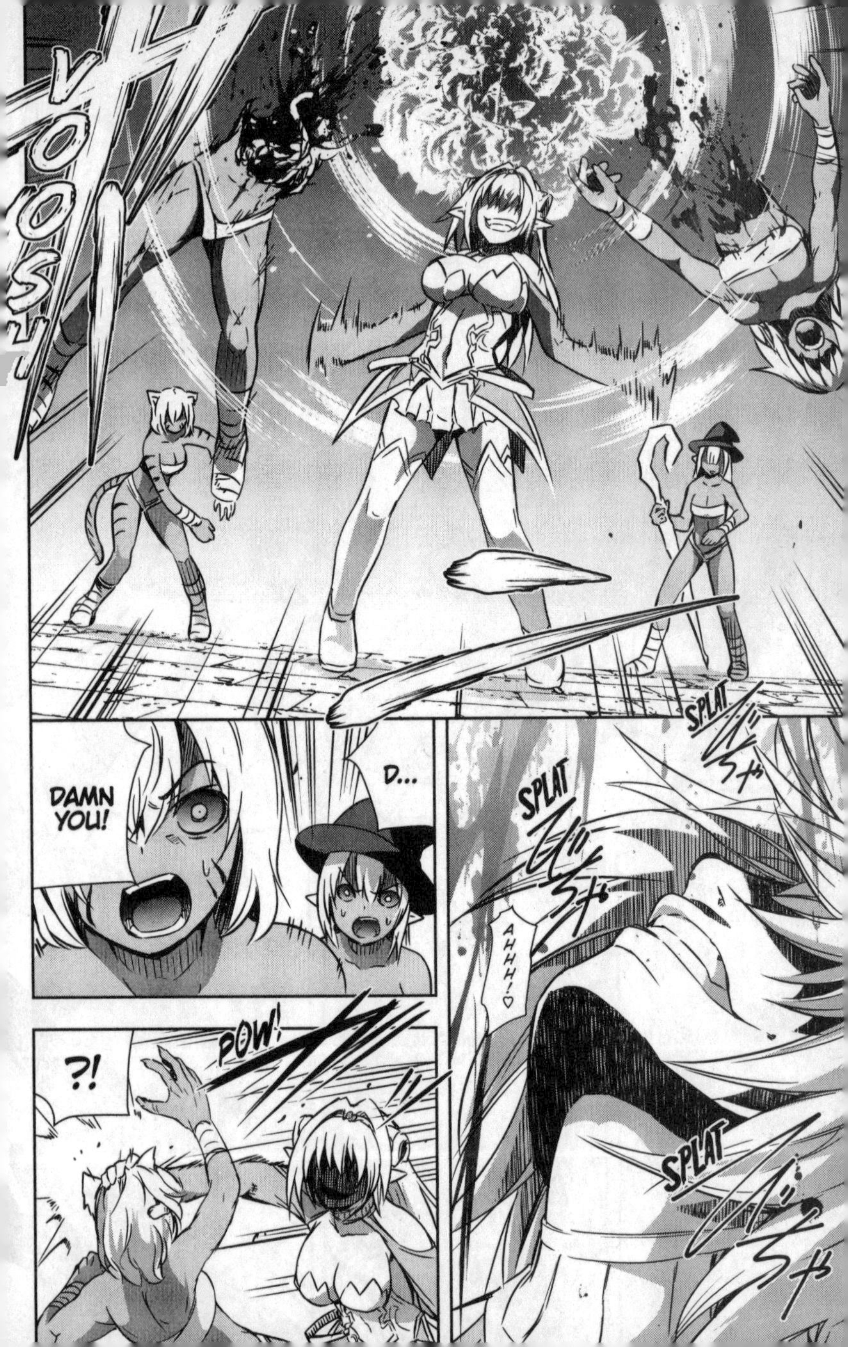

VOOOSH
SPLAT
SPLAT
AHHHH!♡
SPLAT
D...
DAMN YOU!
POW!
?!

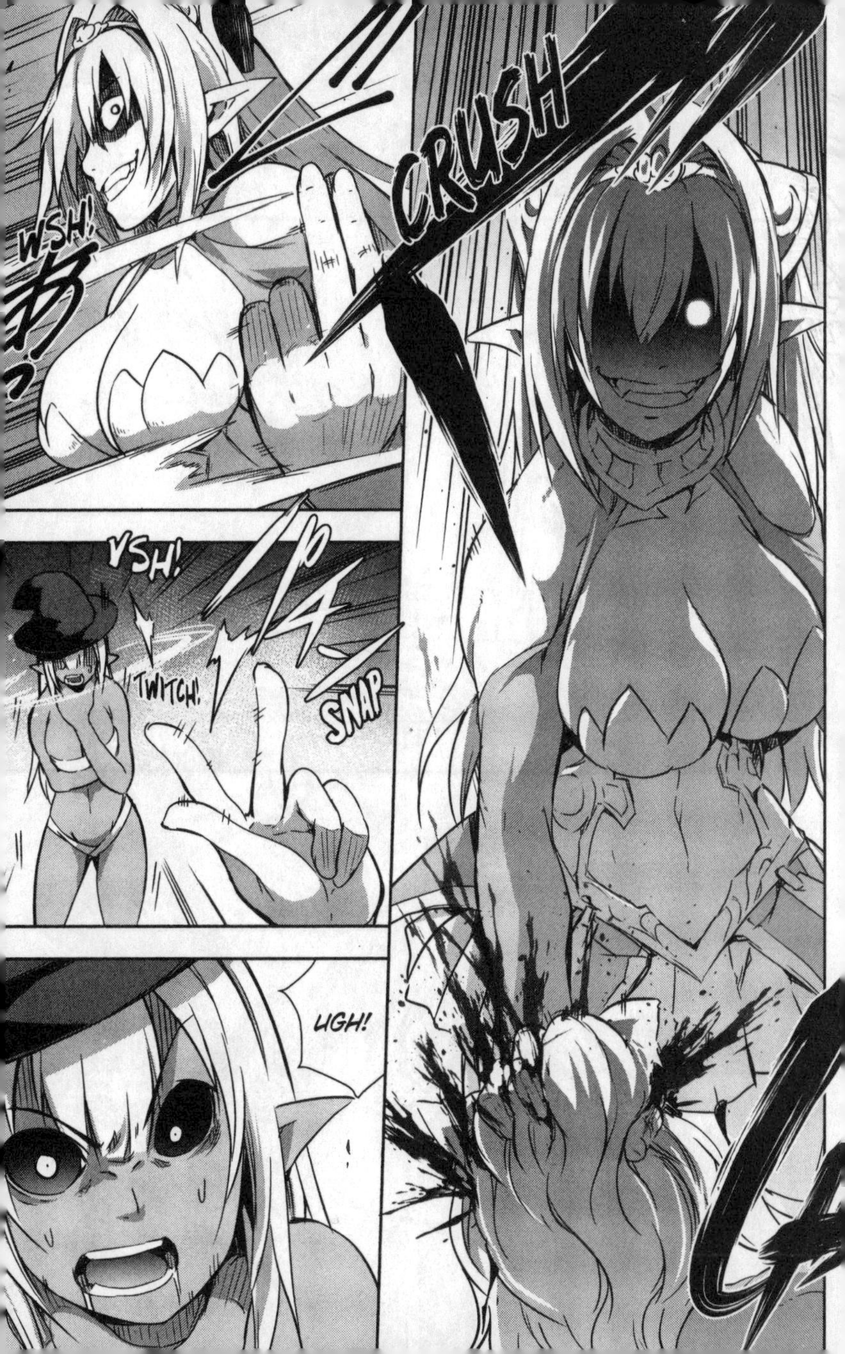
CRUSH
WSH!
VSH!
TWITCH!
SNAP
UGH!

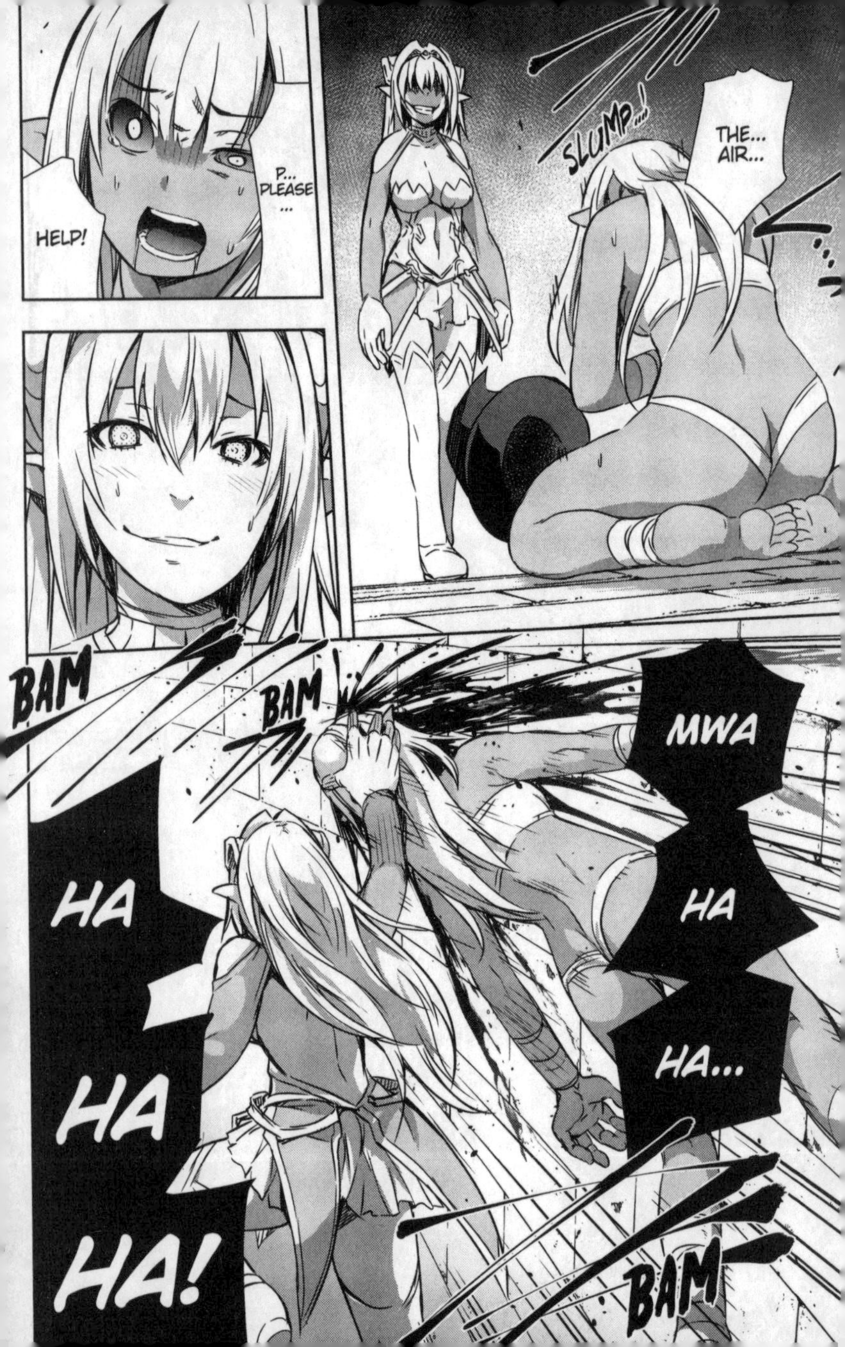
THE... AIR...
SLUMP..!
P... PLEASE ...
HELP!
MWA
HA
HA...
BAM
BAM
HA
HA
HA!
BAM

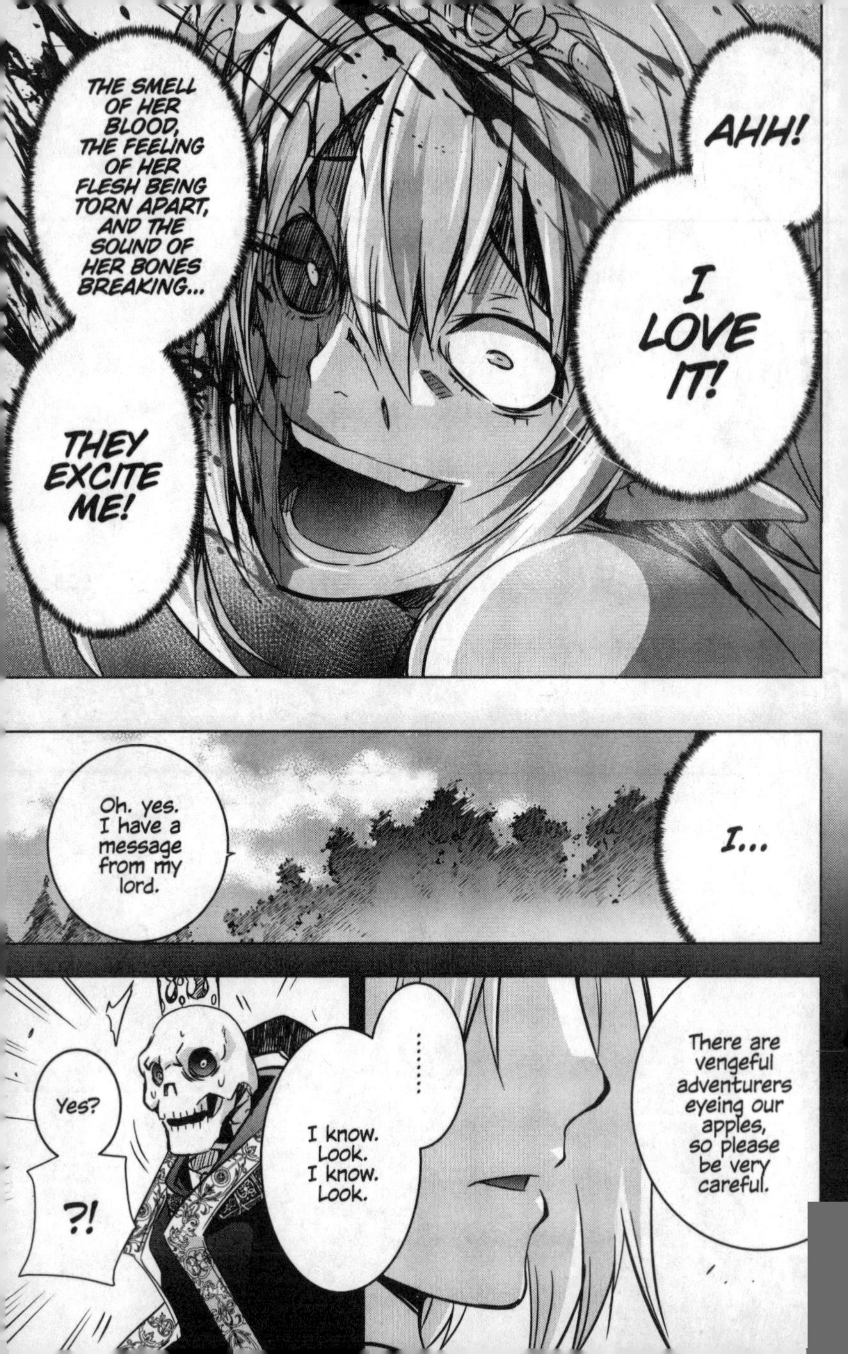
AHH!
I LOVE IT!
THE SMELL OF HER BLOOD, THE FEELING OF HER FLESH BEING TORN APART, AND THE SOUND OF HER BONES BREAKING...
THEY EXCITE ME!
I...
Oh. yes. I have a message from my lord.
There are vengeful adventurers eyeing our apples, so please be very careful.
......
I know. Look. I know. Look.
Yes?
?!

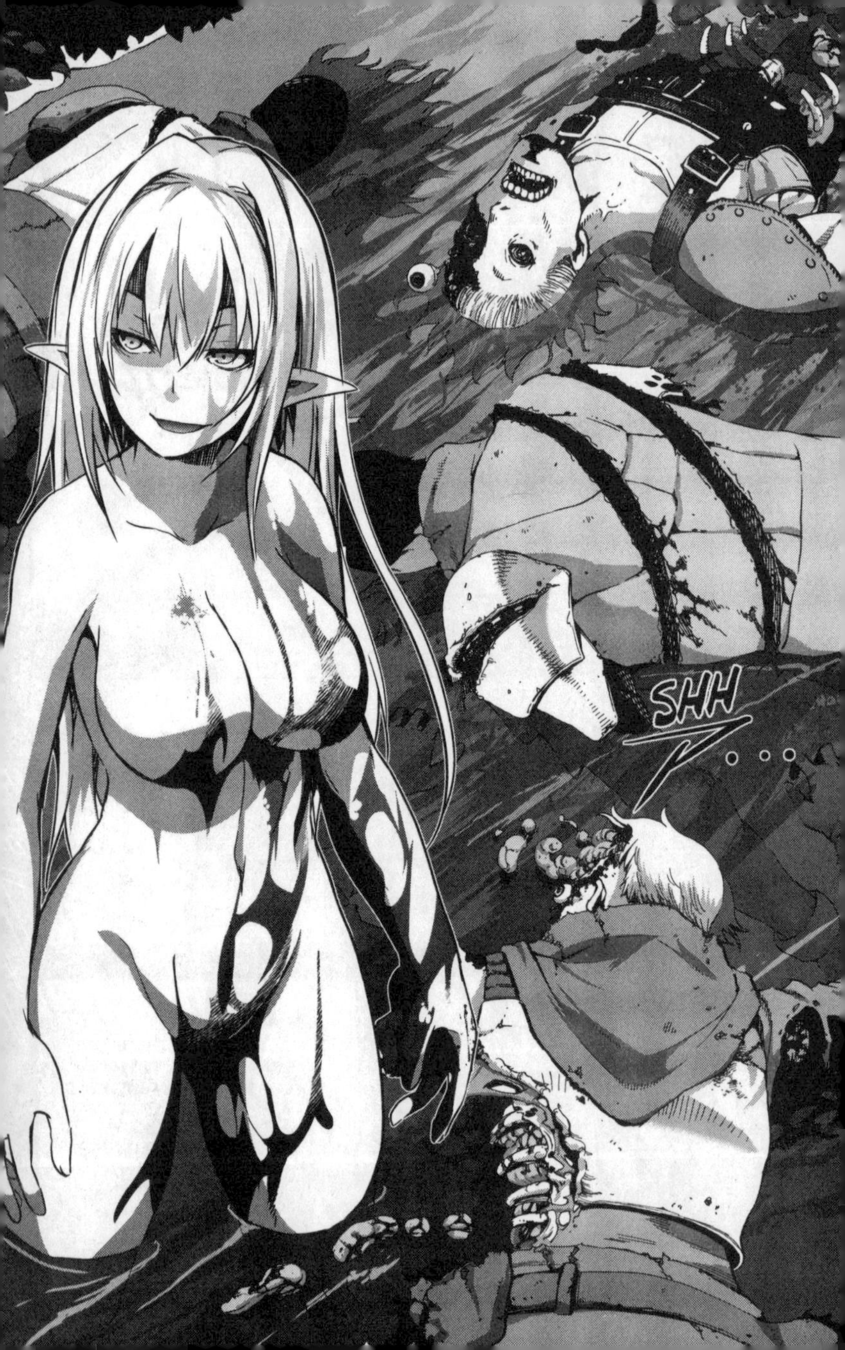
SHH...

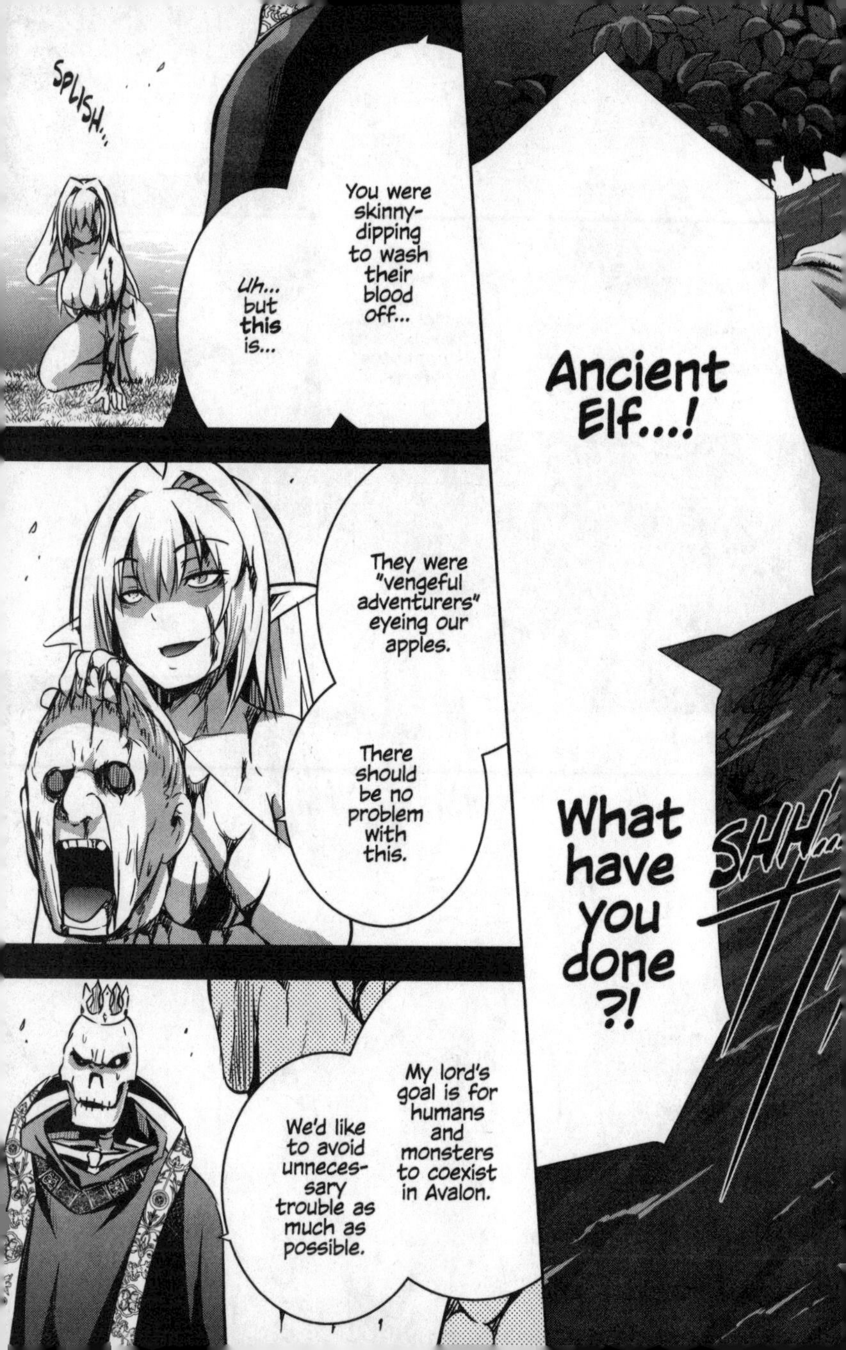

Ancient Elf...!
What have you done ?!
SHH...
You were skinny-dipping to wash their blood off...
Uh... but this is...
SPLISH...
They were "vengeful adventurers" eyeing our apples.
There should be no problem with this.
My lord's goal is for humans and monsters to coexist in Avalon.
We'd like to avoid unneces-sary trouble as much as possible.

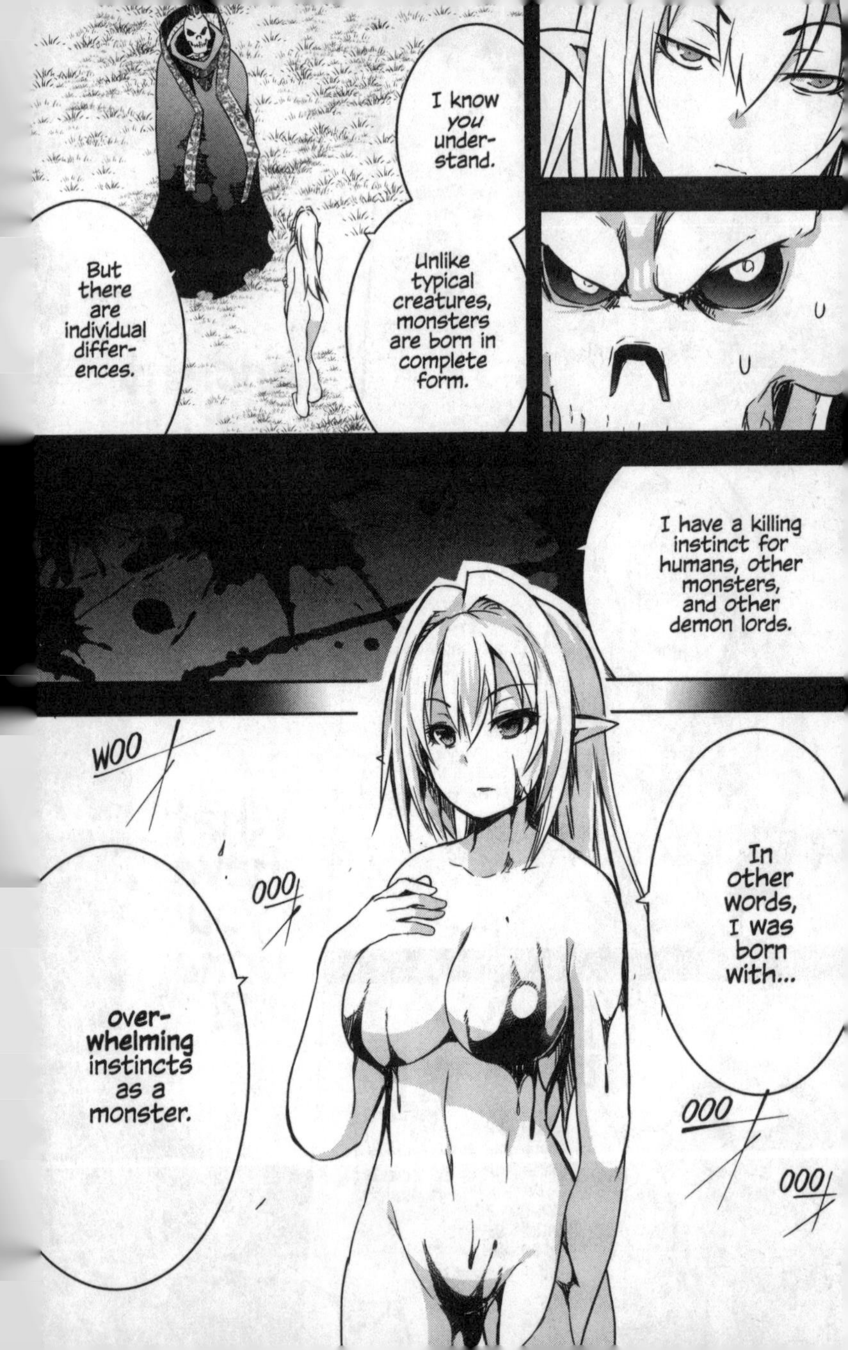
I know *you* under-stand.
Unlike typical creatures, monsters are born in complete form.
But there are individual differ-ences.
I have a killing instinct for humans, other monsters, and other demon lords.
In other words, I was born with...
OOO
OOO
WOO
OOO
over-whelming instincts as a monster.

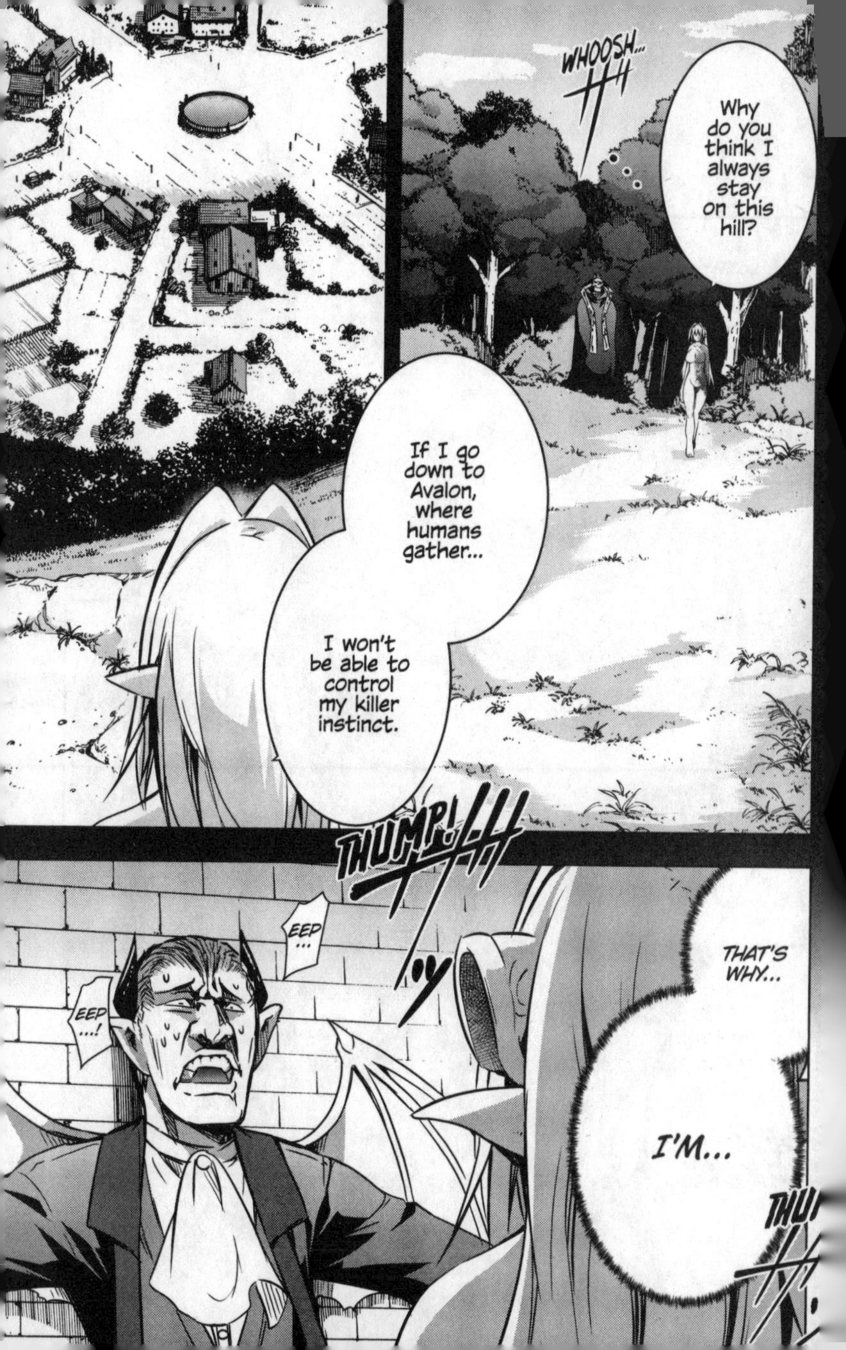
WHOOSH...
Why do you think I always stay on this hill?
If I go down to Avalon, where humans gather...
I won't be able to control my killer instinct.
THUMP!
THAT'S WHY...
I'M...
EEP...
EEP...!

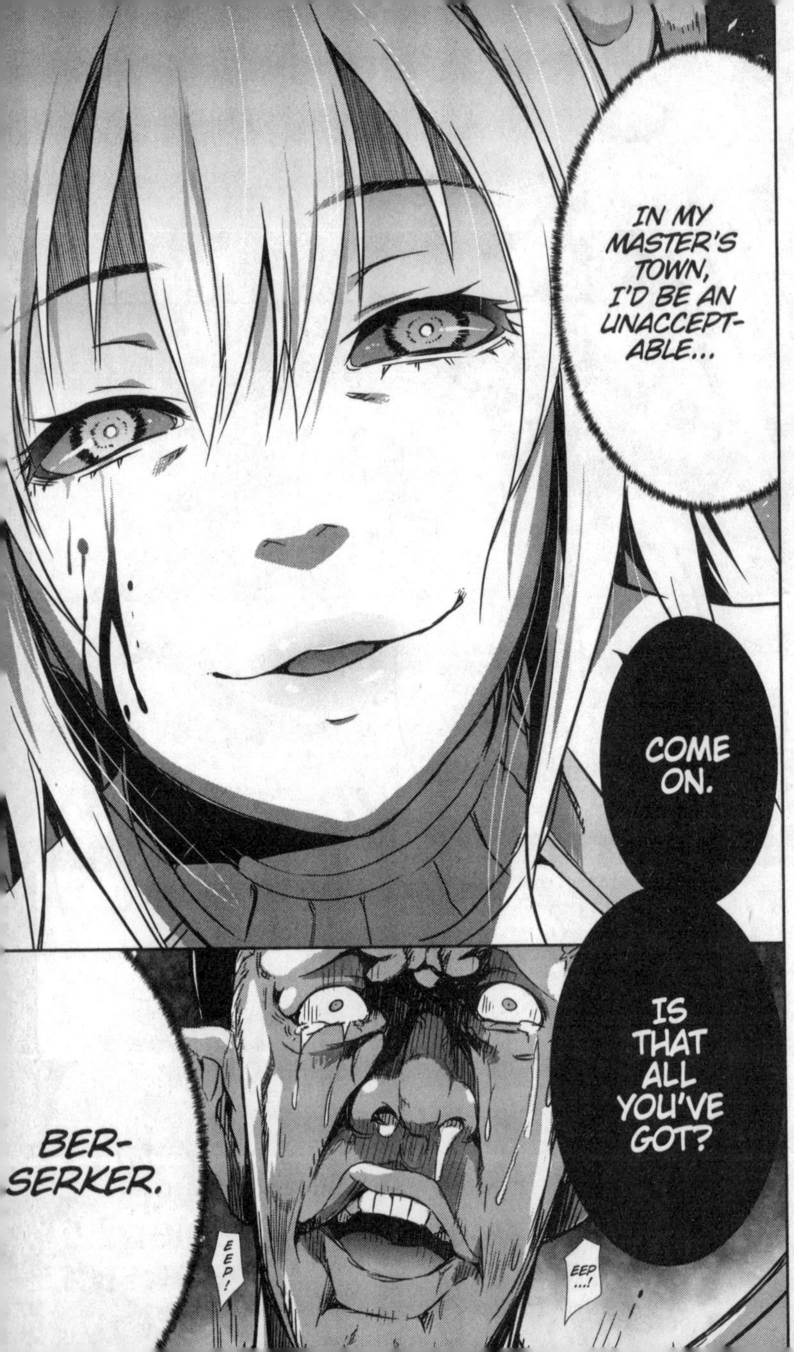
IN MY MASTER'S TOWN, I'D BE AN UNACCEPT-ABLE...
COME ON.
IS THAT ALL YOU'VE GOT?
BER-SERKER.
EEP...!
EEP!

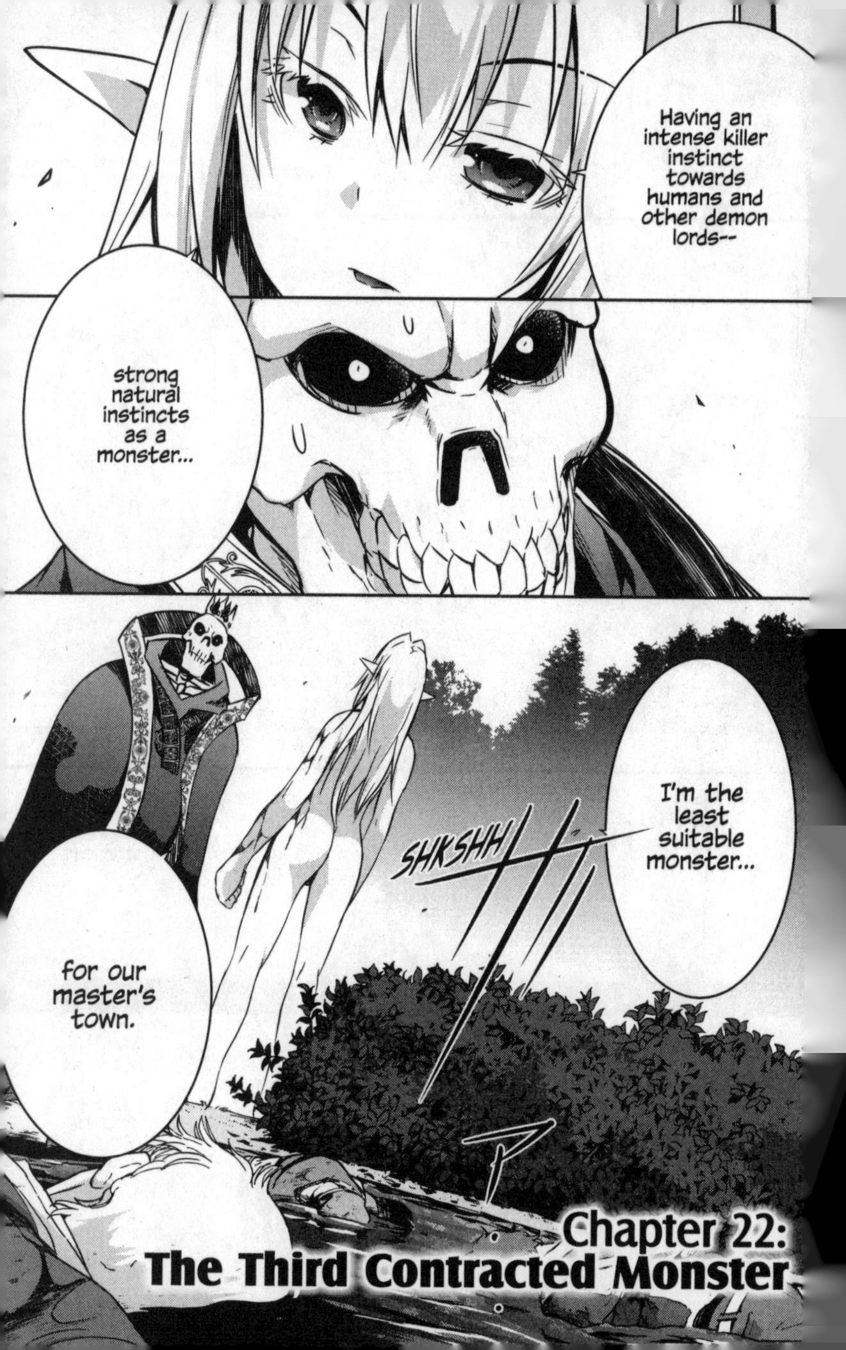
Having an intense killer instinct towards humans and other demon lords--
strong natural instincts as a monster...
I'm the least suitable monster...
SHKSHH
for our master's town.
Chapter 22: The Third Contracted Monster

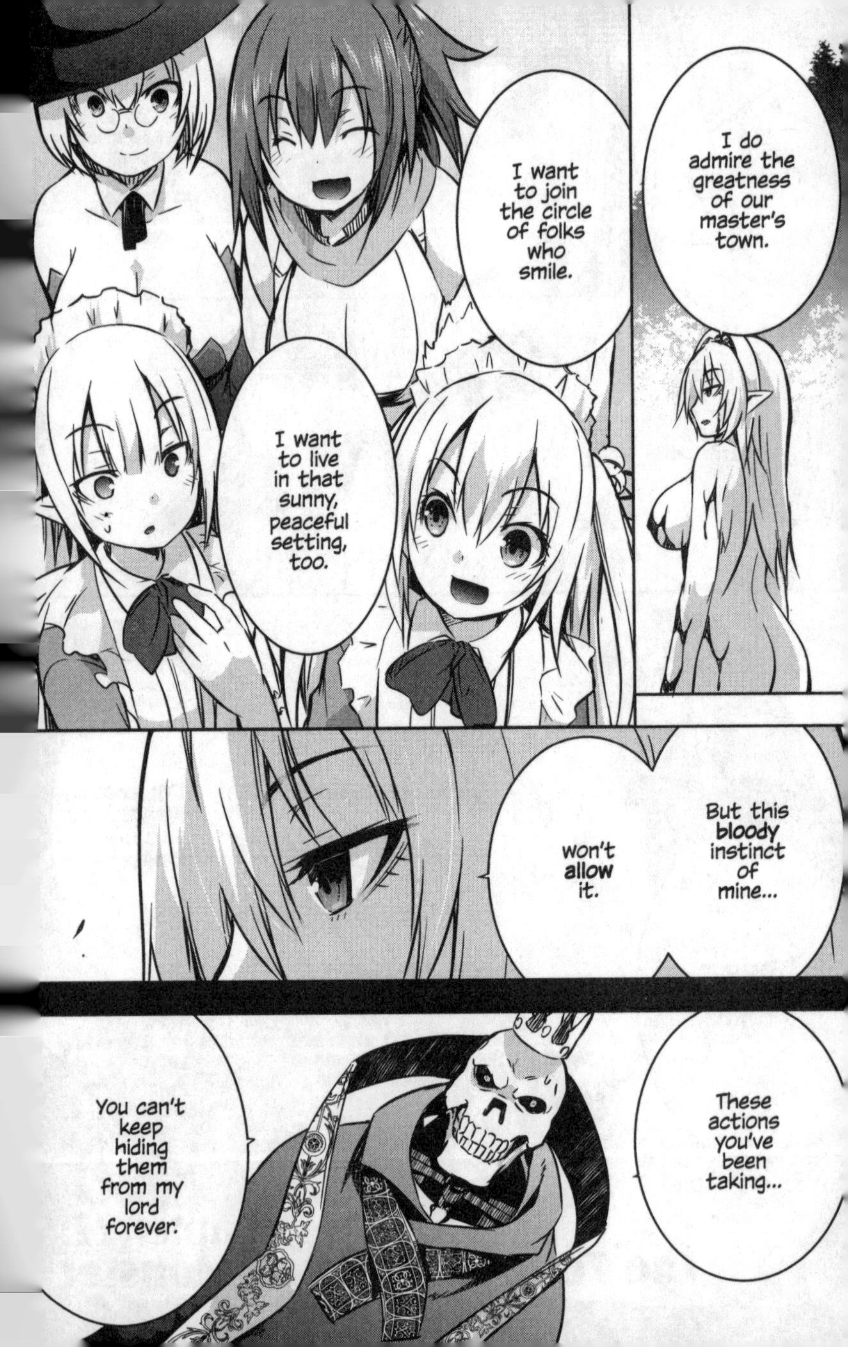
I do admire the greatness of our master's town.
I want to join the circle of folks who smile.
I want to live in that sunny, peaceful setting, too.
But this bloody instinct of mine...
won't allow it.
These actions you've been taking...
You can't keep hiding them from my lord forever.

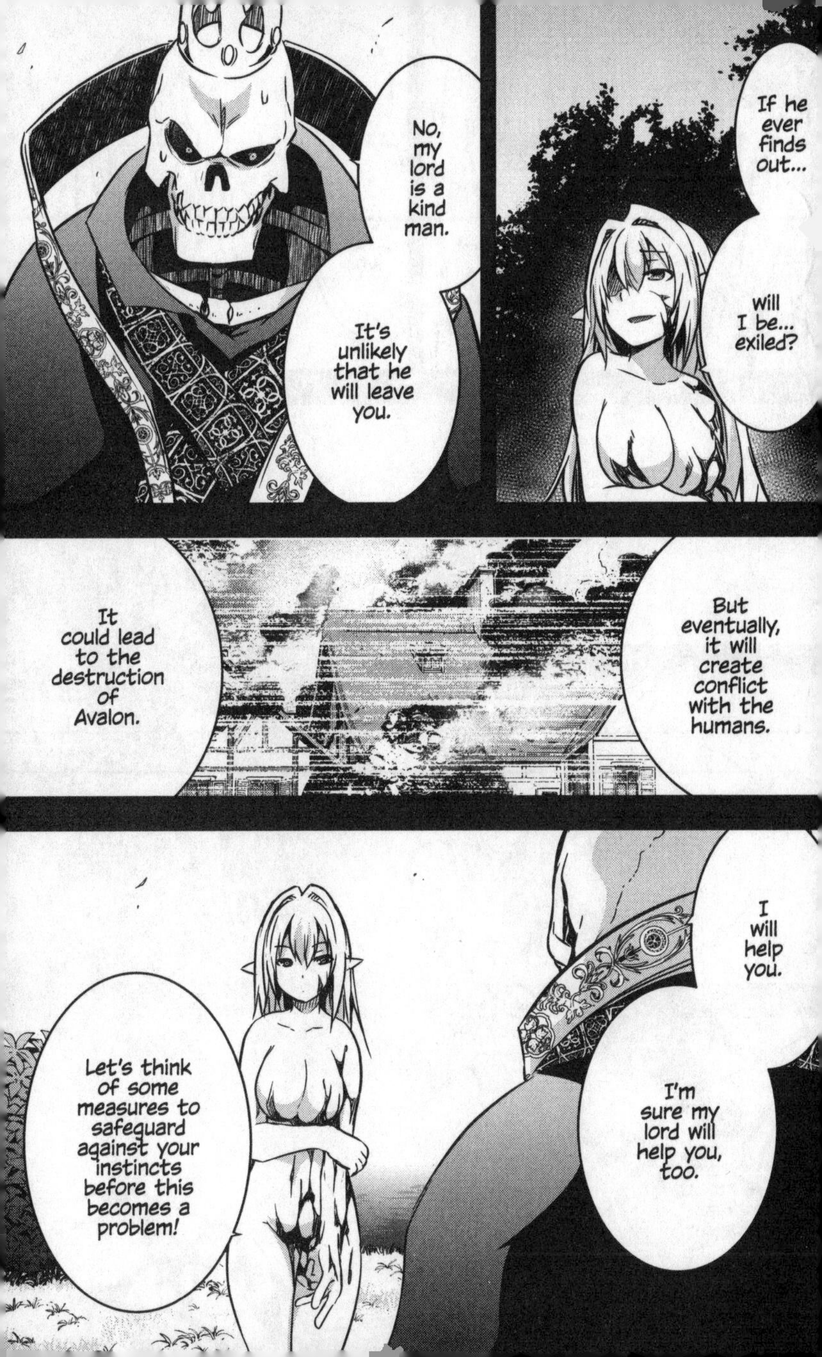
If he ever finds out...
will I be... exiled?
No, my lord is a kind man.
It's unlikely that he will leave you.
But eventually, it will create conflict with the humans.
It could lead to the destruction of Avalon.
I will help you.
I'm sure my lord will help you, too.
Let's think of some measures to safeguard against your instincts before this becomes a problem!

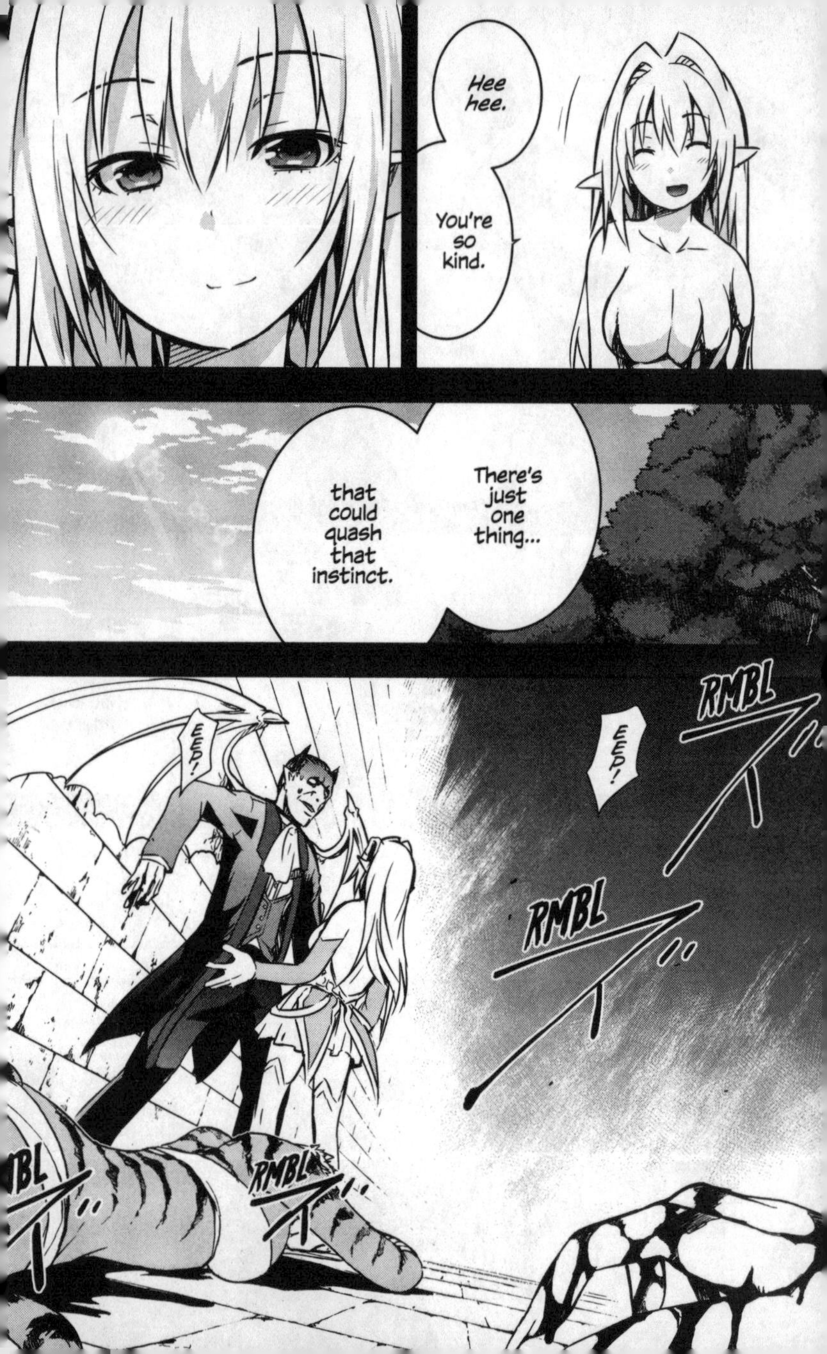
Hee hee.
You're so kind.
There's just one thing...
that could quash that instinct.
RMBL
EEP!
EEP!
RMBL
RMBL
MBL

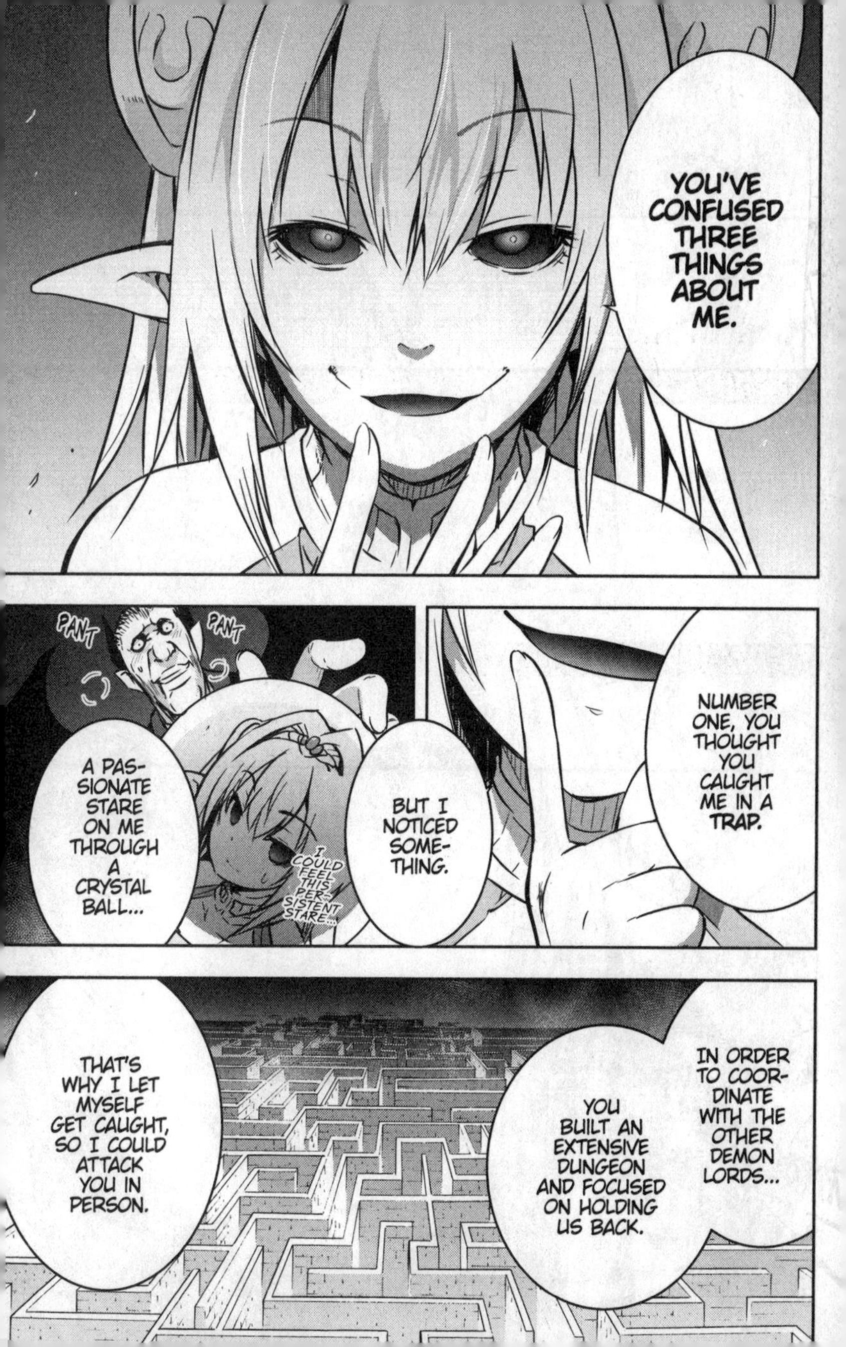
YOU'VE CONFUSED THREE THINGS ABOUT ME.
NUMBER ONE, YOU THOUGHT YOU CAUGHT ME IN A TRAP.
PANT PANT
BUT I NOTICED SOMETHING.
I COULD FEEL THIS PERSISTENT STARE...
A PASSIONATE STARE ON ME THROUGH A CRYSTAL BALL...
IN ORDER TO COORDINATE WITH THE OTHER DEMON LORDS...
YOU BUILT AN EXTENSIVE DUNGEON AND FOCUSED ON HOLDING US BACK.
THAT'S WHY I LET MYSELF GET CAUGHT, SO I COULD ATTACK YOU IN PERSON.

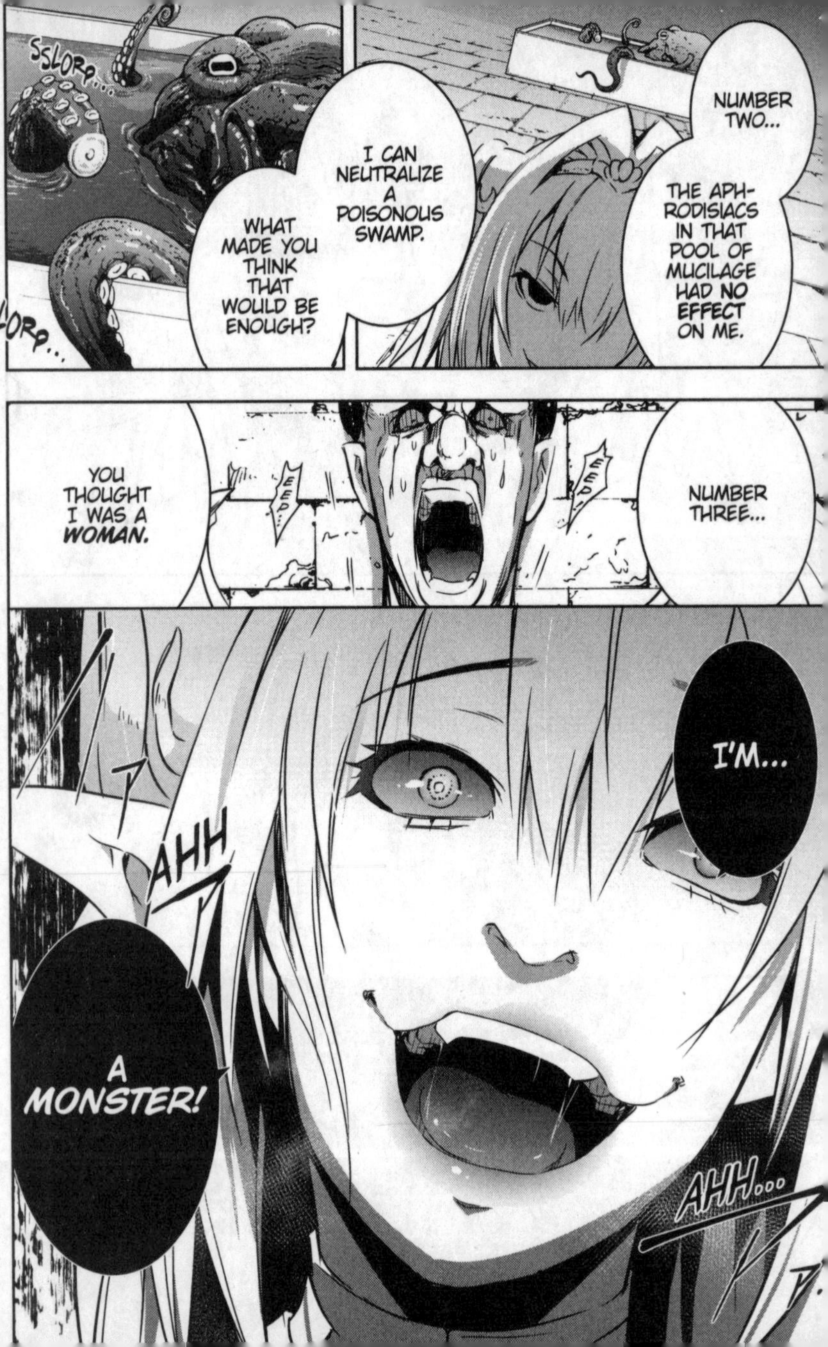
NUMBER TWO...
THE APH-RODISIACS IN THAT POOL OF MUCILAGE HAD NO EFFECT ON ME.
I CAN NEUTRALIZE A POISONOUS SWAMP.
WHAT MADE YOU THINK THAT WOULD BE ENOUGH?
SSLORP...
SLORP...
NUMBER THREE...
EEP...
EEP...
YOU THOUGHT I WAS A *WOMAN.*
I'M...
AHH...
AHH
A *MONSTER!*

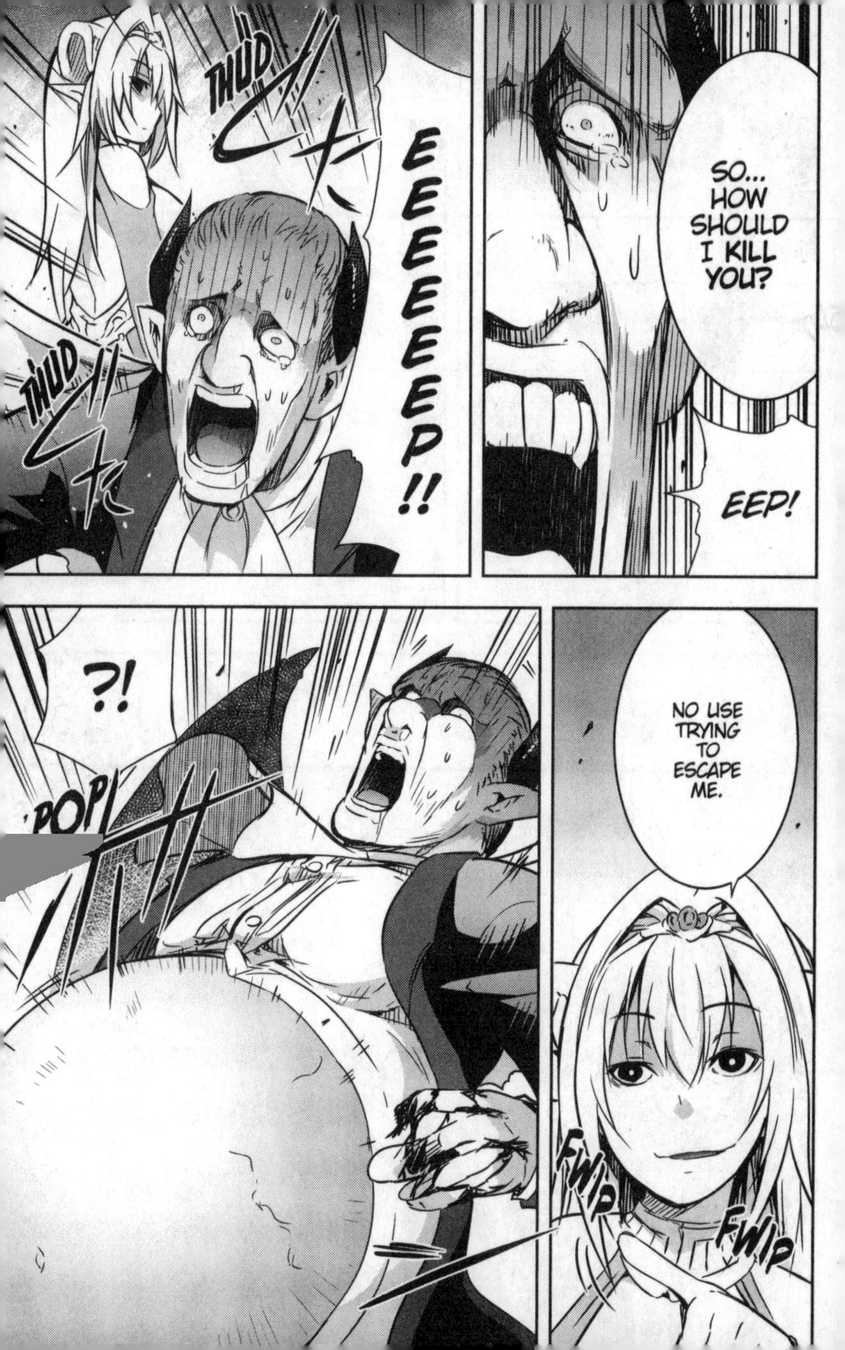
SO... HOW SHOULD I KILL YOU?
EEP!
THUD
EEEEEEEP!!
THUD
NO USE TRYING TO ESCAPE ME.
FWIP
FWIP
?!
POP

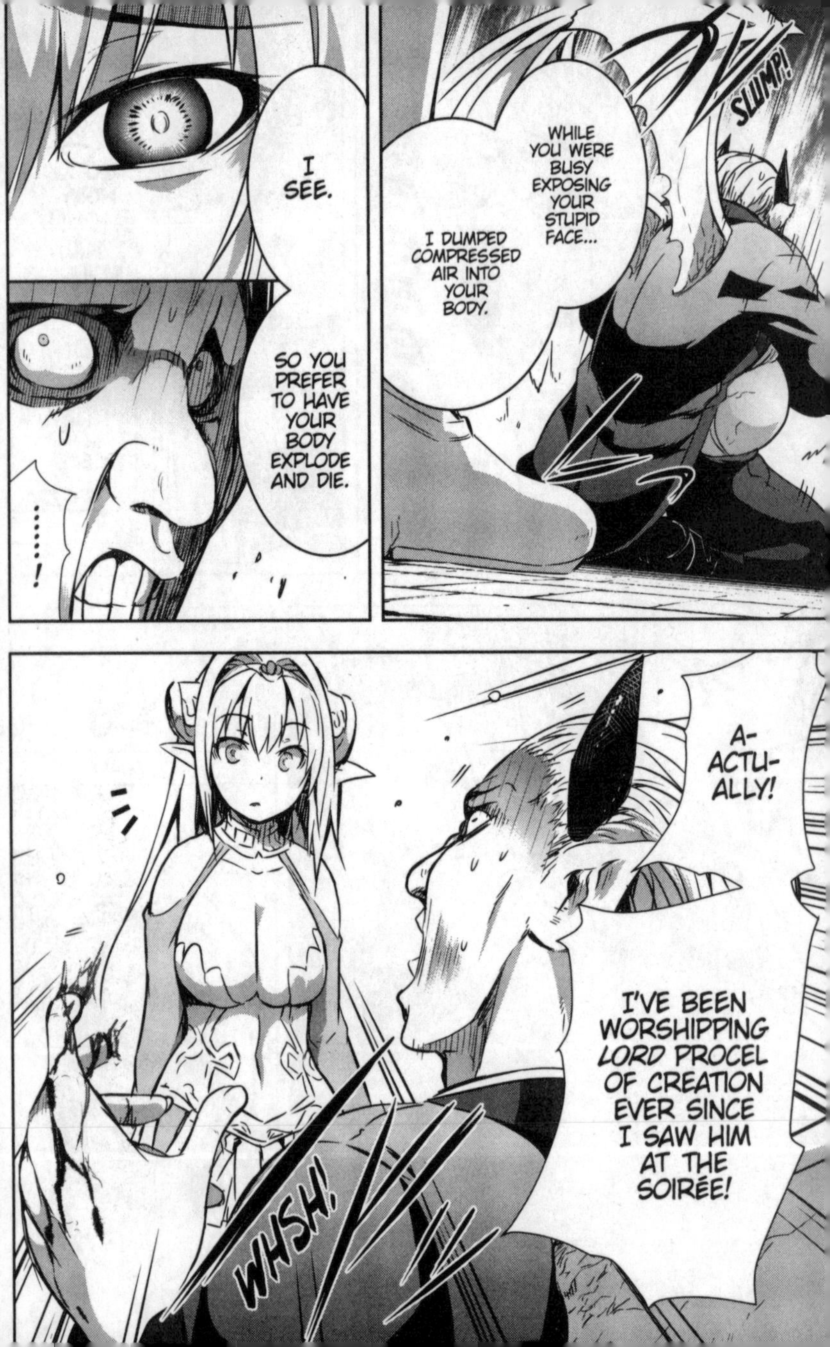
SLUMP!
WHILE YOU WERE BUSY EXPOSING YOUR STUPID FACE...
I DUMPED COMPRESSED AIR INTO YOUR BODY.
I SEE.
SO YOU PREFER TO HAVE YOUR BODY EXPLODE AND DIE.
......!
A- ACTU- ALLY!
I'VE BEEN WORSHIPPING *LORD* PROCEL OF CREATION EVER SINCE I SAW HIM AT THE SOIRÉE!
WHSH!

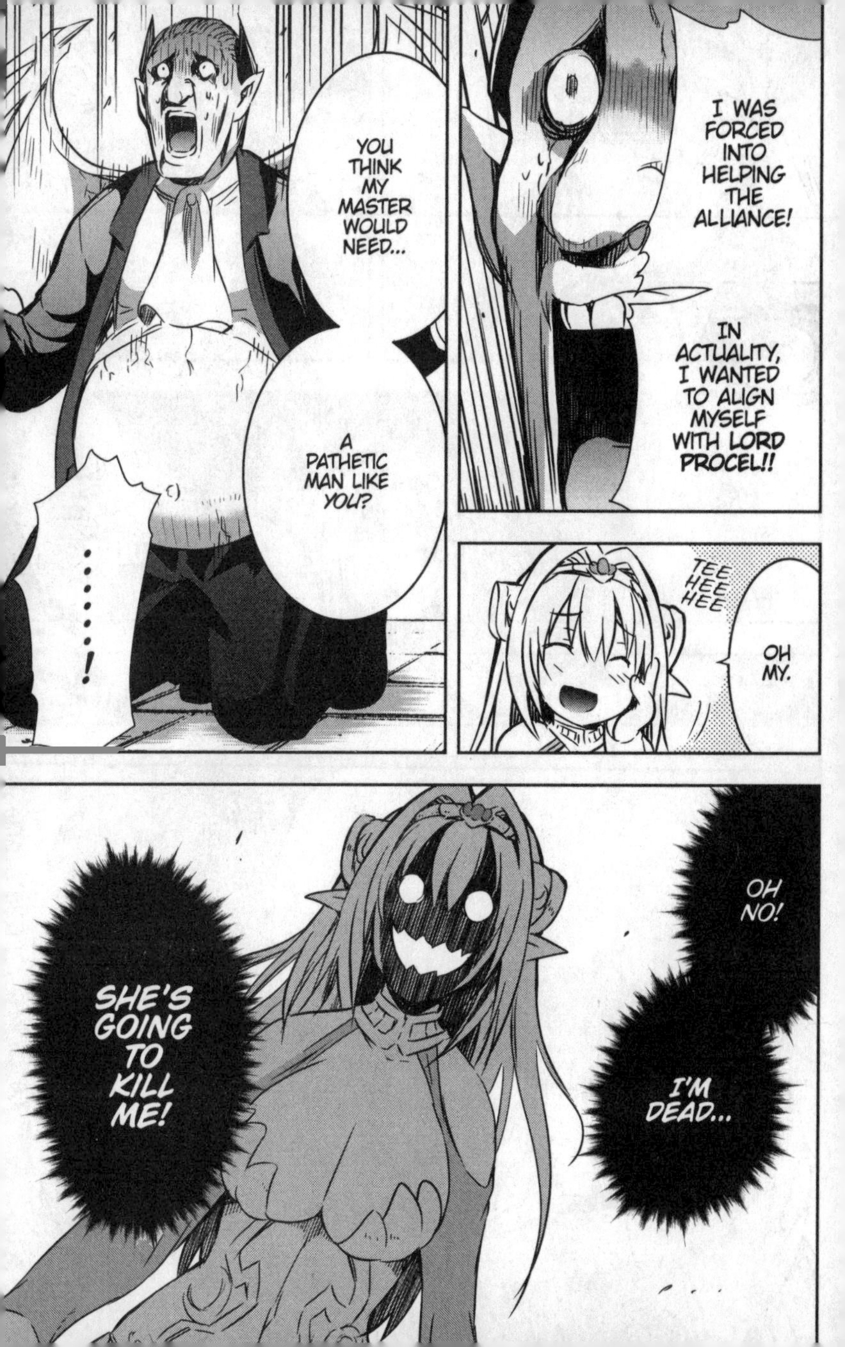
I WAS FORCED INTO HELPING THE ALLIANCE!
IN ACTUALITY, I WANTED TO ALIGN MYSELF WITH LORD PROCEL!!
TEE HEE HEE
OH MY.
YOU THINK MY MASTER WOULD NEED...
A PATHETIC MAN LIKE YOU?
......!
OH NO!
I'M DEAD...
SHE'S GOING TO KILL ME!

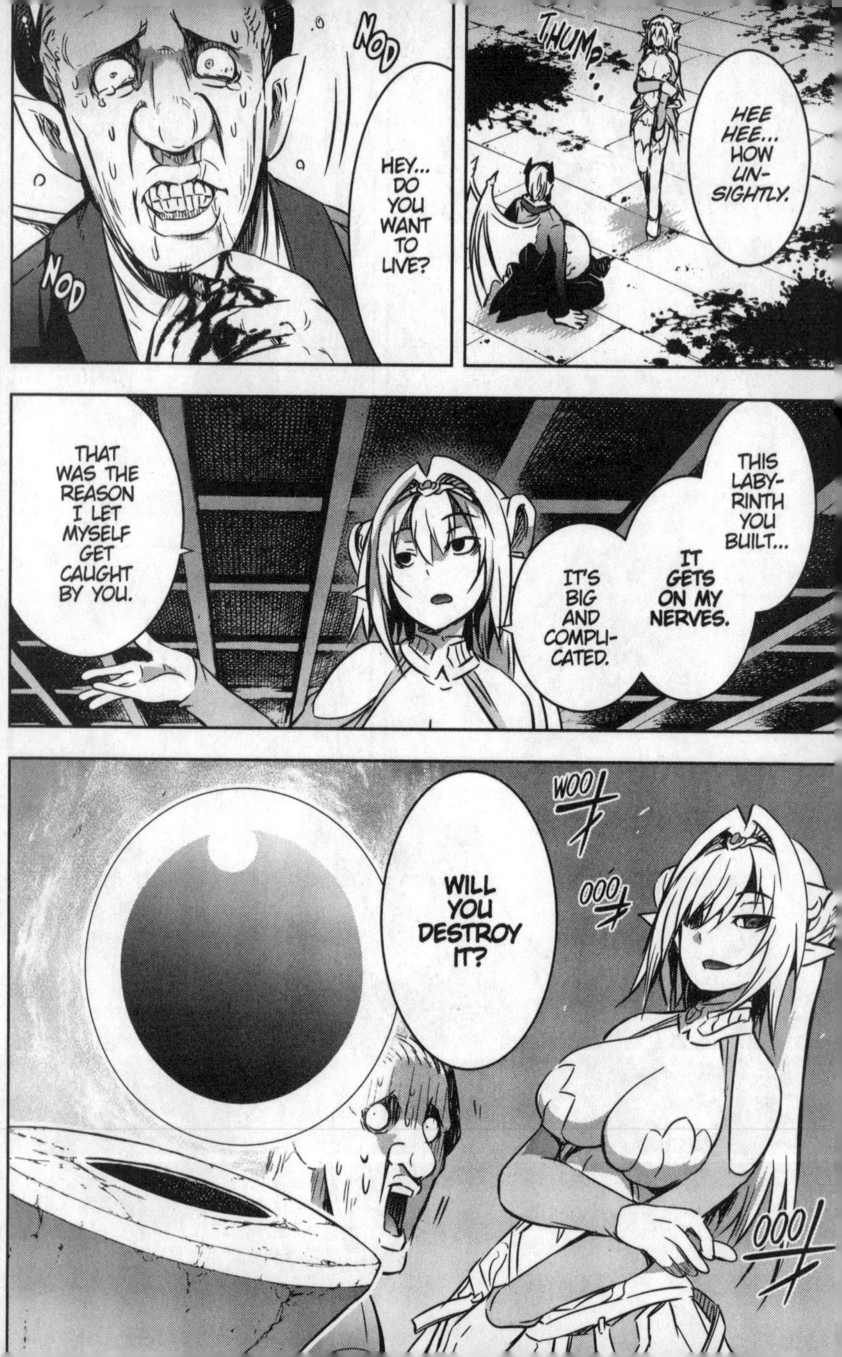
THUMP
HEE HEE... HOW UN-SIGHTLY.
NOD
HEY... DO YOU WANT TO LIVE?
NOD
THIS LABY-RINTH YOU BUILT...
IT GETS ON MY NERVES.
IT'S BIG AND COMPLI-CATED.
THAT WAS THE REASON I LET MYSELF GET CAUGHT BY YOU.
WOO
OOO
WILL YOU DESTROY IT?
OOO

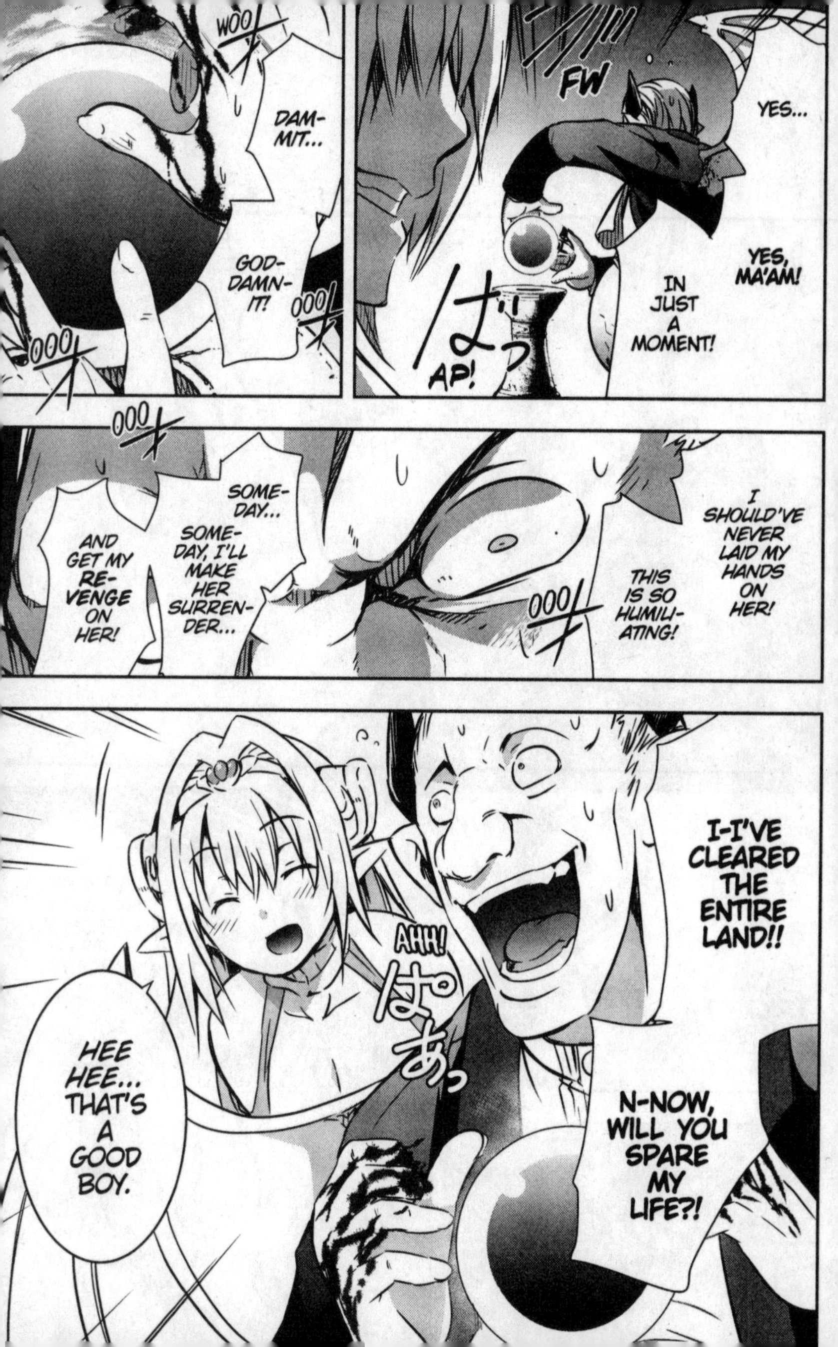
FW
YES...
YES, MA'AM!
IN JUST A MOMENT!
ぱっ AP!
WOO
DAM-MIT...
GOD-DAMN-IT!
OOO
OOO
I SHOULD'VE NEVER LAID MY HANDS ON HER!
THIS IS SO HUMILI-ATING!
OOO
SOME-DAY...
SOME-DAY, I'LL MAKE HER SURREN-DER...
AND GET MY RE-VENGE ON HER!
OOO
I-I'VE CLEARED THE ENTIRE LAND!!
AHH! ぱあっ
N-NOW, WILL YOU SPARE MY LIFE?!
HEE HEE... THAT'S A GOOD BOY.

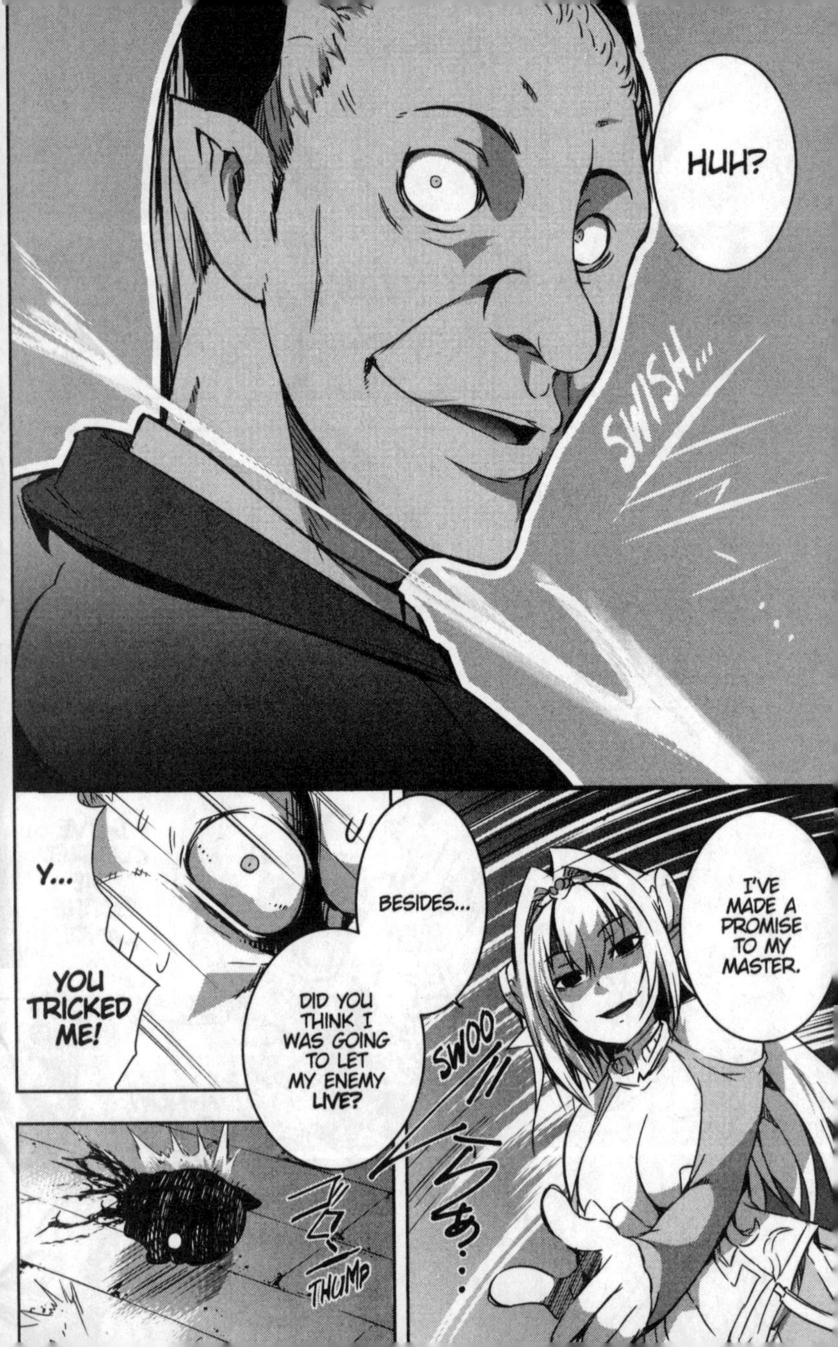
HUH?
SWISH...
I'VE MADE A PROMISE TO MY MASTER.
BESIDES...
DID YOU THINK I WAS GOING TO LET MY ENEMY LIVE?
SWOO
Y...
YOU TRICKED ME!
THUMP

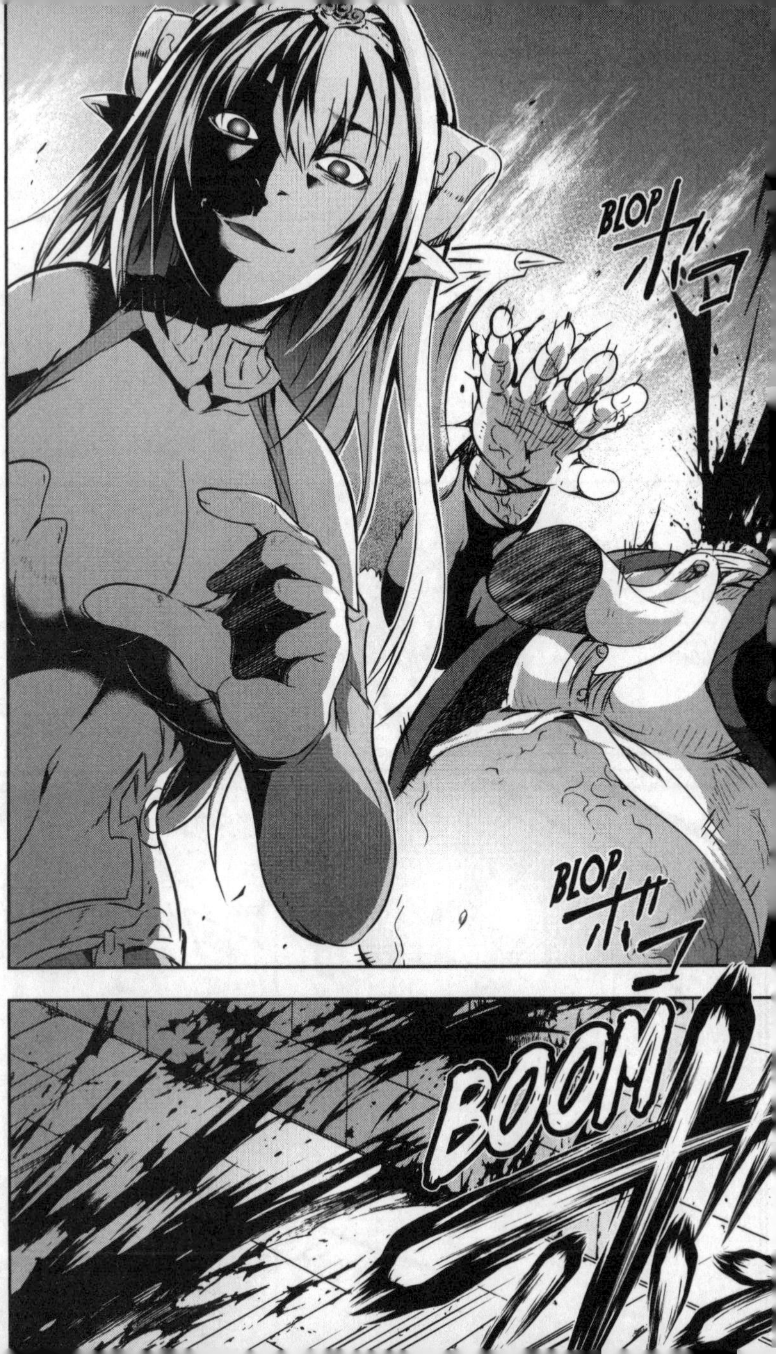
BLOP
BLOP
BOOM

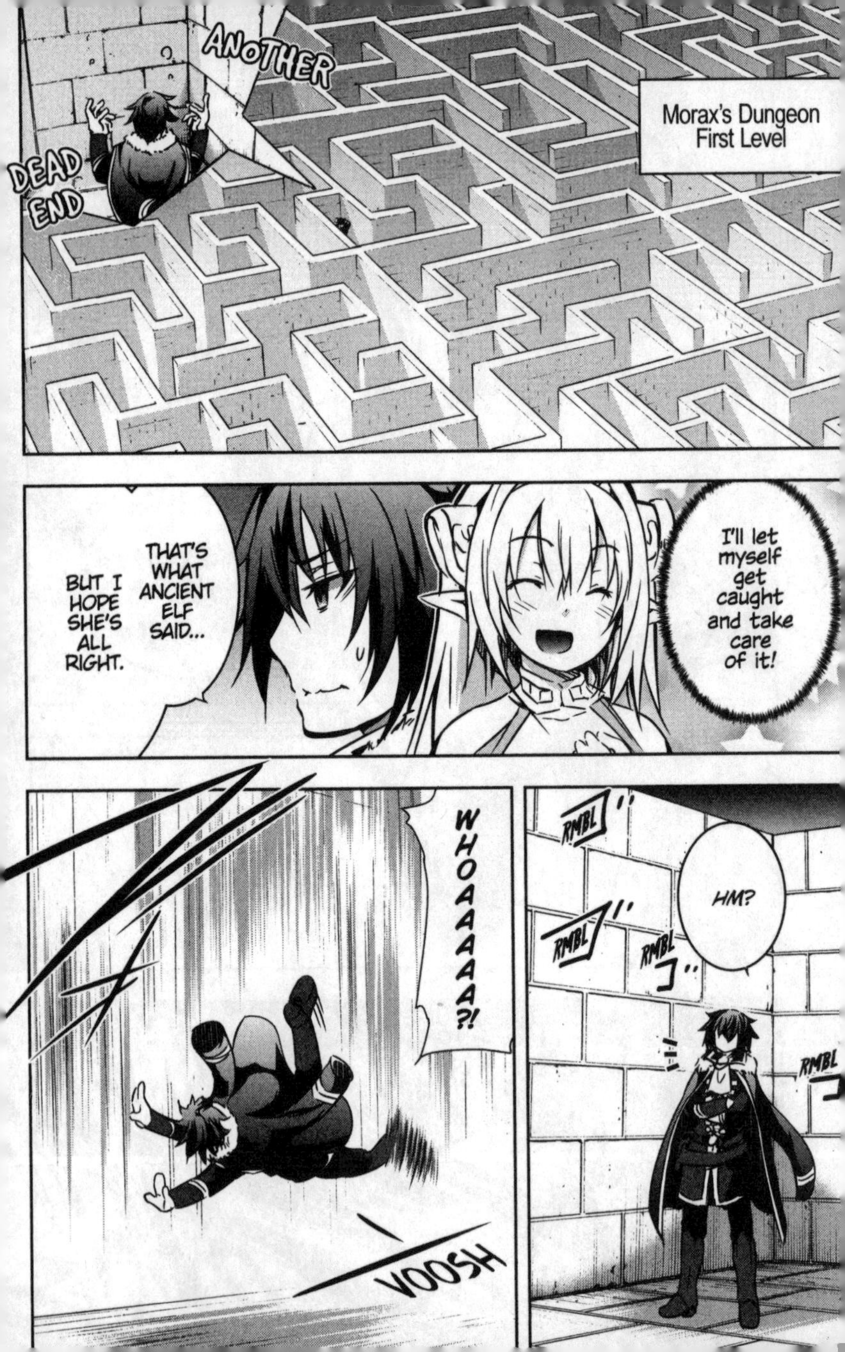
Morax's Dungeon
First Level
ANOTHER
DEAD END
I'll let myself get caught and take care of it!
THAT'S WHAT ANCIENT ELF SAID...
BUT I HOPE SHE'S ALL RIGHT.
RMBL
RMBL
RMBL
HM?
RMBL
WHOAAAAAAA?!
VOOSH

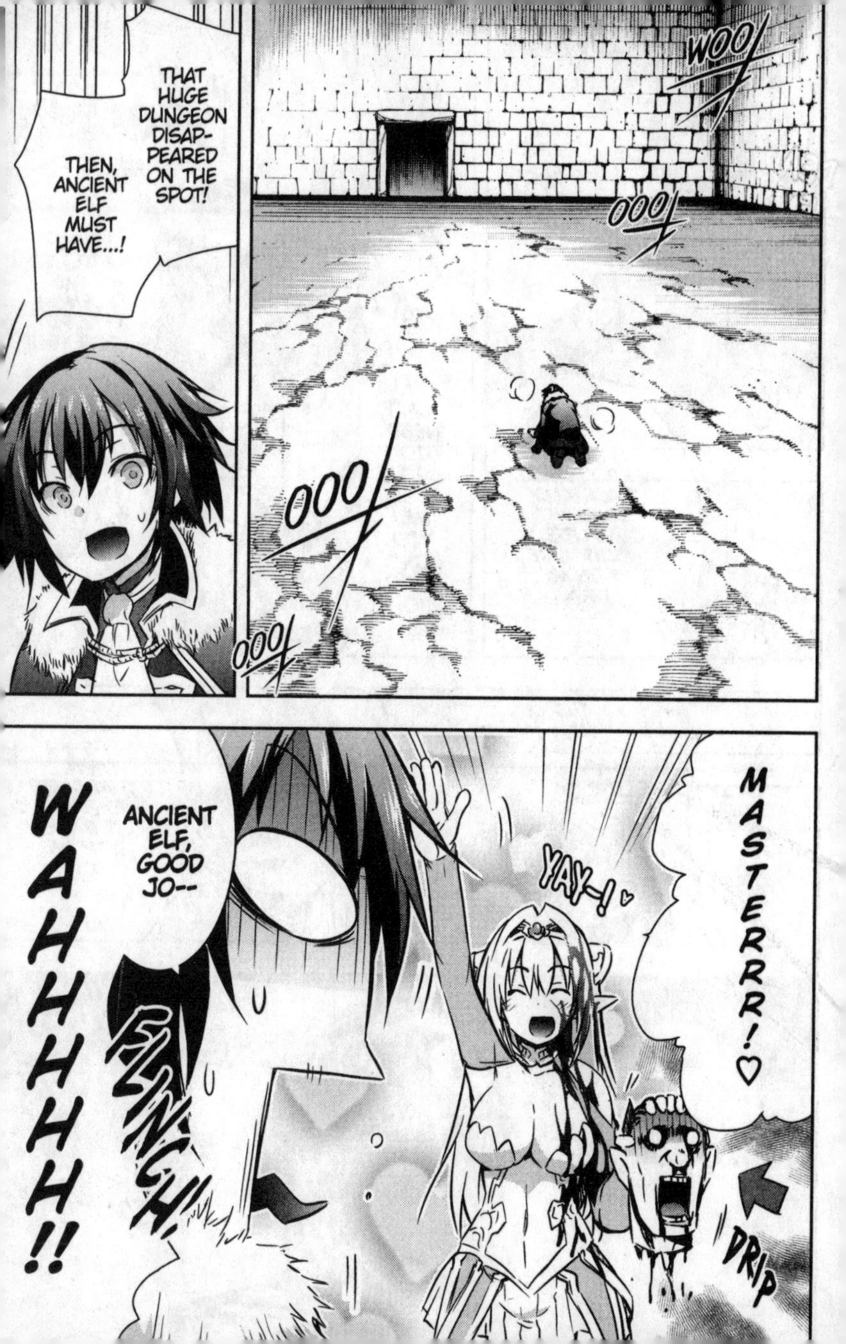
WOO
OOO
OOO
OOO
THAT HUGE DUNGEON DISAPPEARED ON THE SPOT!
THEN, ANCIENT ELF MUST HAVE...!
MASTERRR!♡
YAY-!♡
DRIP
ANCIENT ELF, GOOD JO--
FLINCH
WAHHHHHH!!

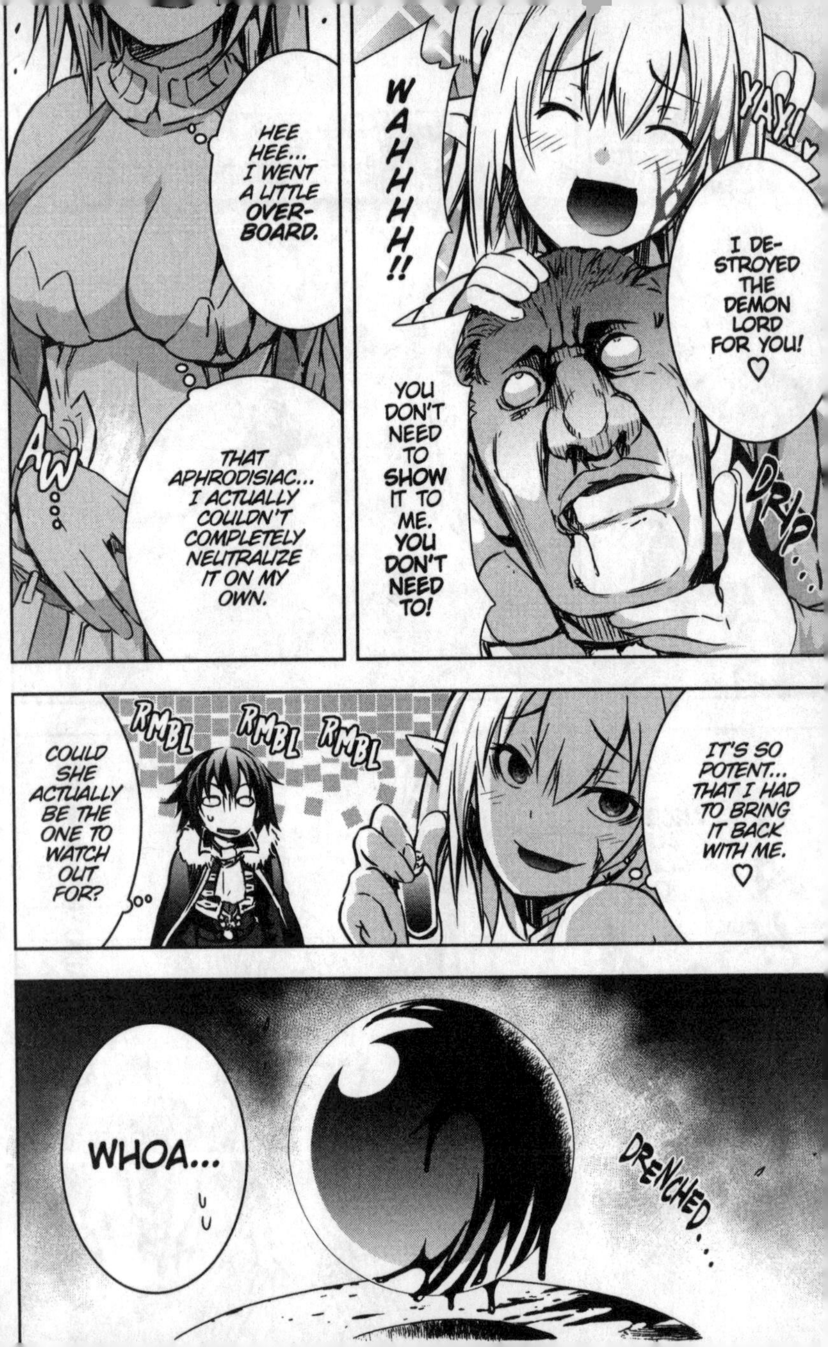
YAY!♥
I DE-STROYED THE DEMON LORD FOR YOU! ♡
WAHHHHH!!
YOU DON'T NEED TO SHOW IT TO ME. YOU DON'T NEED TO!
DRIP...
HEE HEE... I WENT A LITTLE OVER-BOARD.
THAT APHRODISIAC... I ACTUALLY COULDN'T COMPLETELY NEUTRALIZE IT ON MY OWN.
AW
IT'S SO POTENT... THAT I HAD TO BRING IT BACK WITH ME. ♡
RMBL RMBL RMBL
COULD SHE ACTUALLY BE THE ONE TO WATCH OUT FOR?
DRENCHED...
WHOA...

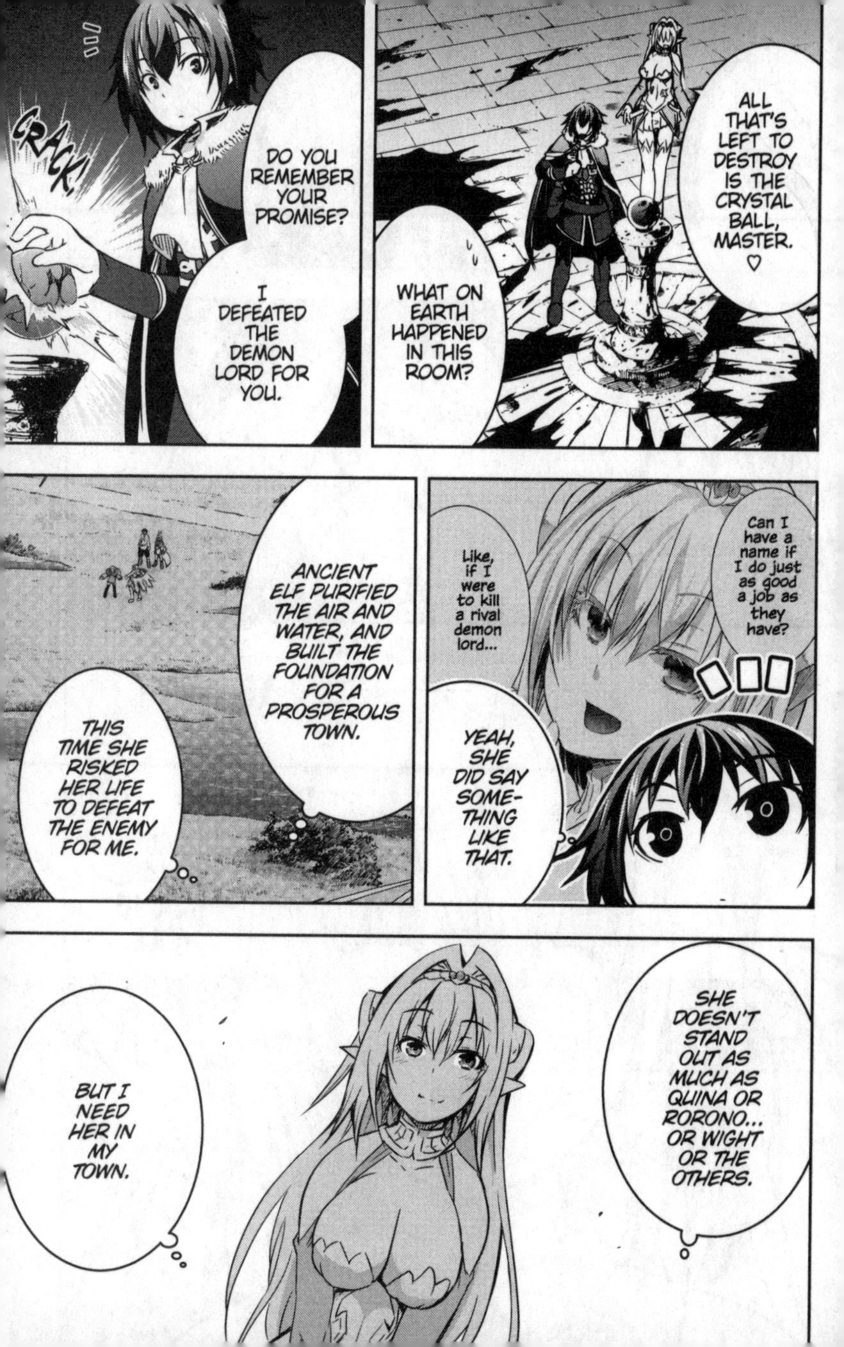
ALL THAT'S LEFT TO DESTROY IS THE CRYSTAL BALL, MASTER. ♡
WHAT ON EARTH HAPPENED IN THIS ROOM?
CRACK
DO YOU REMEMBER YOUR PROMISE?
I DEFEATED THE DEMON LORD FOR YOU.
Can I have a name if I do just as good a job as they have?
Like, if I were to kill a rival demon lord...
YEAH, SHE DID SAY SOMETHING LIKE THAT.
ANCIENT ELF PURIFIED THE AIR AND WATER, AND BUILT THE FOUNDATION FOR A PROSPEROUS TOWN.
THIS TIME SHE RISKED HER LIFE TO DEFEAT THE ENEMY FOR ME.
SHE DOESN'T STAND OUT AS MUCH AS QUINA OR RORONO... OR WIGHT OR THE OTHERS.
BUT I NEED HER IN MY TOWN.

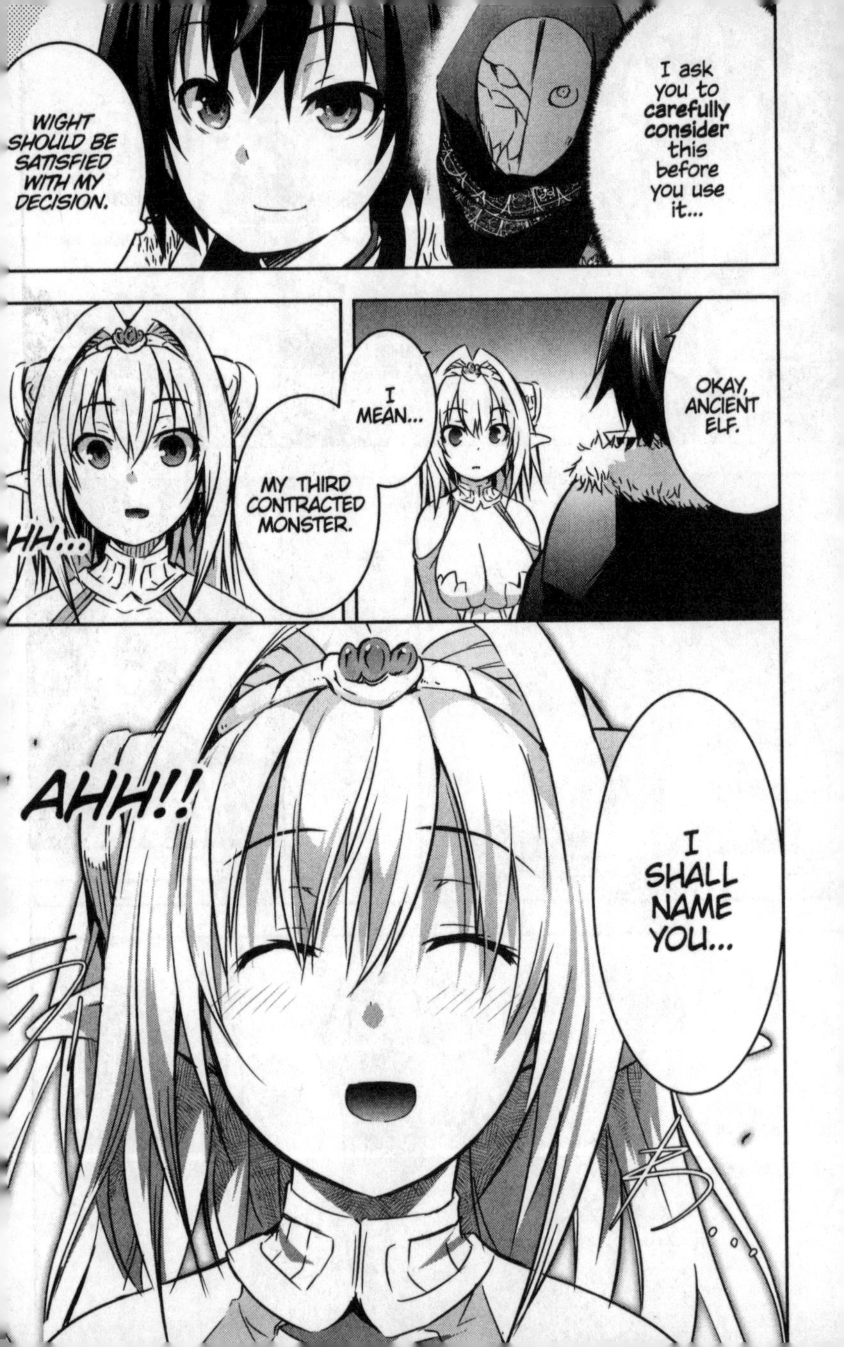
I ask you to carefully consider this before you use it...
WIGHT SHOULD BE SATISFIED WITH MY DECISION.
OKAY, ANCIENT ELF.
I MEAN...
MY THIRD CONTRACTED MONSTER.
HH...
I SHALL NAME YOU...
AHH!!

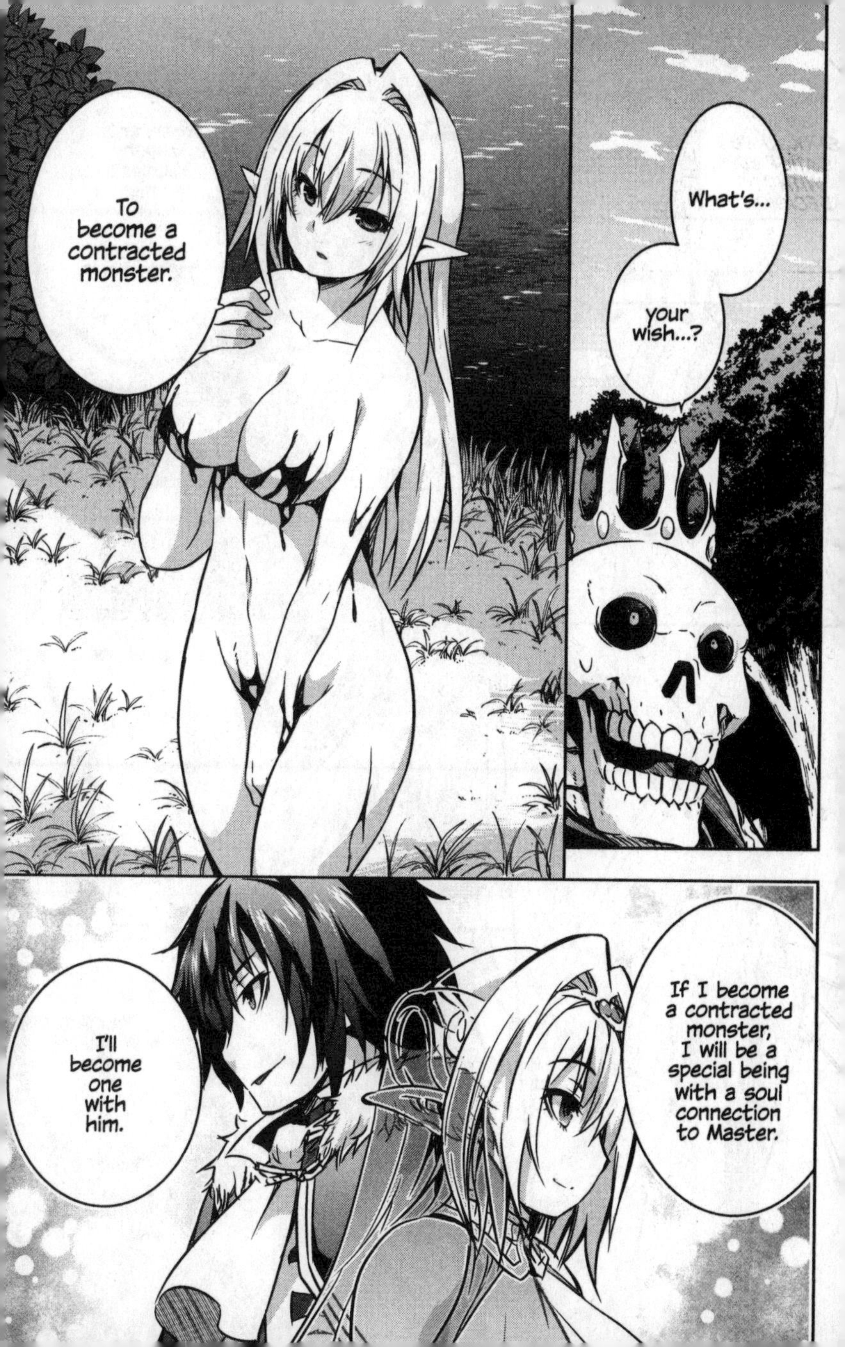
What's...
your wish...?
To become a contracted monster.
If I become a contracted monster, I will be a special being with a soul connection to Master.
I'll become one with him.

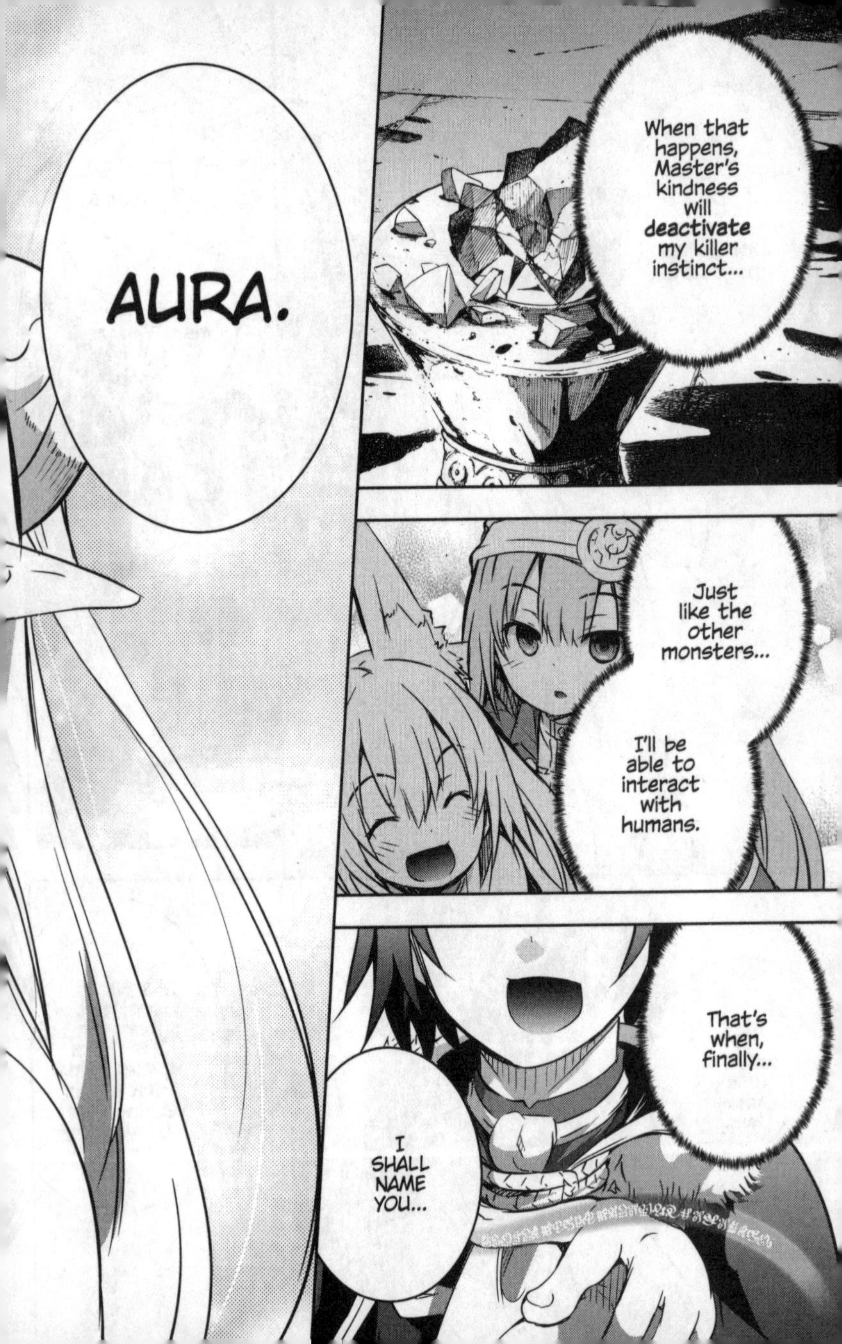
When that happens, Master's kindness will deactivate my killer instinct...
Just like the other monsters...
I'll be able to interact with humans.
That's when, finally...
I SHALL NAME YOU...
AURA.

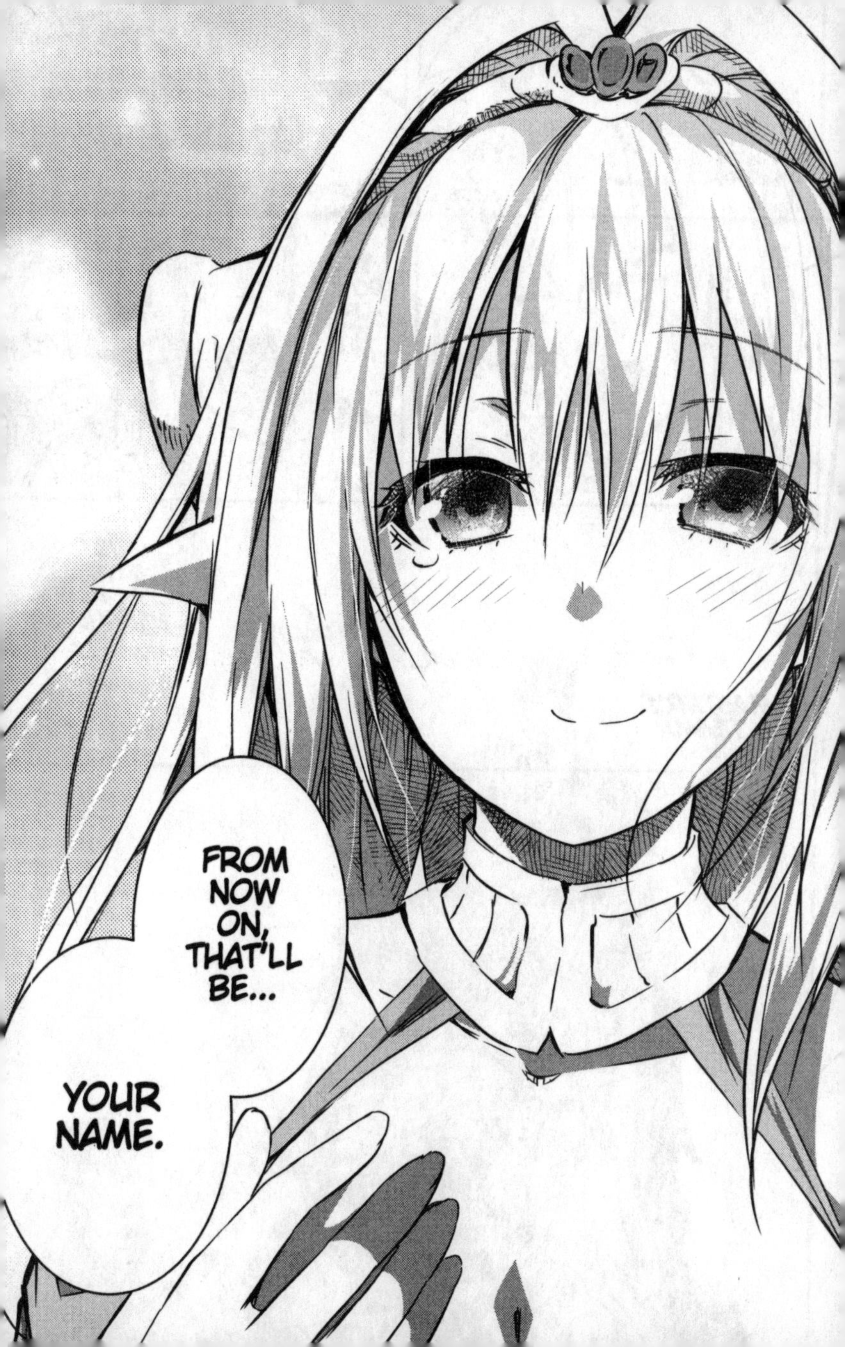
FROM NOW ON, THAT'LL BE...
YOUR NAME.

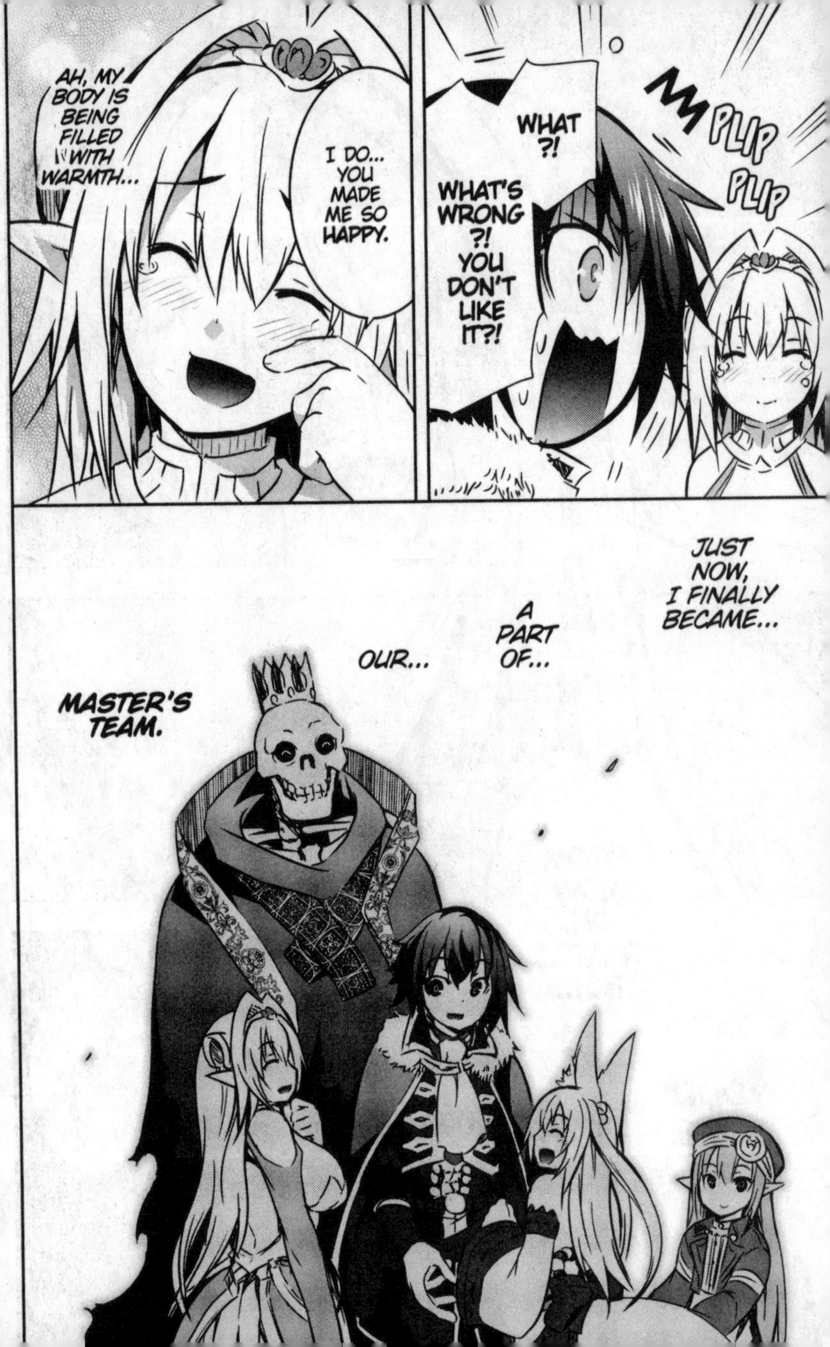
PLIP PLIP
WHAT?!
WHAT'S WRONG?! YOU DON'T LIKE IT?!
I DO... YOU MADE ME SO HAPPY.
AH, MY BODY IS BEING FILLED WITH WARMTH...
JUST NOW, I FINALLY BECAME...
A PART OF...
OUR...
MASTER'S TEAM.

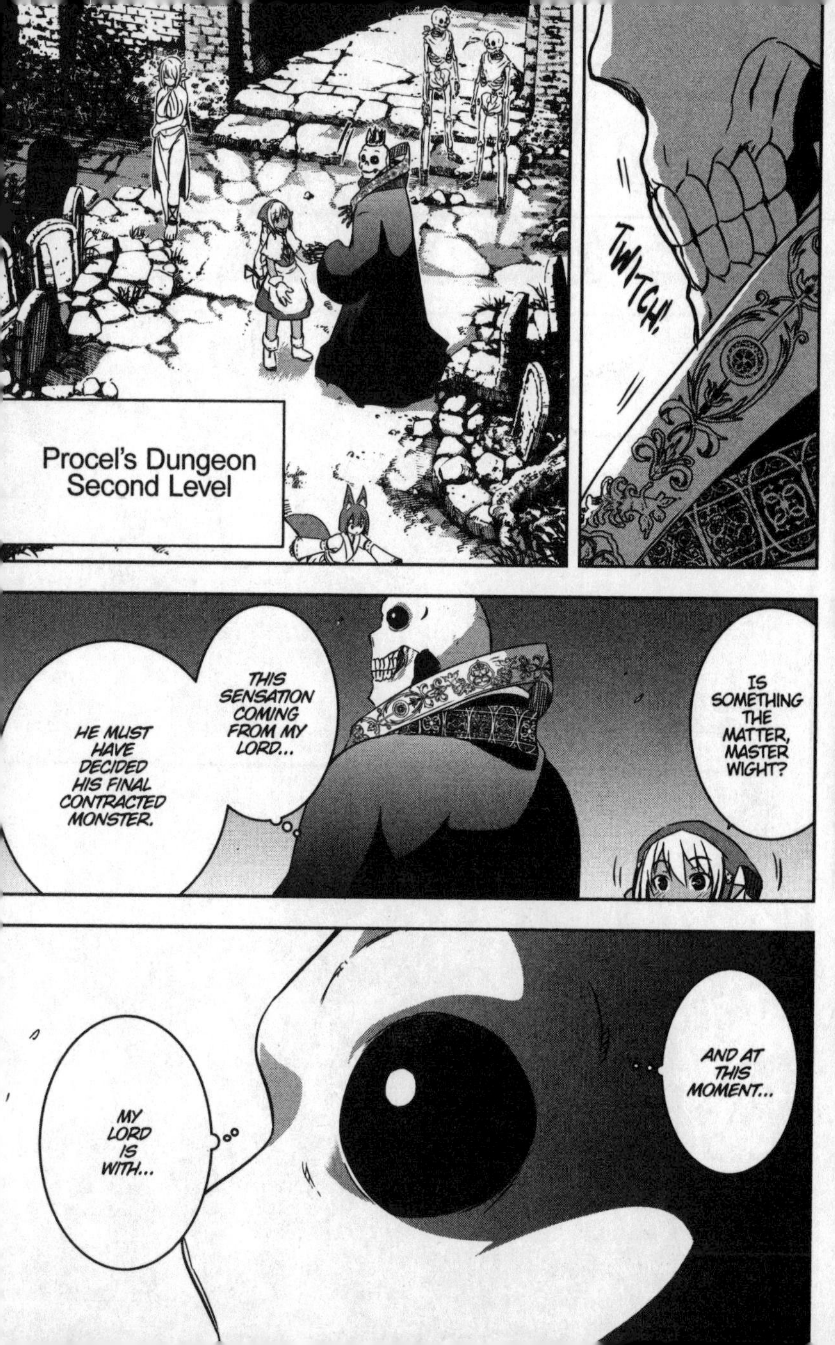
TWITCH!
Procel's Dungeon Second Level
IS SOMETHING THE MATTER, MASTER WIGHT?
THIS SENSATION COMING FROM MY LORD...
HE MUST HAVE DECIDED HIS FINAL CONTRACTED MONSTER.
AND AT THIS MOMENT...
MY LORD IS WITH...

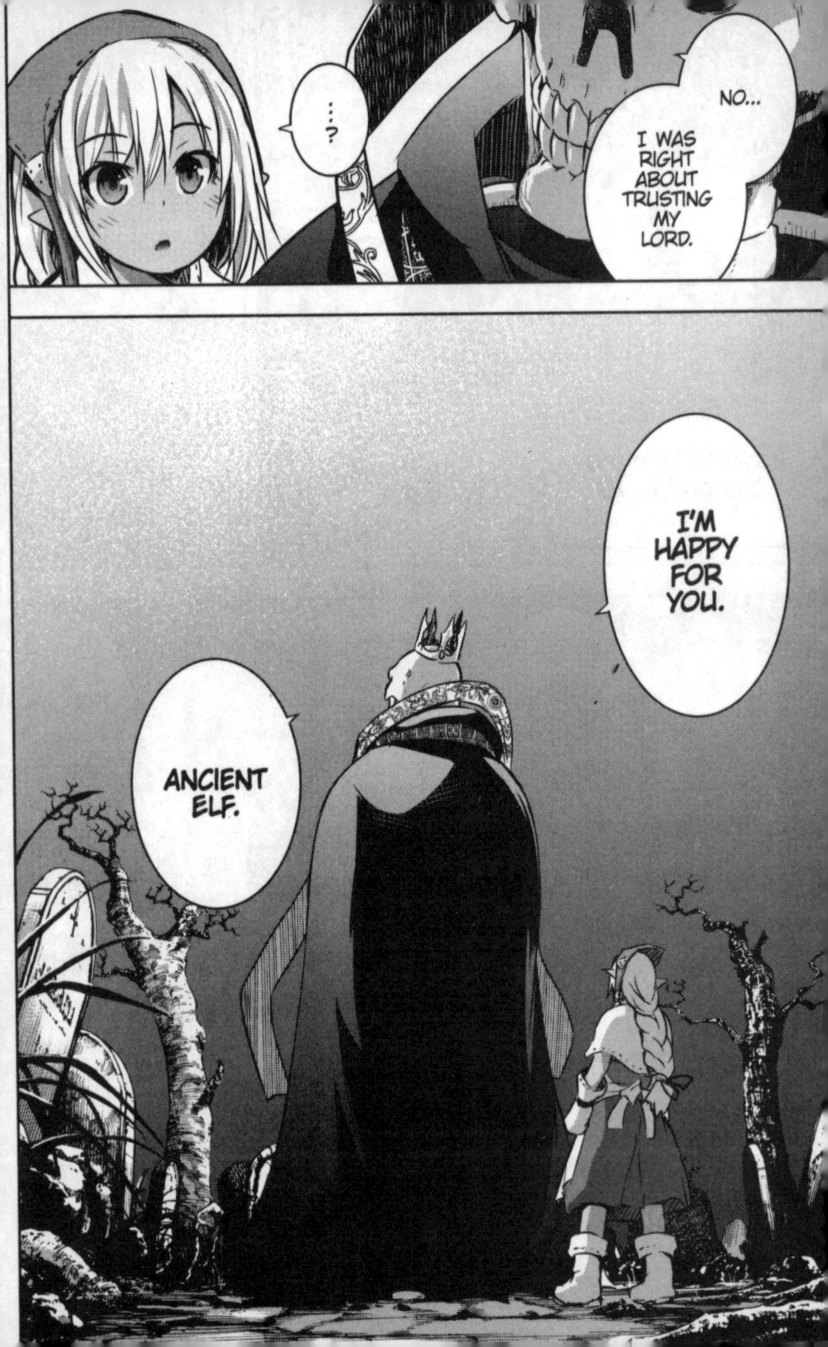
NO...
I WAS RIGHT ABOUT TRUSTING MY LORD.
...?
I'M HAPPY FOR YOU.
ANCIENT ELF.

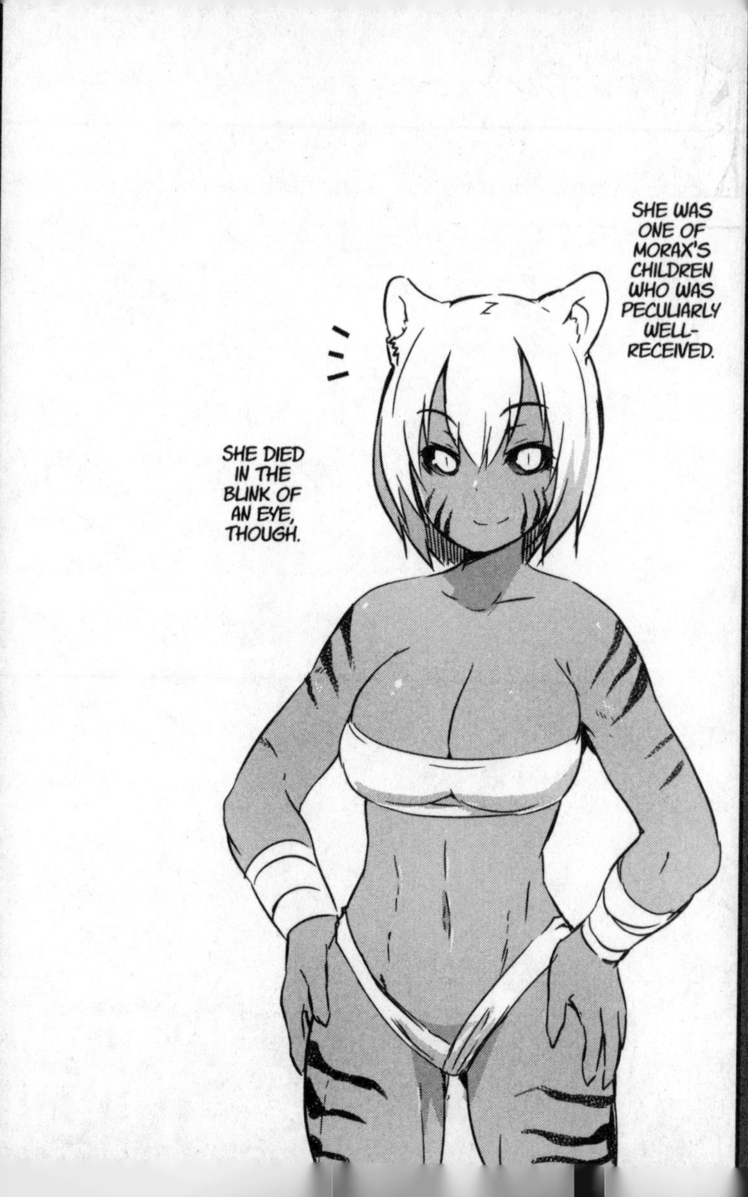
SHE WAS ONE OF MORAX'S CHILDREN WHO WAS PECULIARLY WELL-RECEIVED.
SHE DIED IN THE BLINK OF AN EYE, THOUGH.

DUNGEON BUILDER:
THE DEMON KING'S LABYRINTH IS A MODERN CITY!

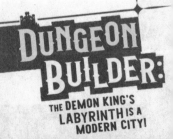

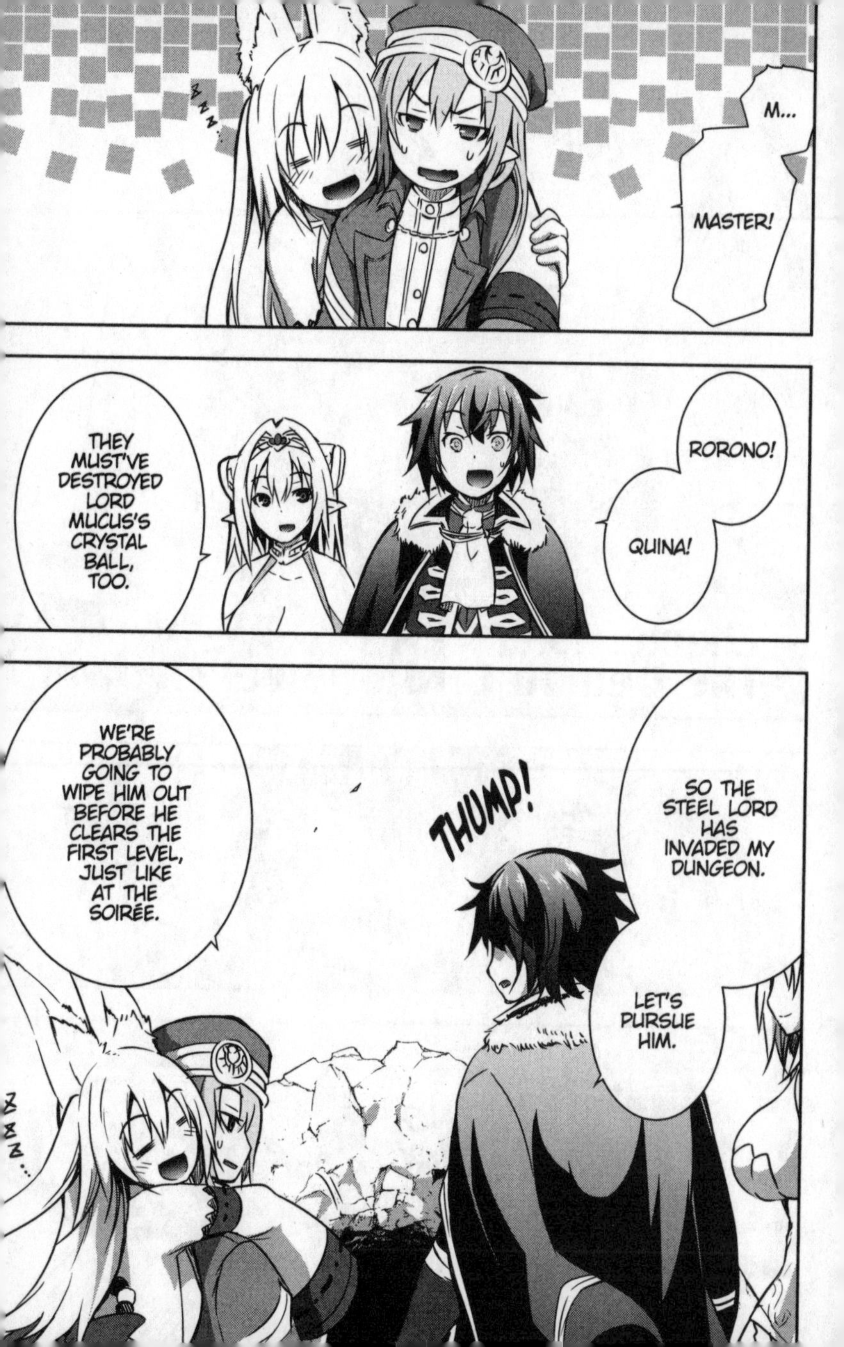
M...
MASTER!
ZZZ...
RORONO!
QUINA!
THEY MUST'VE DESTROYED LORD MUCUS'S CRYSTAL BALL, TOO.
SO THE STEEL LORD HAS INVADED MY DUNGEON.
LET'S PURSUE HIM.
THUMP!
WE'RE PROBABLY GOING TO WIPE HIM OUT BEFORE HE CLEARS THE FIRST LEVEL, JUST LIKE AT THE SOIRÉE.
ZZZ...

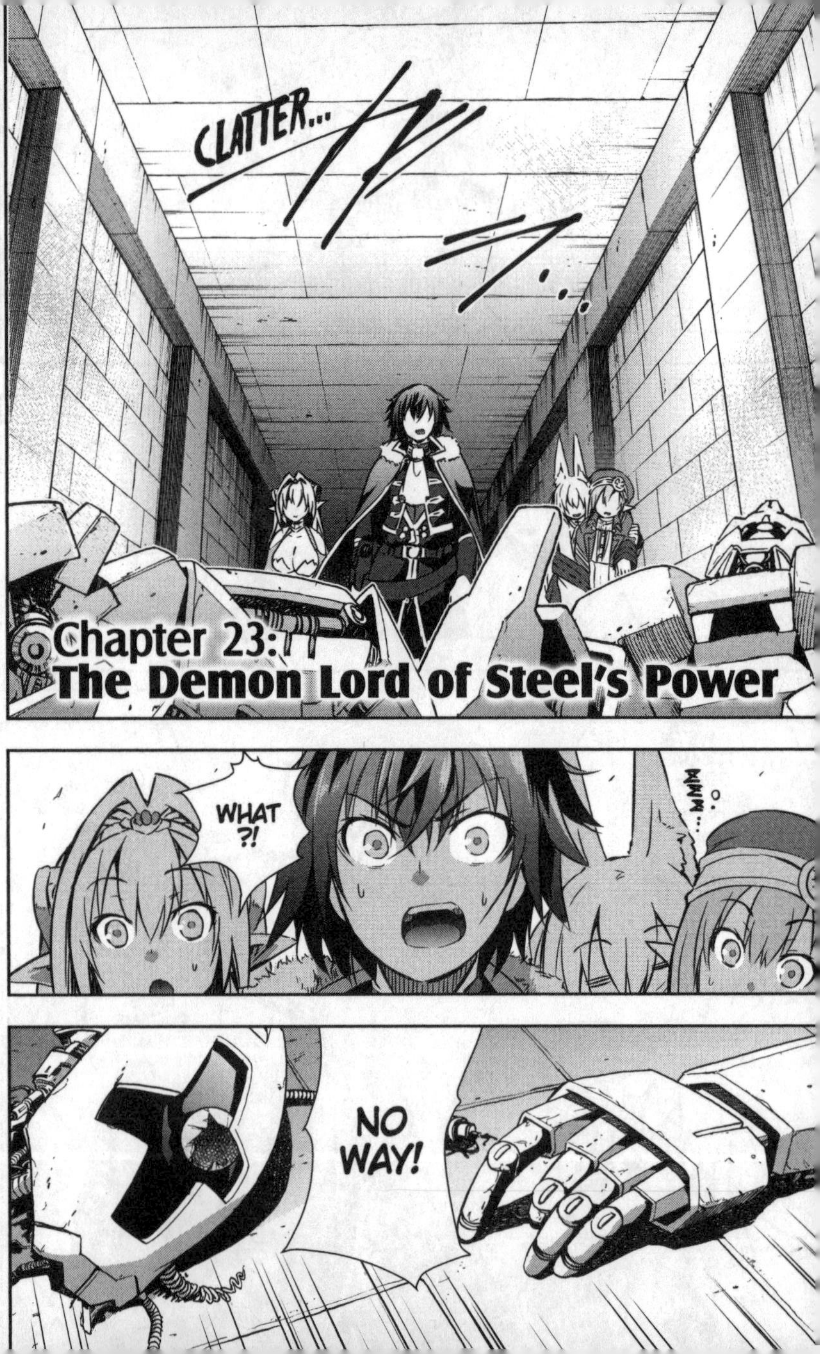
CLATTER...
Chapter 23:
The Demon Lord of Steel's Power
MMM...
WHAT ?!
NO WAY!

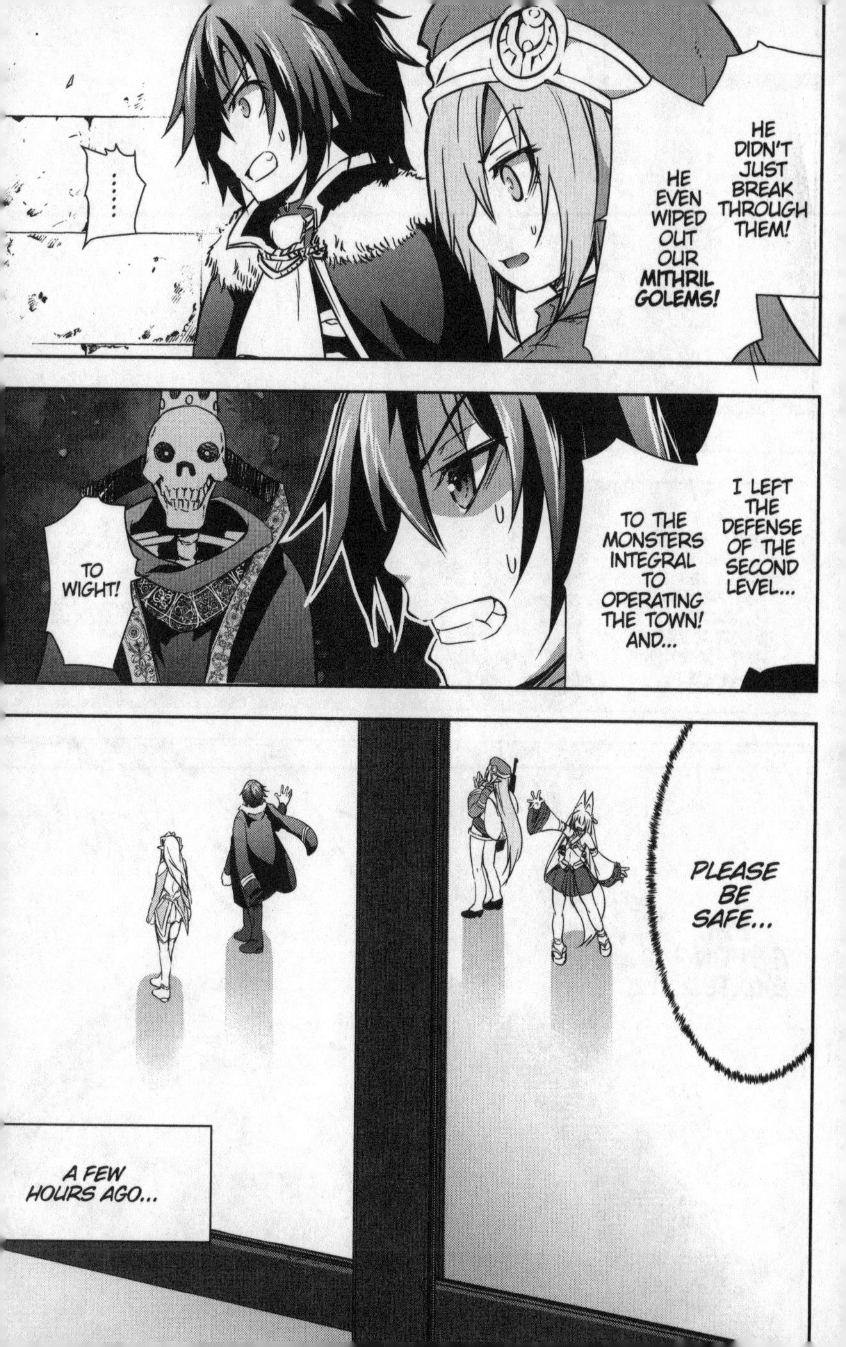
HE DIDN'T JUST BREAK THROUGH THEM!
HE EVEN WIPED OUT OUR MITHRIL GOLEMS!
......
I LEFT THE DEFENSE OF THE SECOND LEVEL...
TO THE MONSTERS INTEGRAL TO OPERATING THE TOWN! AND...
TO WIGHT!
PLEASE BE SAFE...
A FEW HOURS AGO...

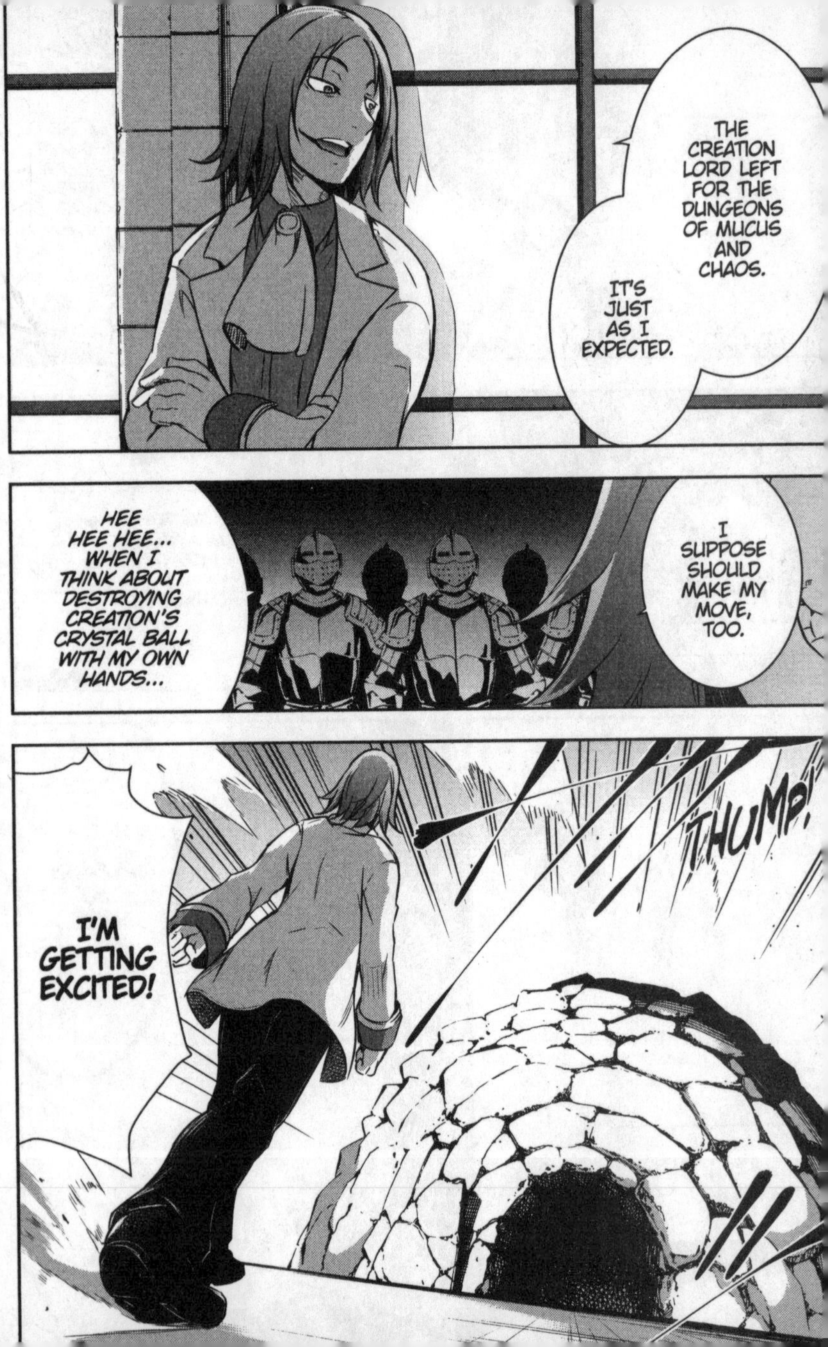
THE CREATION LORD LEFT FOR THE DUNGEONS OF MUCUS AND CHAOS.
IT'S JUST AS I EXPECTED.
I SUPPOSE SHOULD MAKE MY MOVE, TOO.
HEE HEE HEE... WHEN I THINK ABOUT DESTROYING CREATION'S CRYSTAL BALL WITH MY OWN HANDS...
THUMP!
I'M GETTING EXCITED!

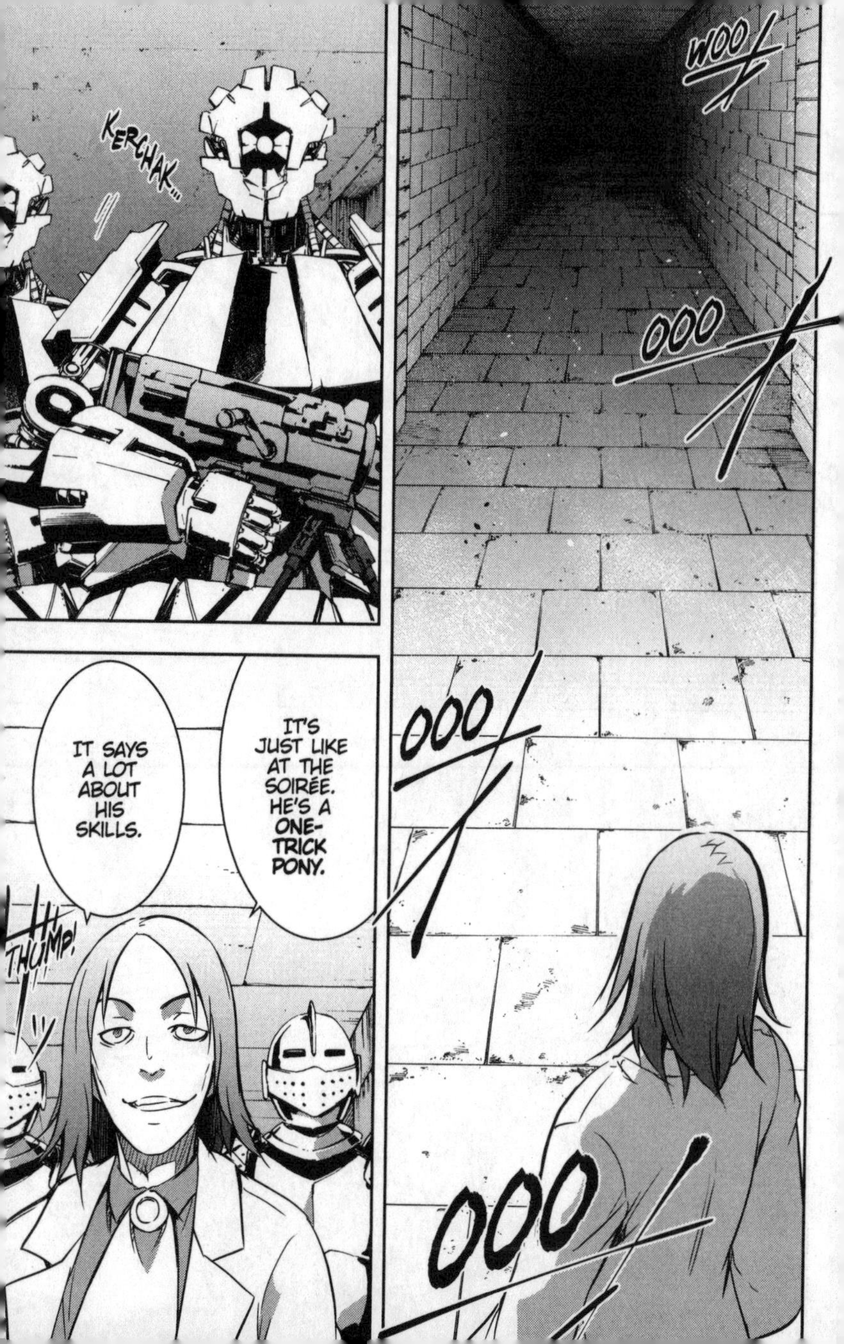
WOOO
OOO
OOO
OOO
KERCHAK...
IT'S JUST LIKE AT THE SOIRÉE. HE'S A ONE-TRICK PONY.
IT SAYS A LOT ABOUT HIS SKILLS.
THUMP!

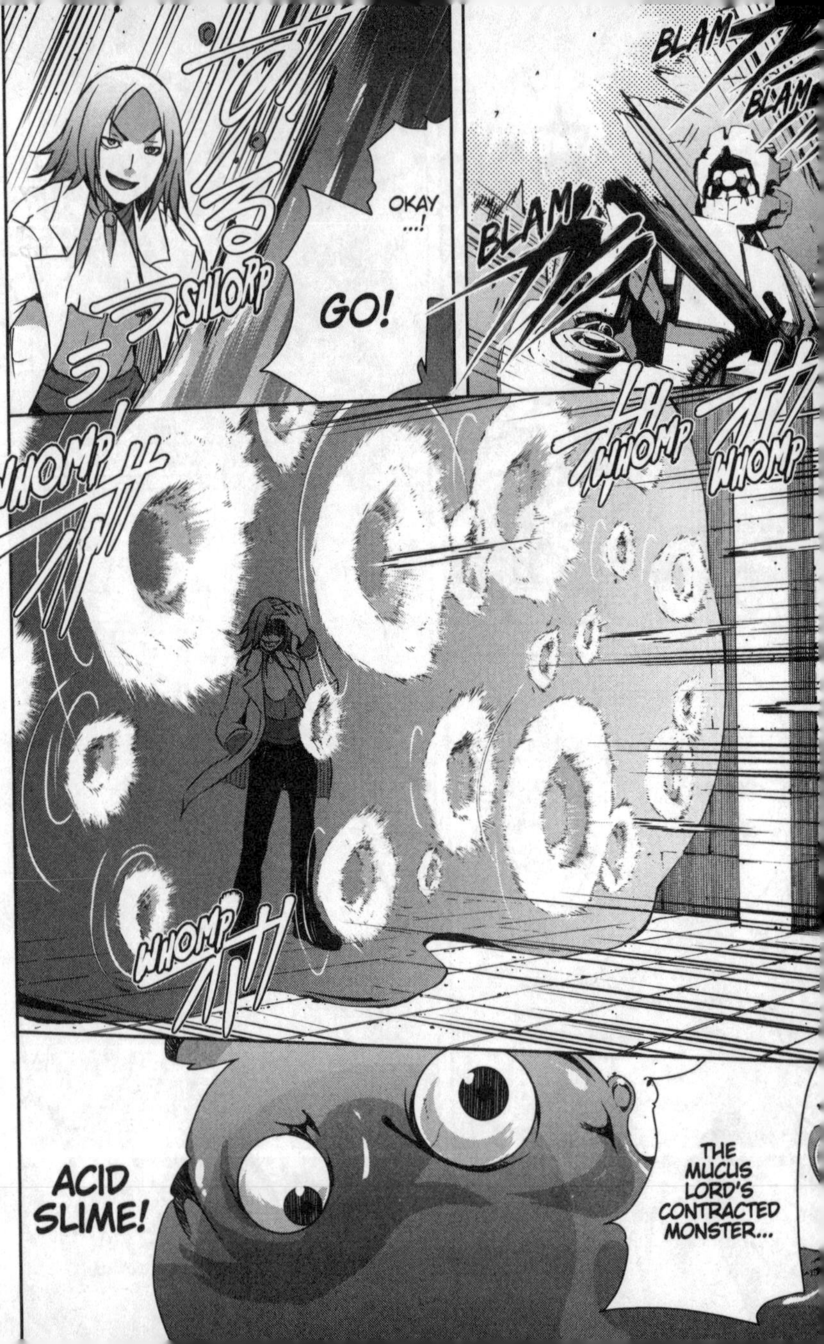

BLAM
BLAM
BLAM
OKAY ...!
GO!
SHLORP
WHOMP
WHOMP
WHOMP
WHOMP
THE MUCUS LORD'S CONTRACTED MONSTER...
ACID SLIME!

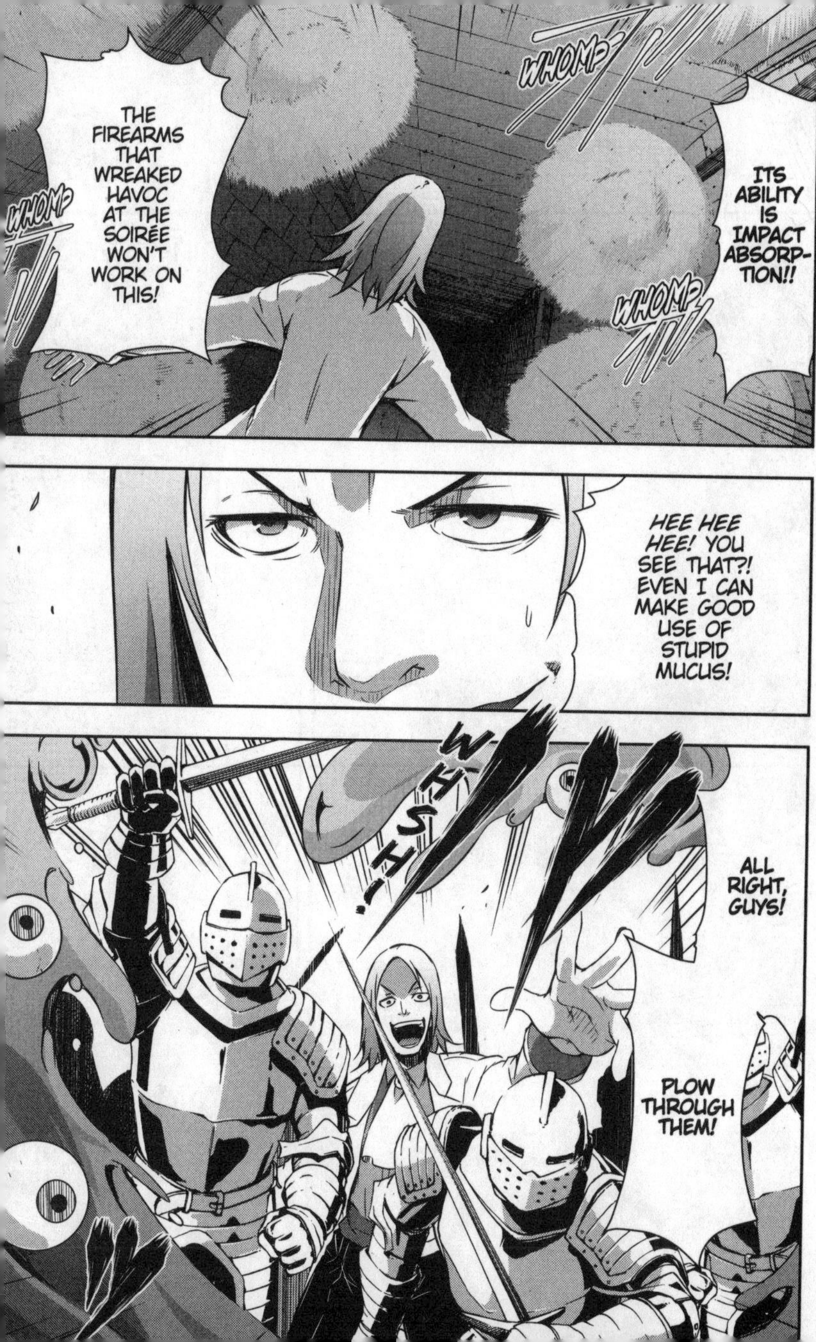
WHOMP
ITS ABILITY IS IMPACT ABSORPTION!!
WHOMP
THE FIREARMS THAT WREAKED HAVOC AT THE SOIRÉE WON'T WORK ON THIS!
WHOMP
HEE HEE HEE! YOU SEE THAT?! EVEN I CAN MAKE GOOD USE OF STUPID MUCUS!
ALL RIGHT, GUYS!
PLOW THROUGH THEM!
WHSH!

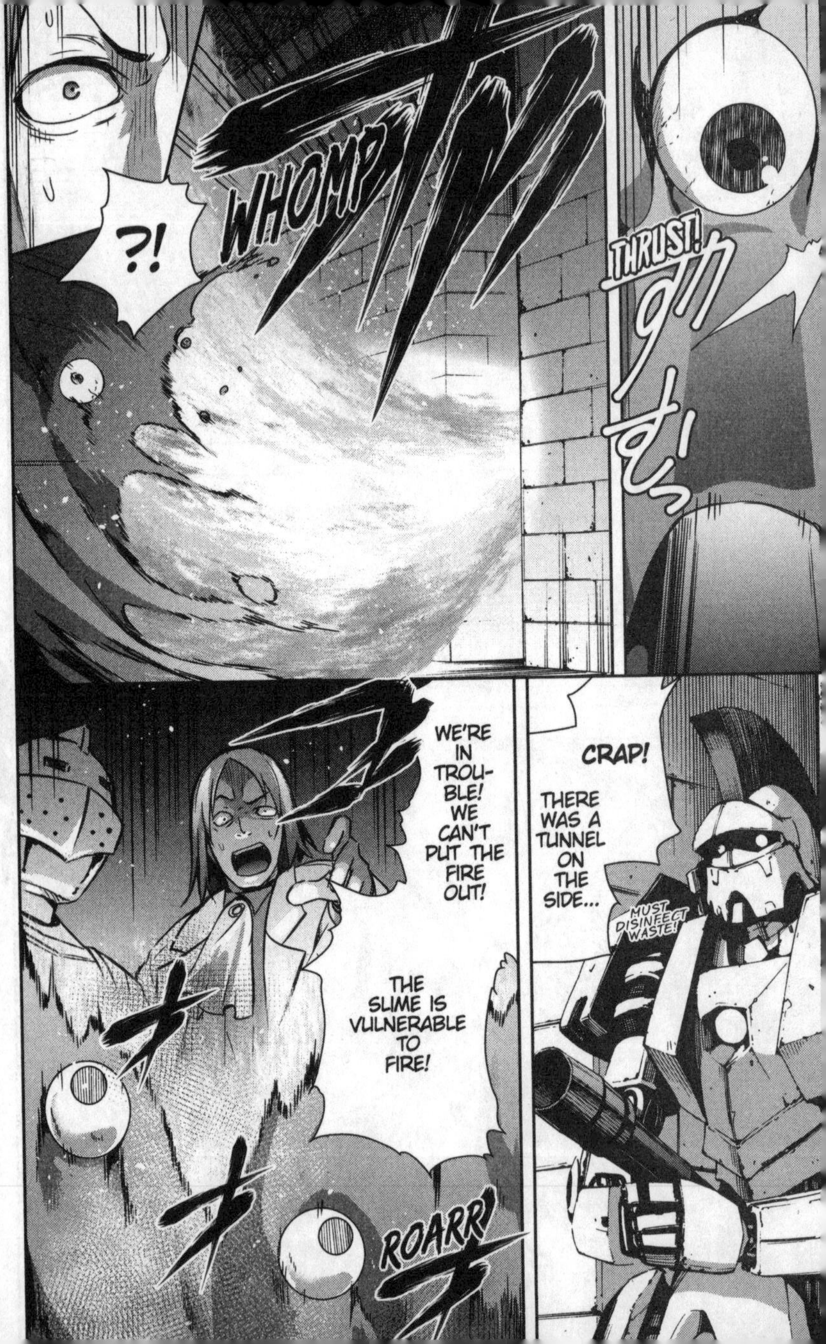
THRUST!
?!
WHOMP
CRAP!
THERE WAS A TUNNEL ON THE SIDE...
MUST DISINFECT WASTE!
WE'RE IN TROUBLE! WE CAN'T PUT THE FIRE OUT!
THE SLIME IS VULNERABLE TO FIRE!
ROARR

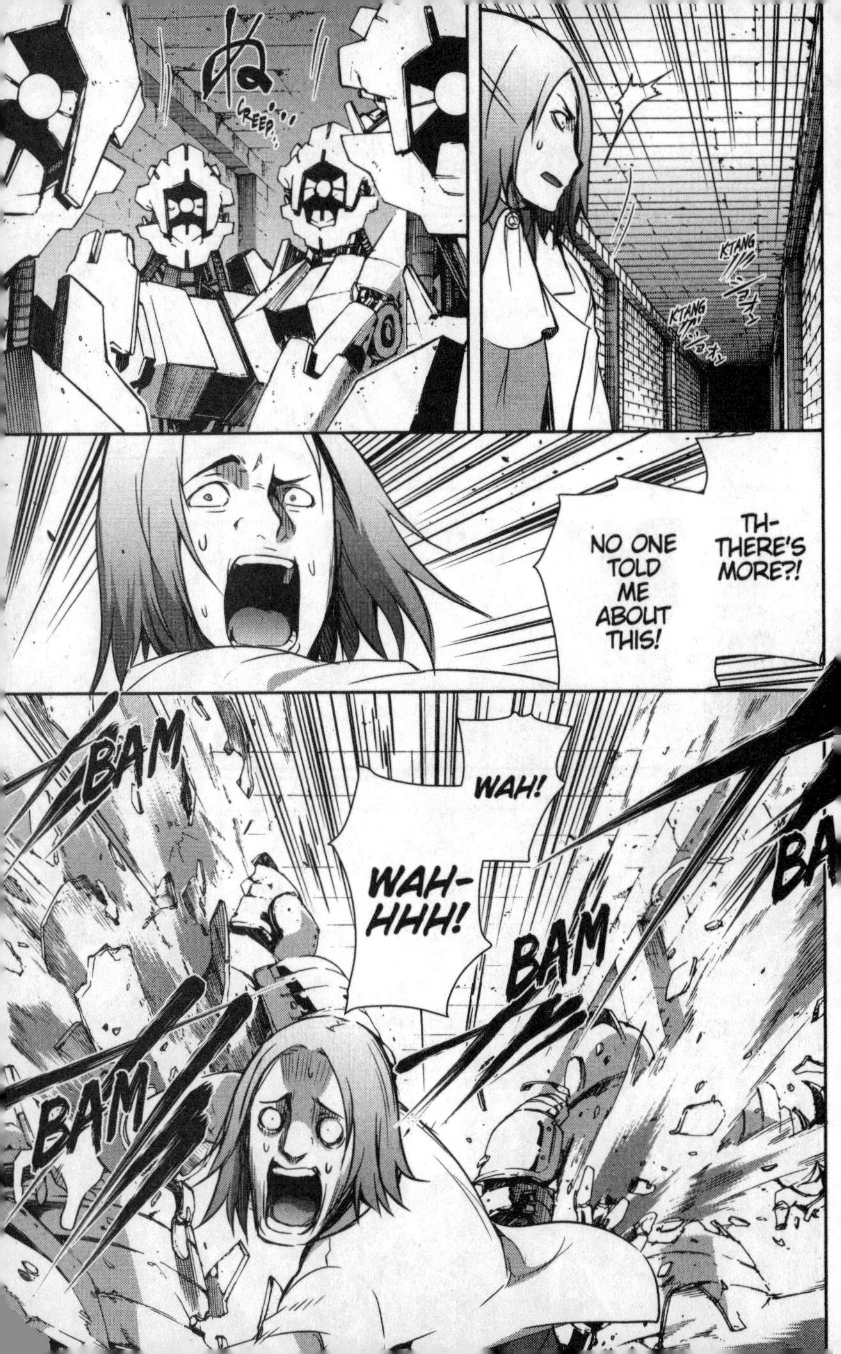
KTANG
KTANG
ぬ
CREEP...
TH- THERE'S MORE?!
NO ONE TOLD ME ABOUT THIS!
BAM
WAH!
WAH-HHH!
BAM
BAM

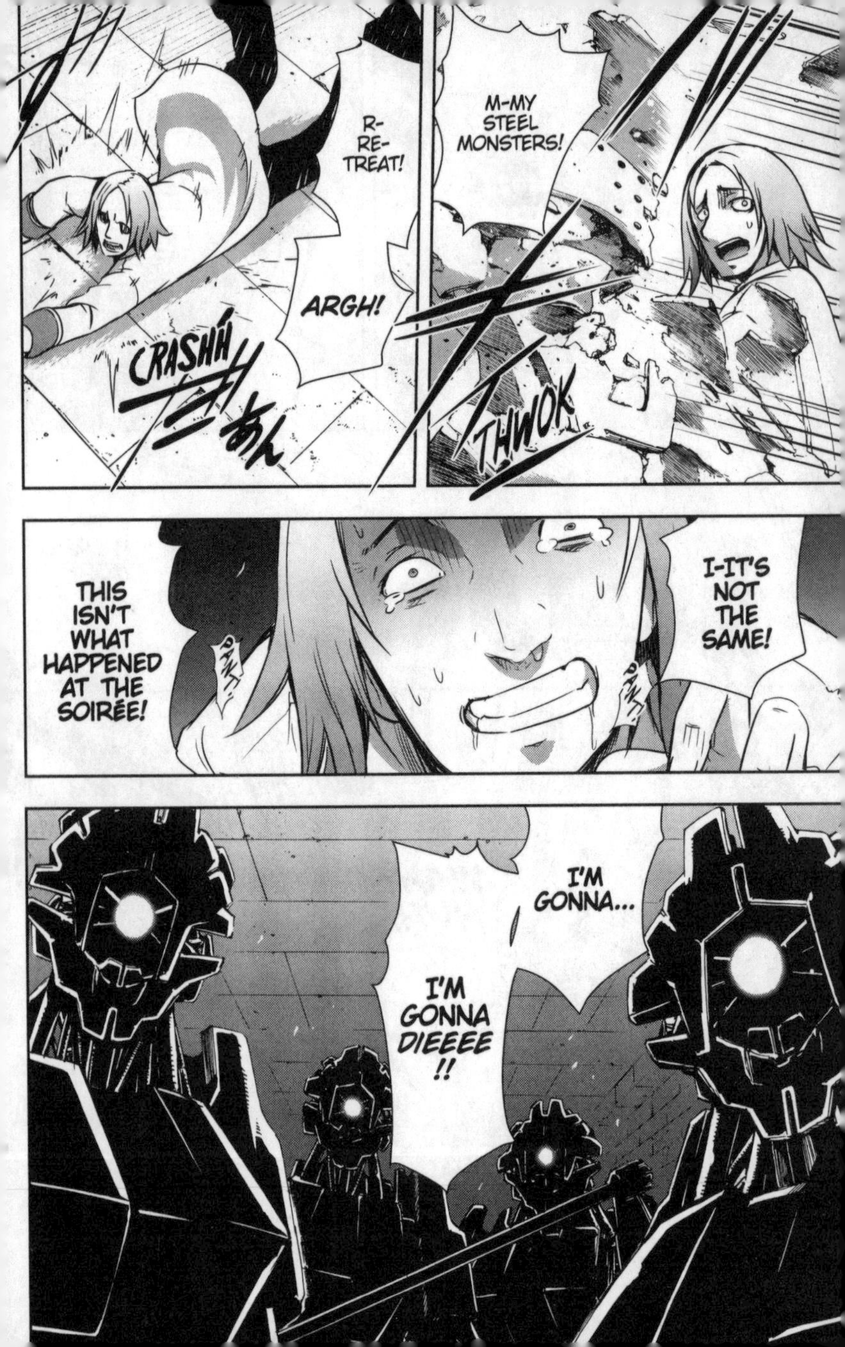

M-MY STEEL MONSTERS!
THWOK
R-RE-TREAT!
ARGH!
CRASHH
I-IT'S NOT THE SAME!
PANT
THIS ISN'T WHAT HAPPENED AT THE SOIRÉE!
PANT
I'M GONNA...
I'M GONNA DIEEEE!!

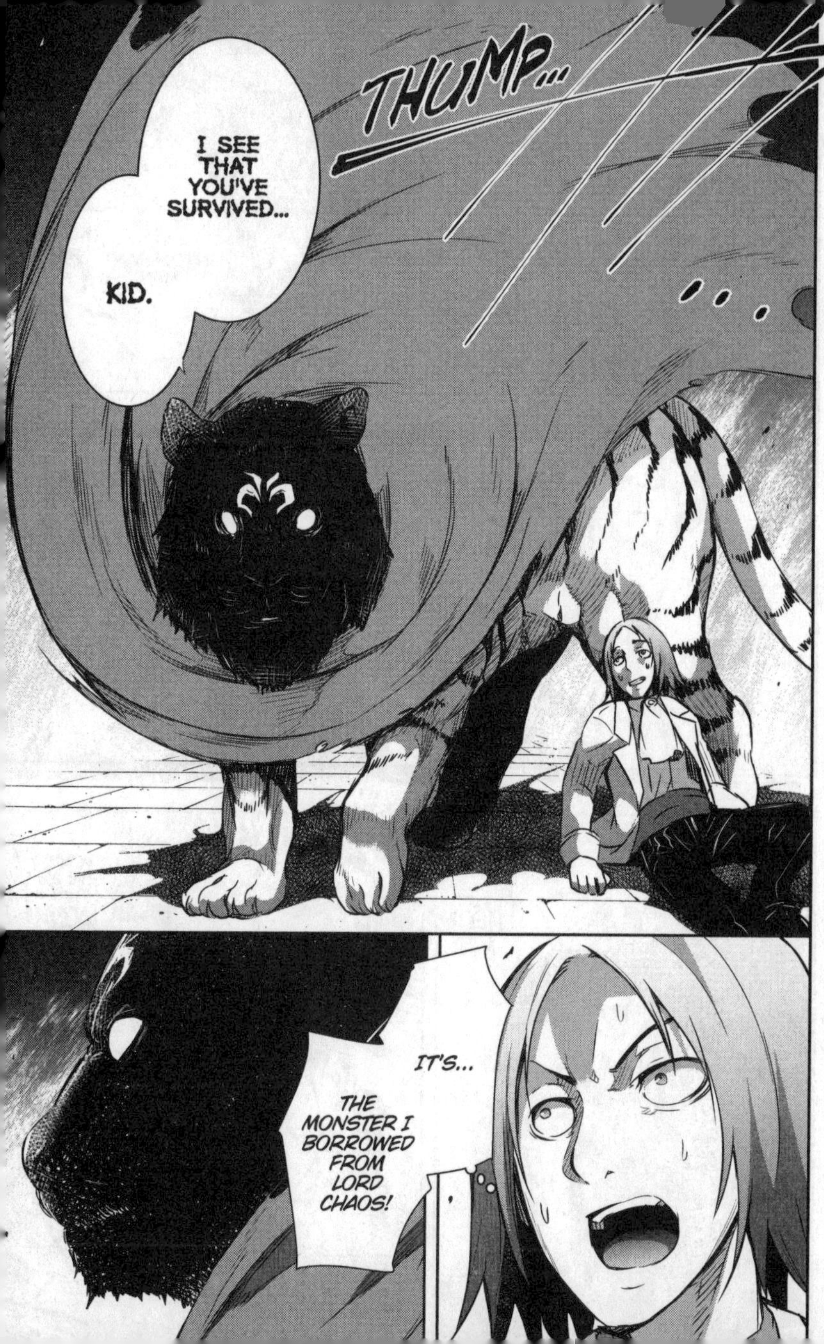
THUMP...
...
I SEE THAT YOU'VE SURVIVED...
KID.
IT'S...
THE MONSTER I BORROWED FROM LORD CHAOS!

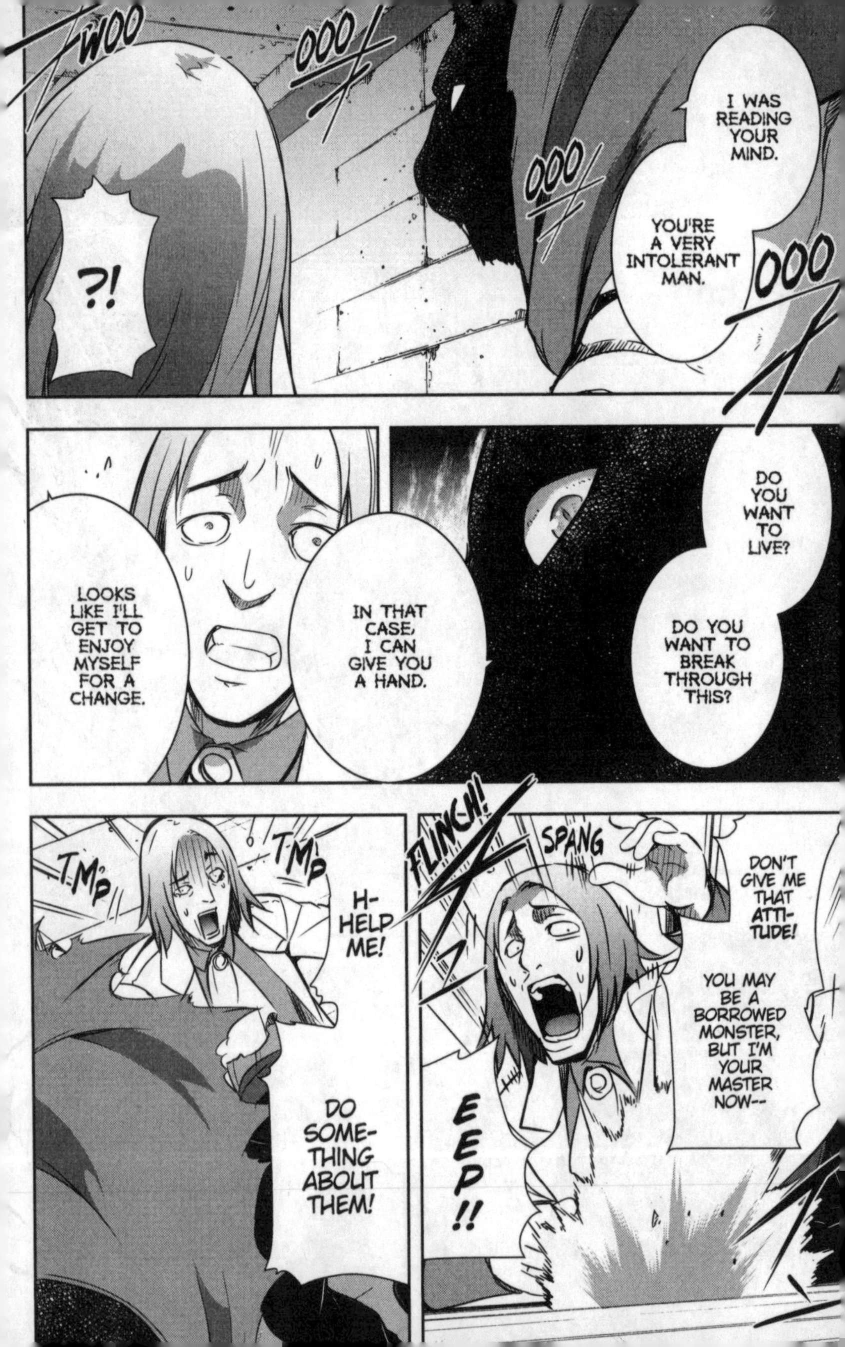
TWOOOOO
OOO
OOO
I WAS READING YOUR MIND.
YOU'RE A VERY INTOLERANT MAN.
?!
DO YOU WANT TO LIVE?
DO YOU WANT TO BREAK THROUGH THIS?
IN THAT CASE, I CAN GIVE YOU A HAND.
LOOKS LIKE I'LL GET TO ENJOY MYSELF FOR A CHANGE.
SPANG
DON'T GIVE ME THAT ATTI-TUDE!
YOU MAY BE A BORROWED MONSTER, BUT I'M YOUR MASTER NOW--
FLINCH!
EEP!!
T-MP
T-MP
H-HELP ME!
DO SOME-THING ABOUT THEM!

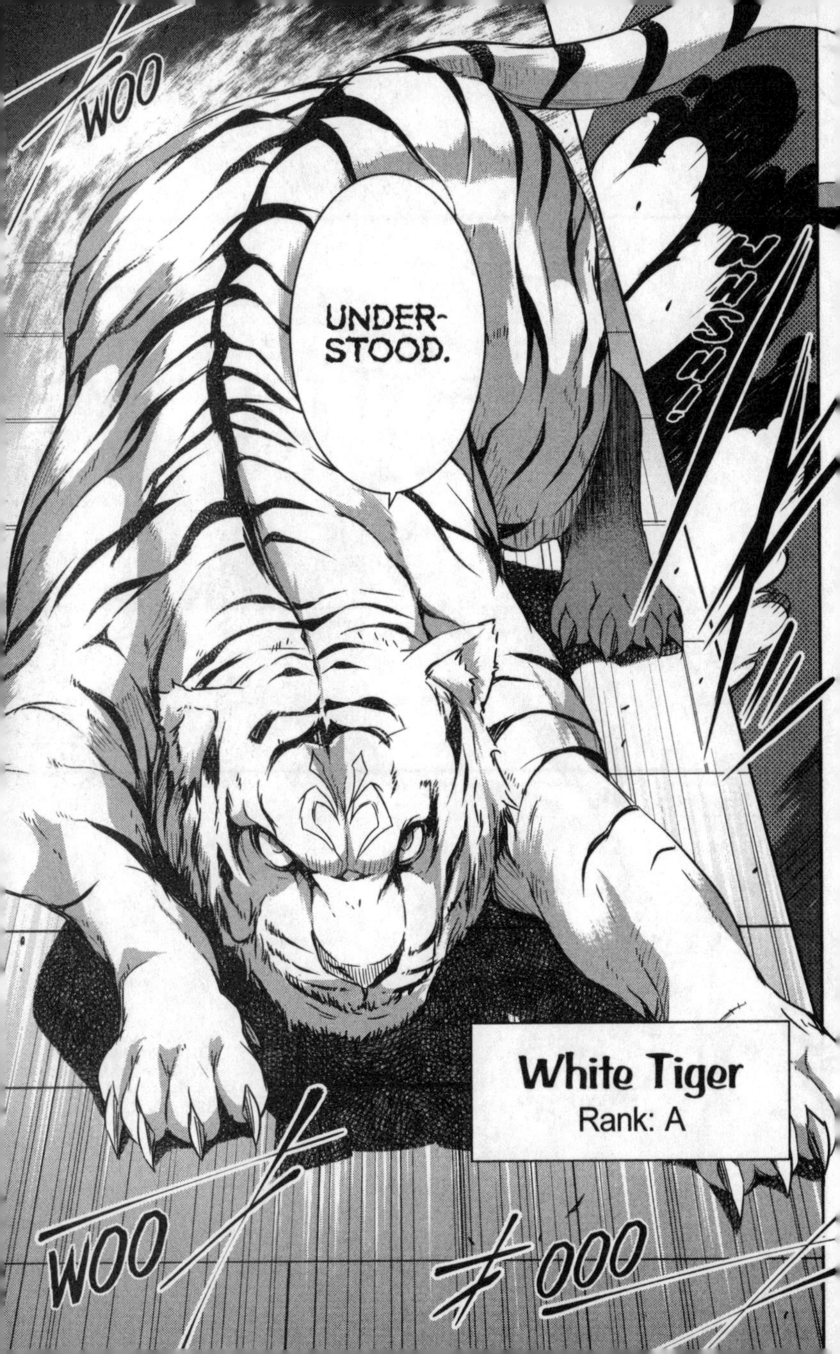
WHSH!
WOO
UNDER-STOOD.
White Tiger
Rank: A
OOO
WOO

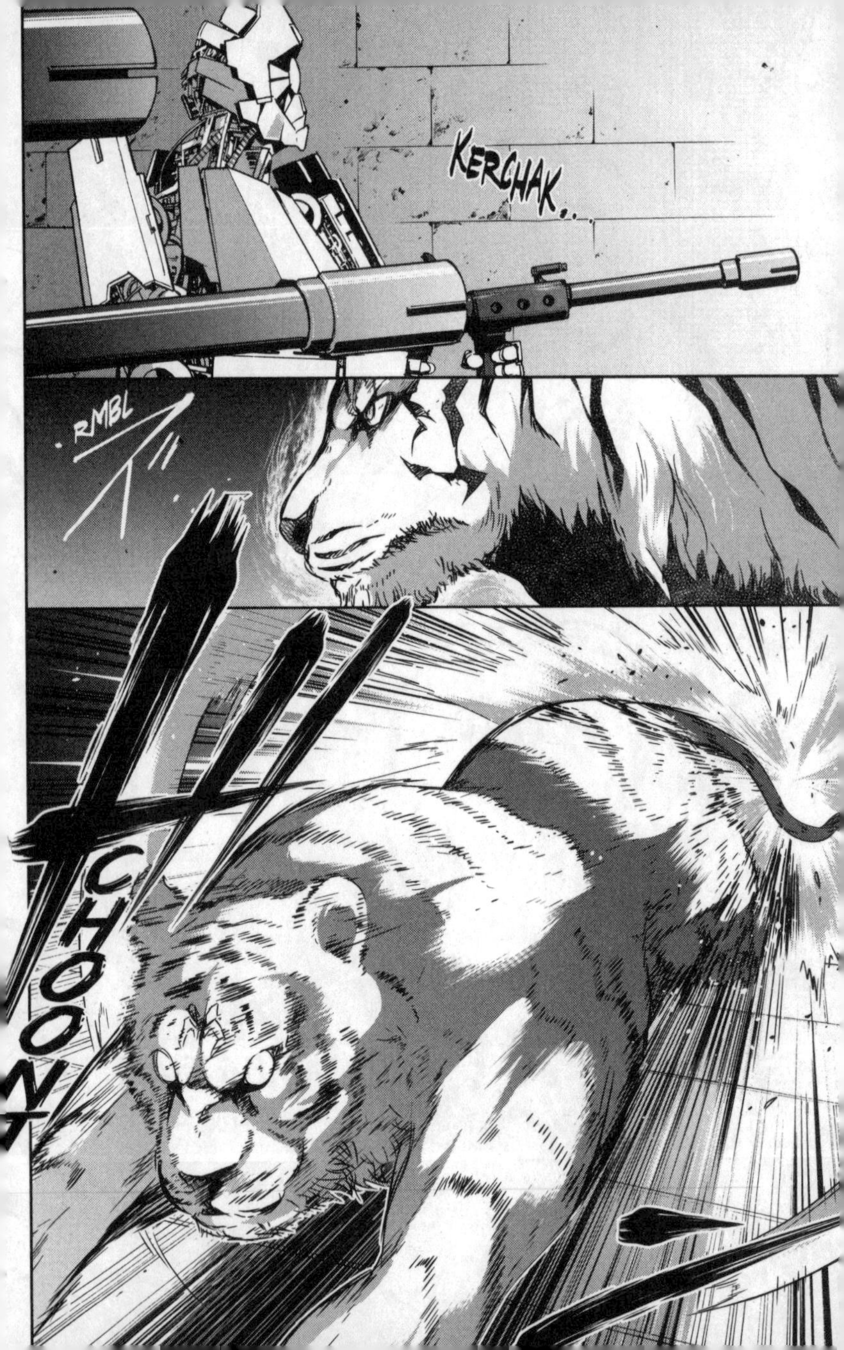
KERCHAK...
RMBL
CHOOON

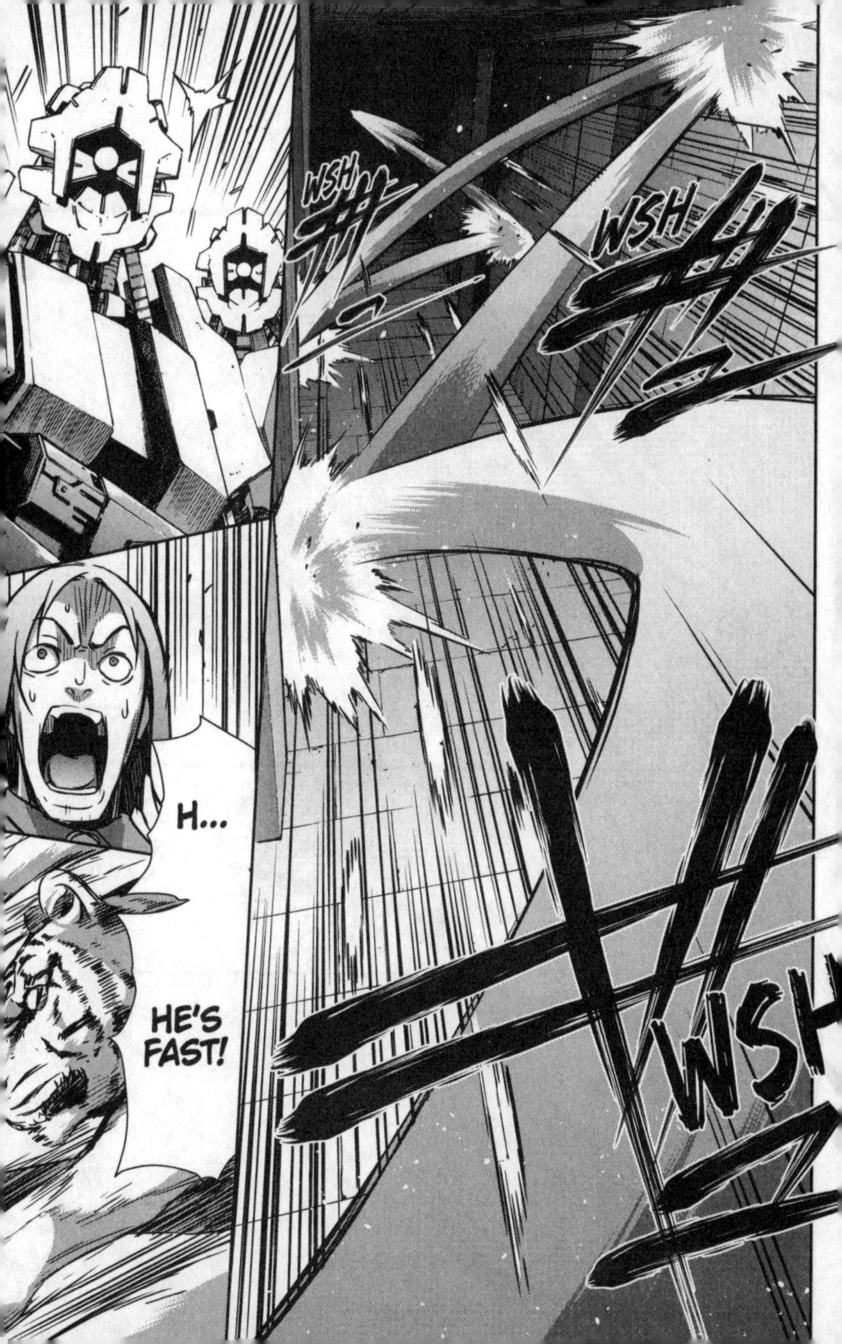
WSH
WSH
WSH
H...
HE'S FAST!

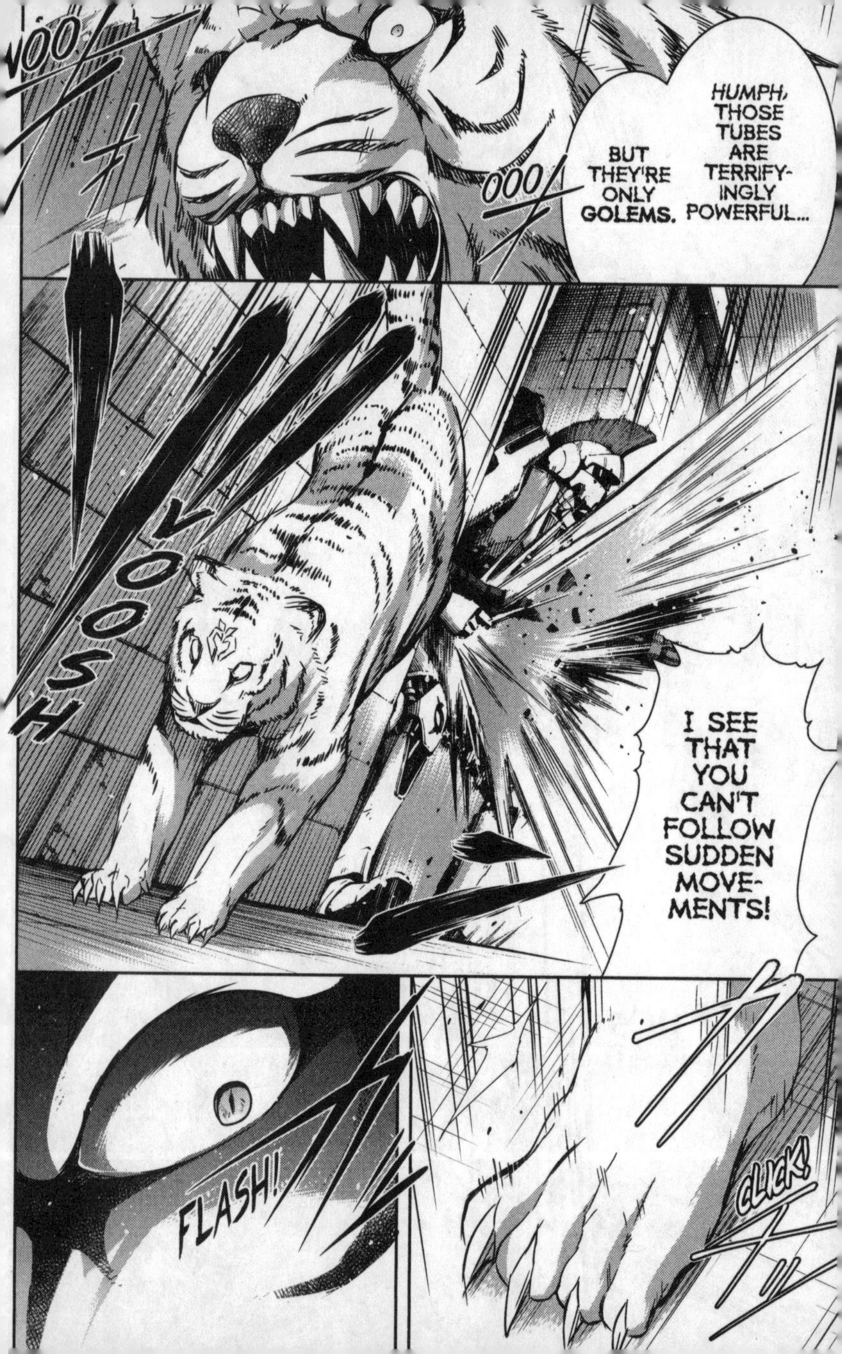
HUMPH, THOSE TUBES ARE TERRIFY-INGLY POWERFUL...
BUT THEY'RE ONLY GOLEMS.
VOOO
OOO
I SEE THAT YOU CAN'T FOLLOW SUDDEN MOVE-MENTS!
VOOOSH
CLICK!
FLASH!

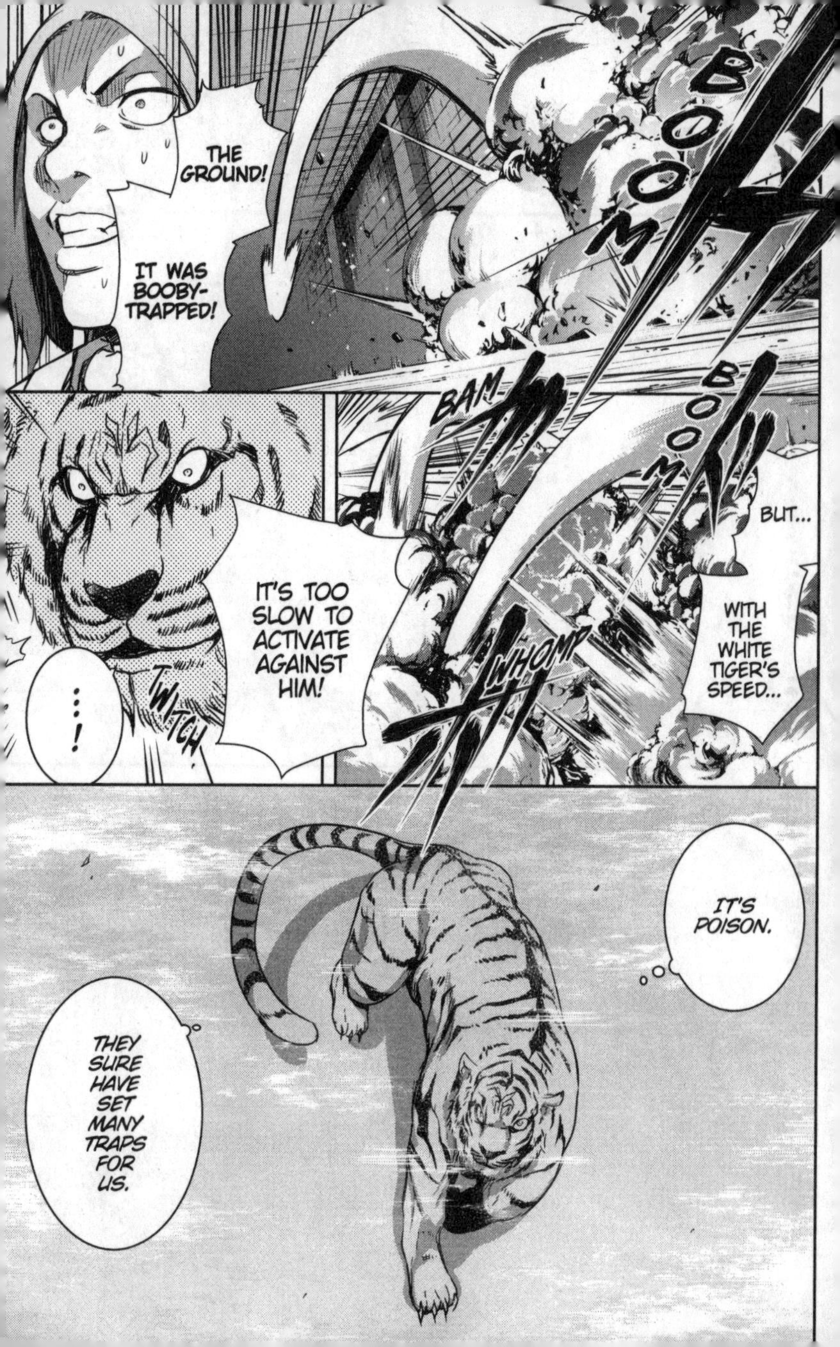
BOOM
THE GROUND!
IT WAS BOOBY-TRAPPED!
BOOM
BAM
BUT...
WITH THE WHITE TIGER'S SPEED...
WHOMP
IT'S TOO SLOW TO ACTIVATE AGAINST HIM!
TWITCH
...!
IT'S POISON.
THEY SURE HAVE SET MANY TRAPS FOR US.

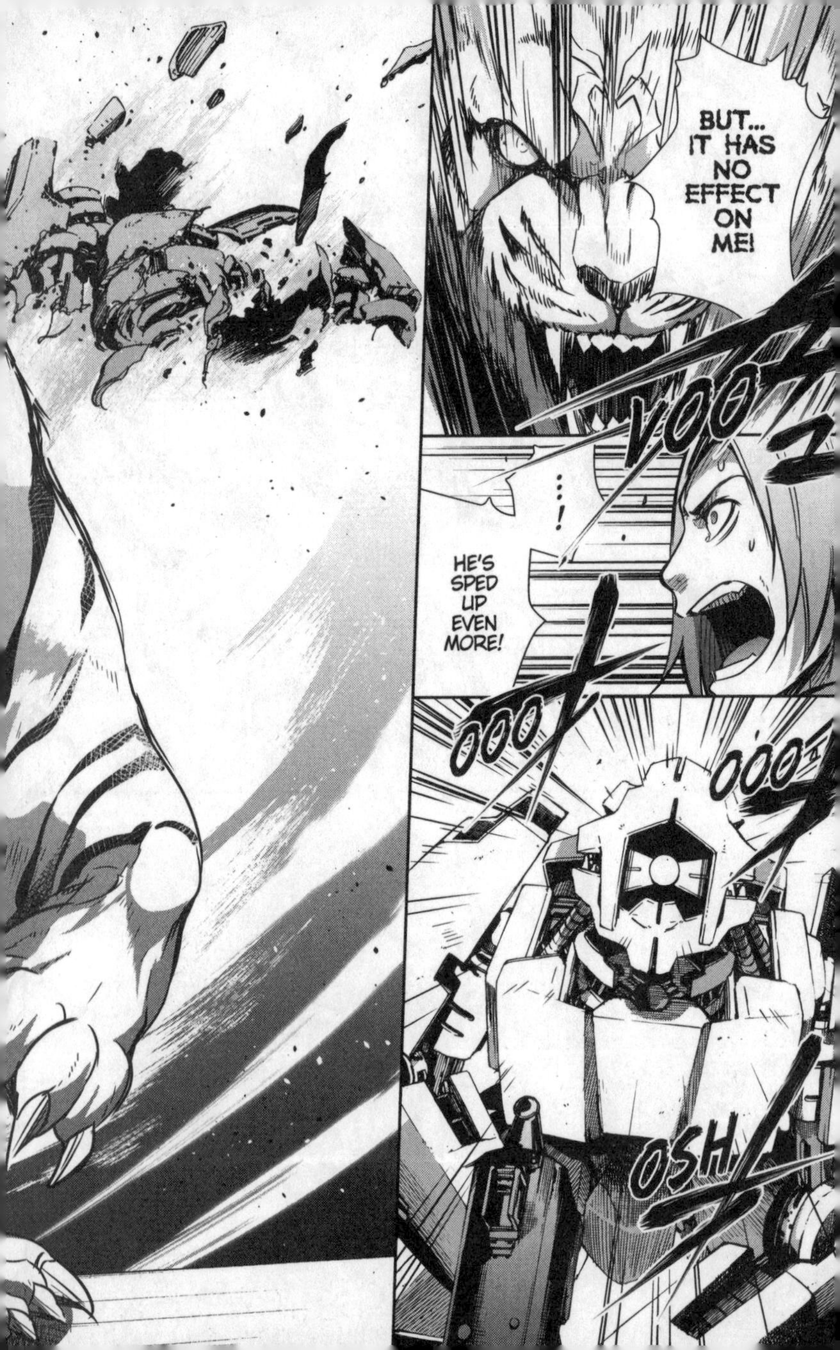
BUT... IT HAS NO EFFECT ON ME!
VOOO
...!
HE'S SPED UP EVEN MORE!
OOO
OOO
OSH

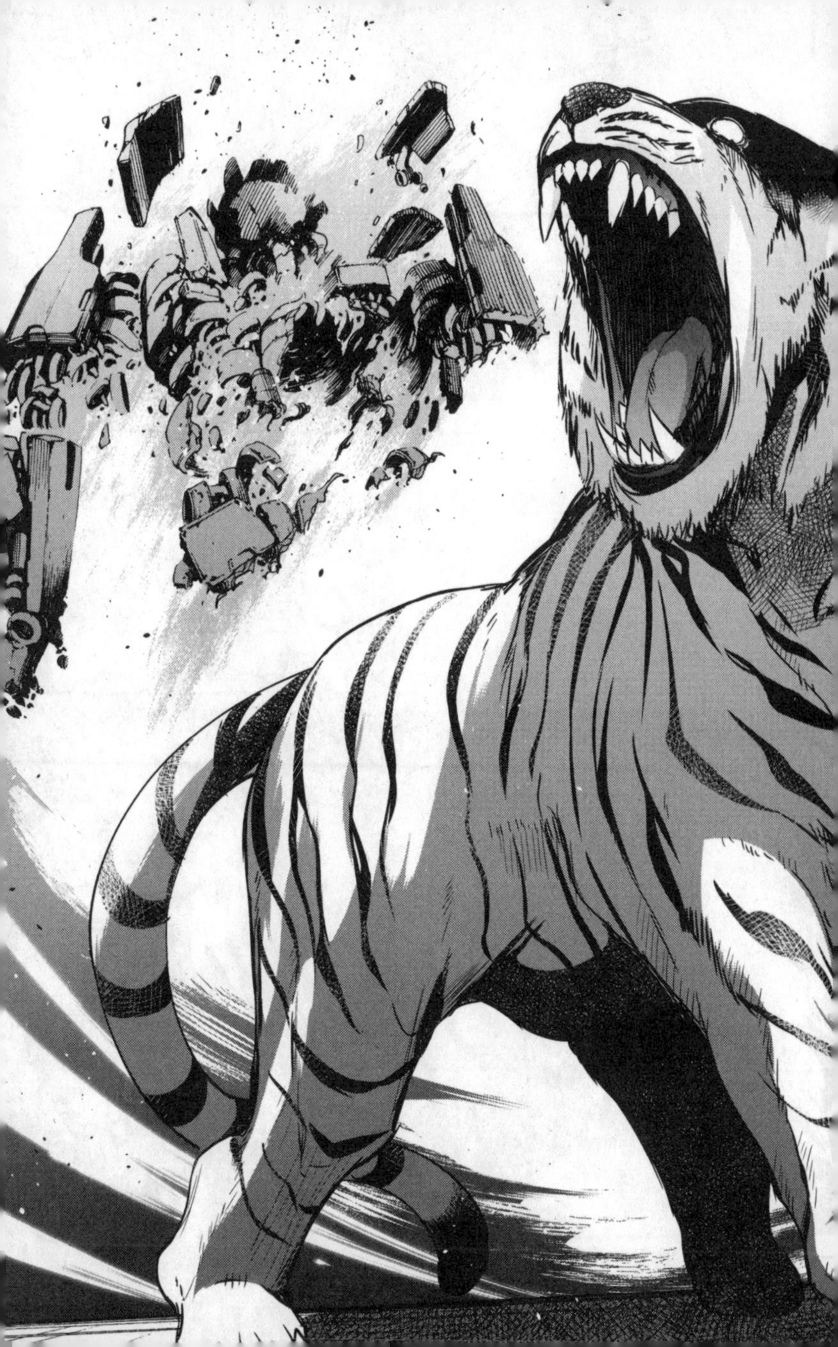

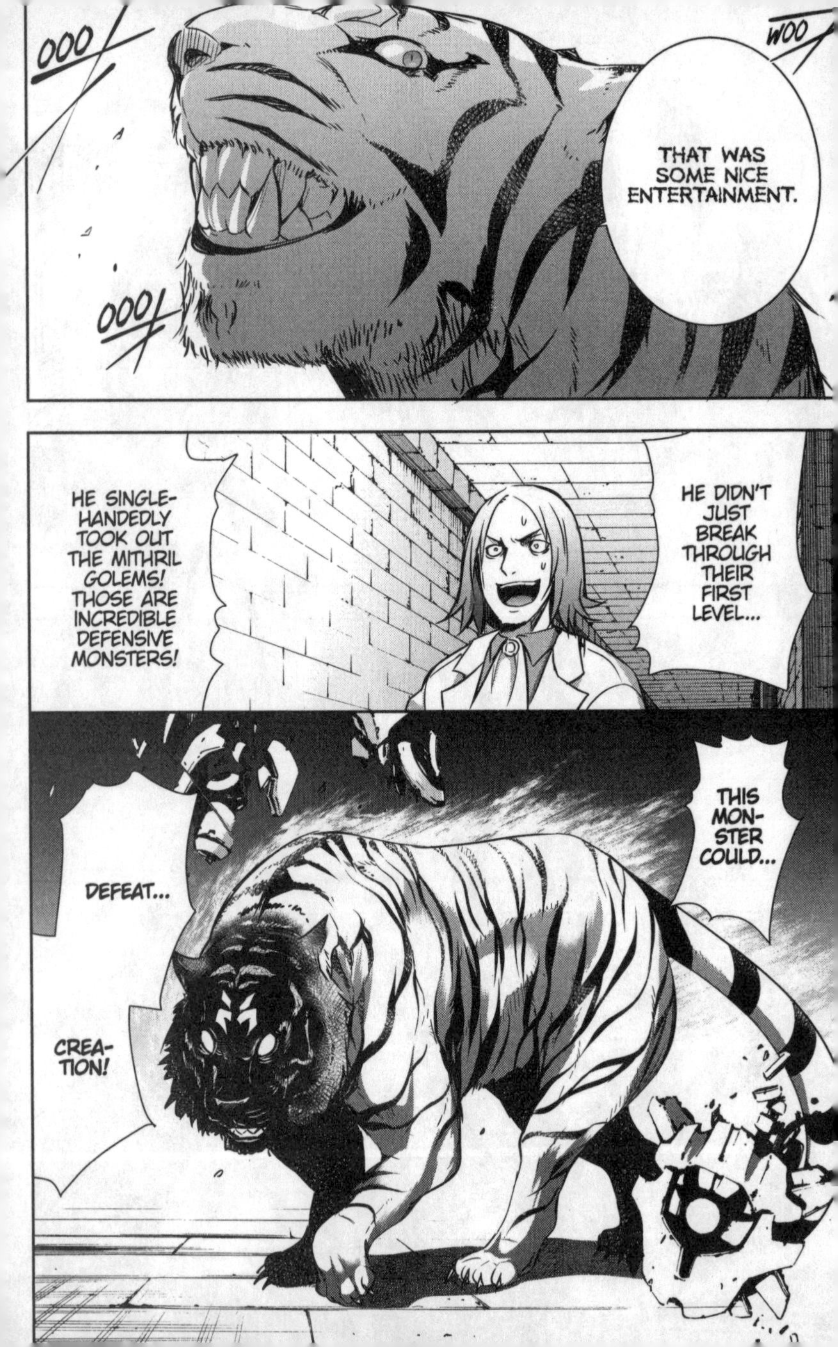
WOO
THAT WAS SOME NICE ENTERTAINMENT.
OOO
OOO
HE DIDN'T JUST BREAK THROUGH THEIR FIRST LEVEL...
HE SINGLE-HANDEDLY TOOK OUT THE MITHRIL GOLEMS! THOSE ARE INCREDIBLE DEFENSIVE MONSTERS!
THIS MON-STER COULD...
DEFEAT...
CREA-TION!

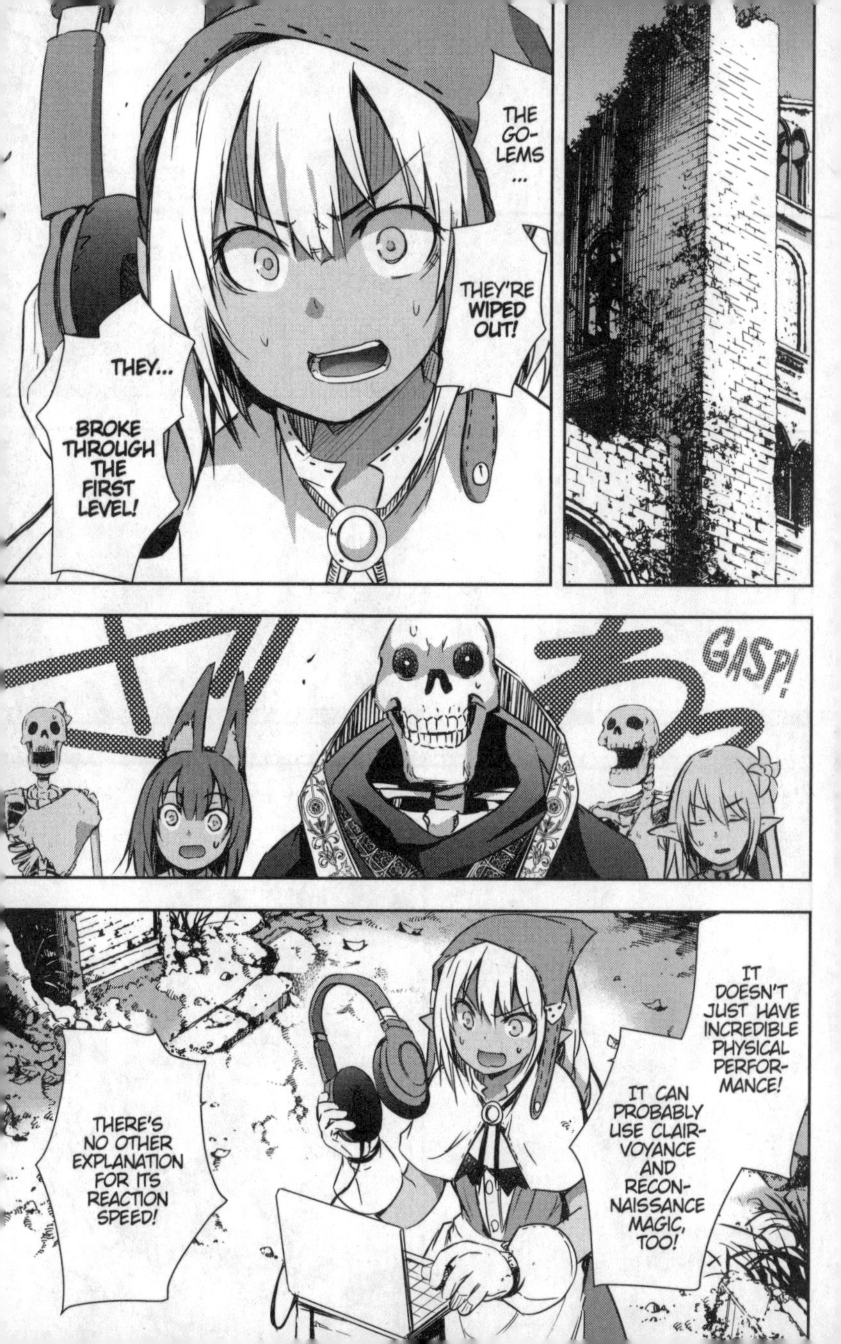
THE GO-LEMS ...
THEY'RE WIPED OUT!
THEY...
BROKE THROUGH THE FIRST LEVEL!
GASP!
IT DOESN'T JUST HAVE INCREDIBLE PHYSICAL PERFOR-MANCE!
IT CAN PROBABLY USE CLAIR-VOYANCE AND RECON-NAISSANCE MAGIC, TOO!
THERE'S NO OTHER EXPLANATION FOR ITS REACTION SPEED!

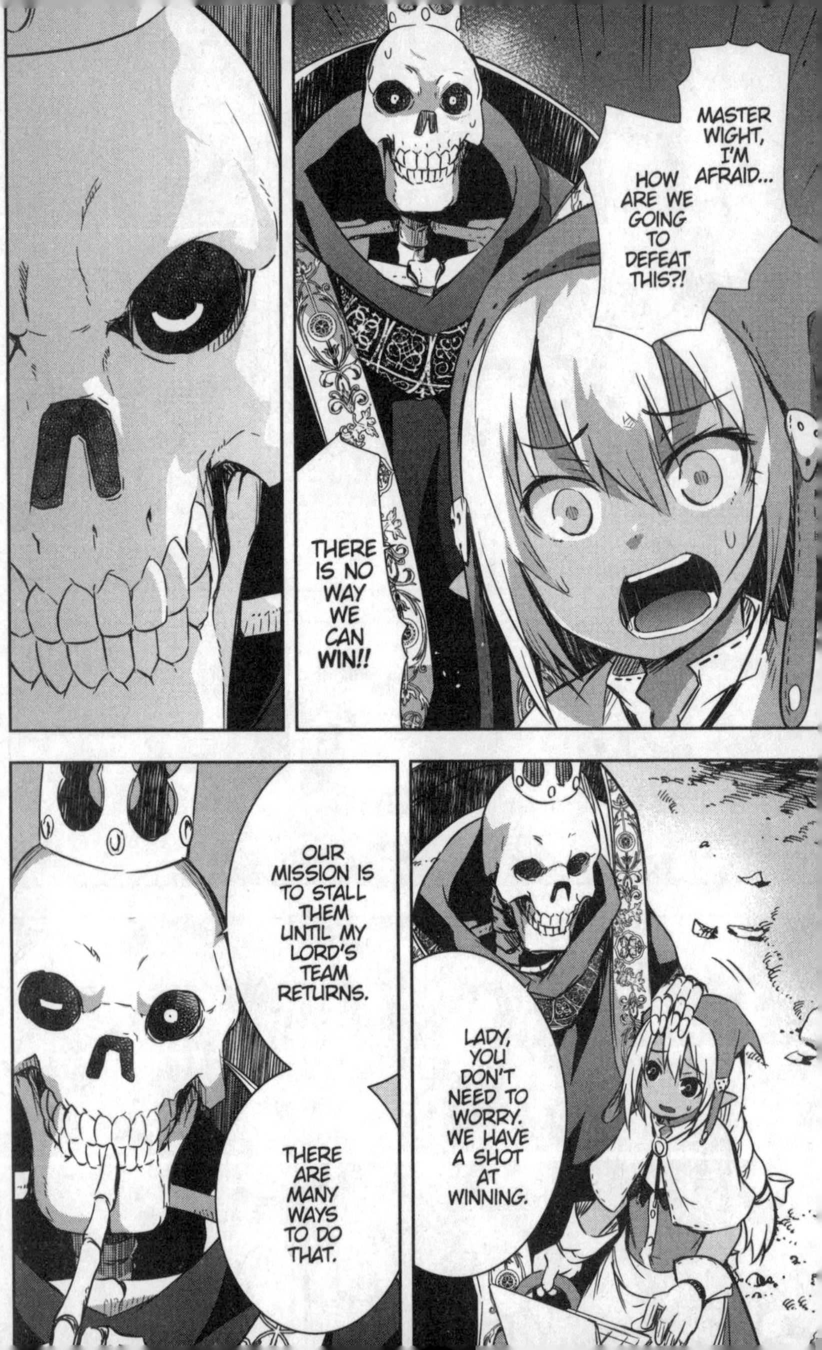
MASTER WIGHT, I'M AFRAID...
HOW ARE WE GOING TO DEFEAT THIS?!
THERE IS NO WAY WE CAN WIN!!
LADY, YOU DON'T NEED TO WORRY. WE HAVE A SHOT AT WINNING.
OUR MISSION IS TO STALL THEM UNTIL MY LORD'S TEAM RETURNS.
THERE ARE MANY WAYS TO DO THAT.

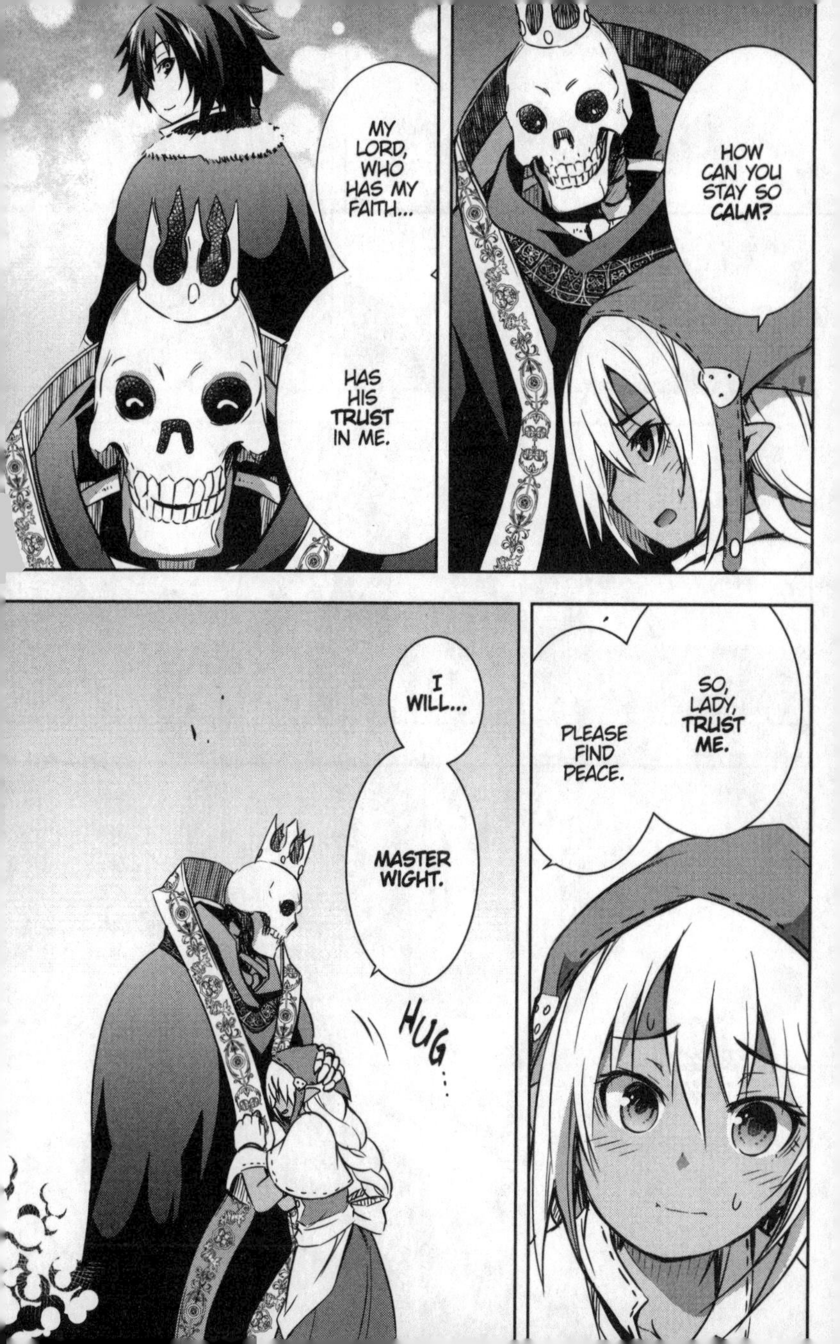
HOW CAN YOU STAY SO CALM?
MY LORD, WHO HAS MY FAITH...
HAS HIS TRUST IN ME.
SO, LADY, TRUST ME.
PLEASE FIND PEACE.
I WILL...
MASTER WIGHT.
HUG...

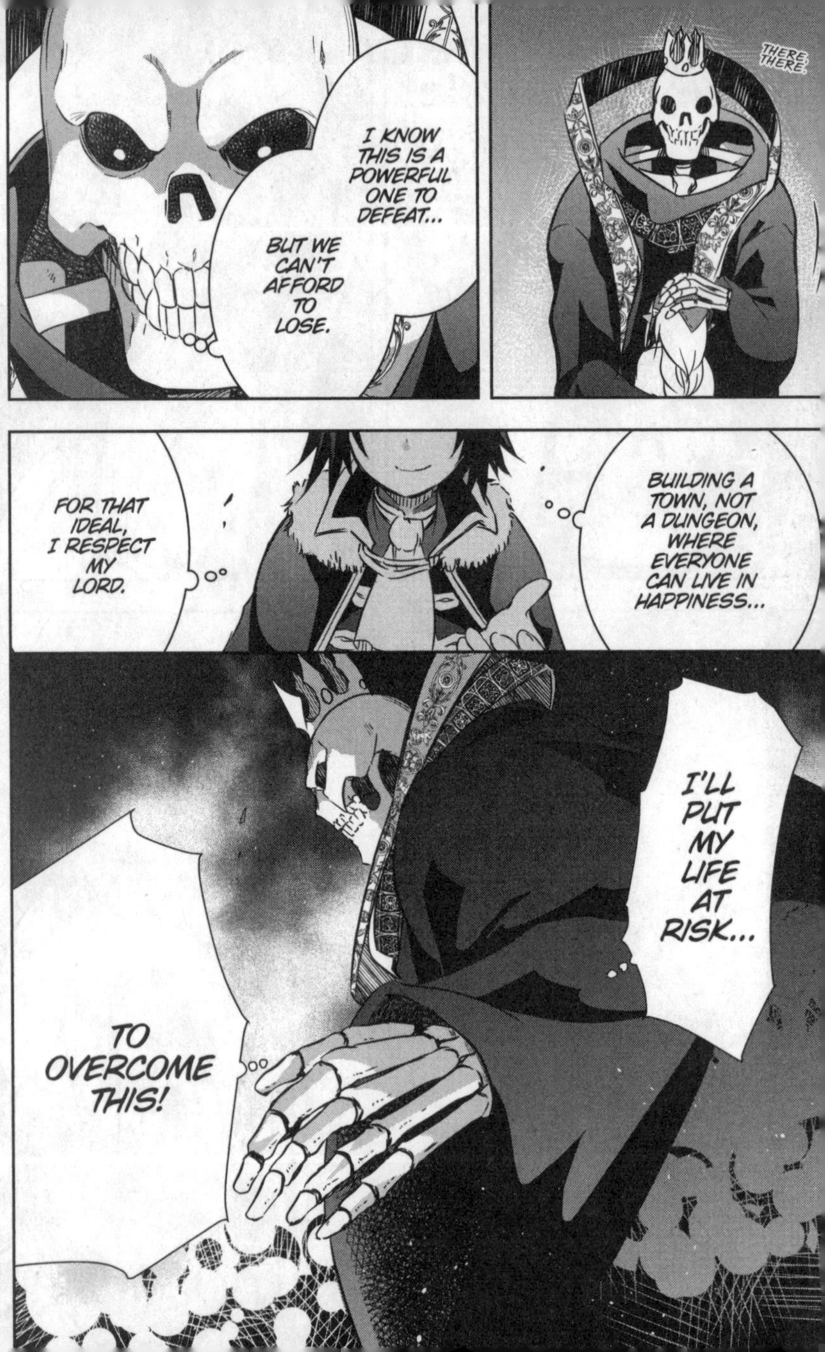
THERE, THERE.
I KNOW THIS IS A POWERFUL ONE TO DEFEAT...
BUT WE CAN'T AFFORD TO LOSE.
BUILDING A TOWN, NOT A DUNGEON, WHERE EVERYONE CAN LIVE IN HAPPINESS...
FOR THAT IDEAL, I RESPECT MY LORD.
I'LL PUT MY LIFE AT RISK...
TO OVERCOME THIS!

Chapter 24: The Caliber of the Commander

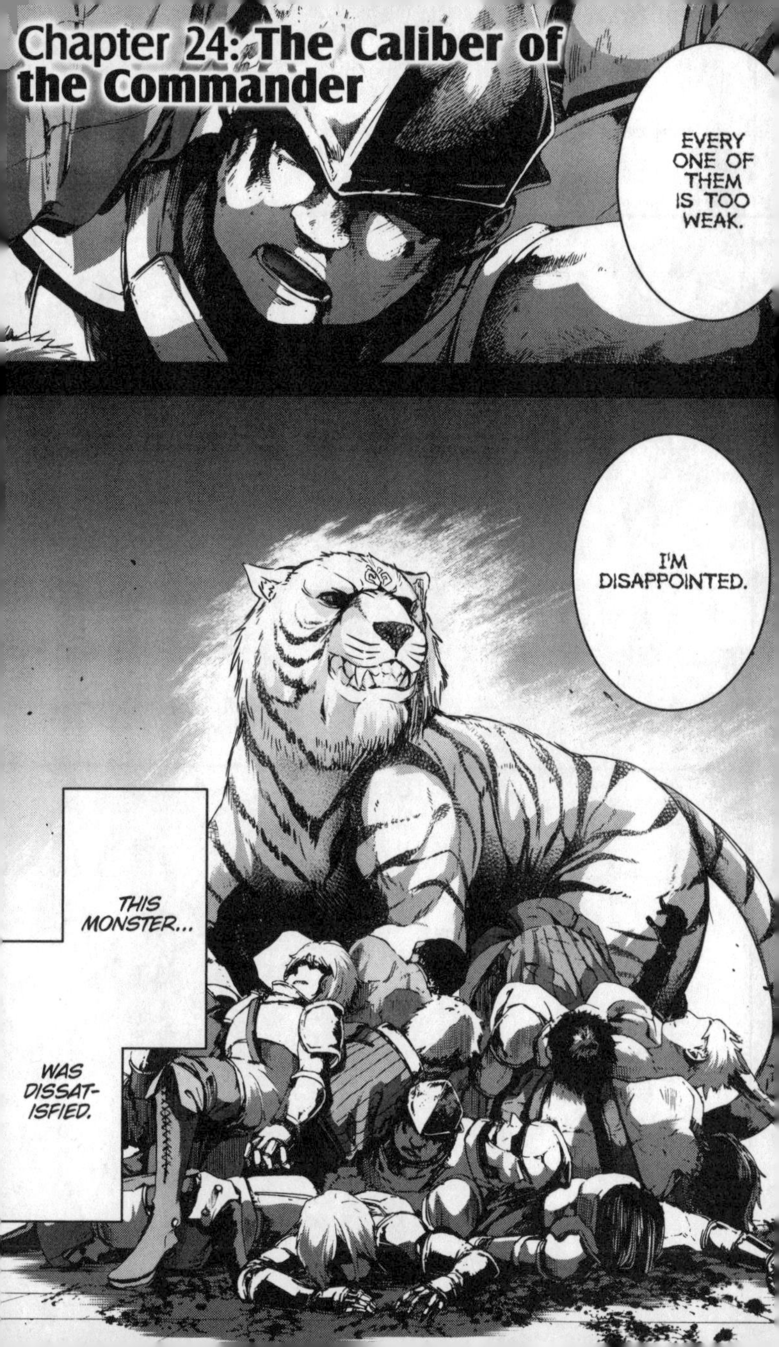
EVERY ONE OF THEM IS TOO WEAK.
I'M DISAPPOINTED.
THIS MONSTER...
WAS DISSAT- ISFIED.

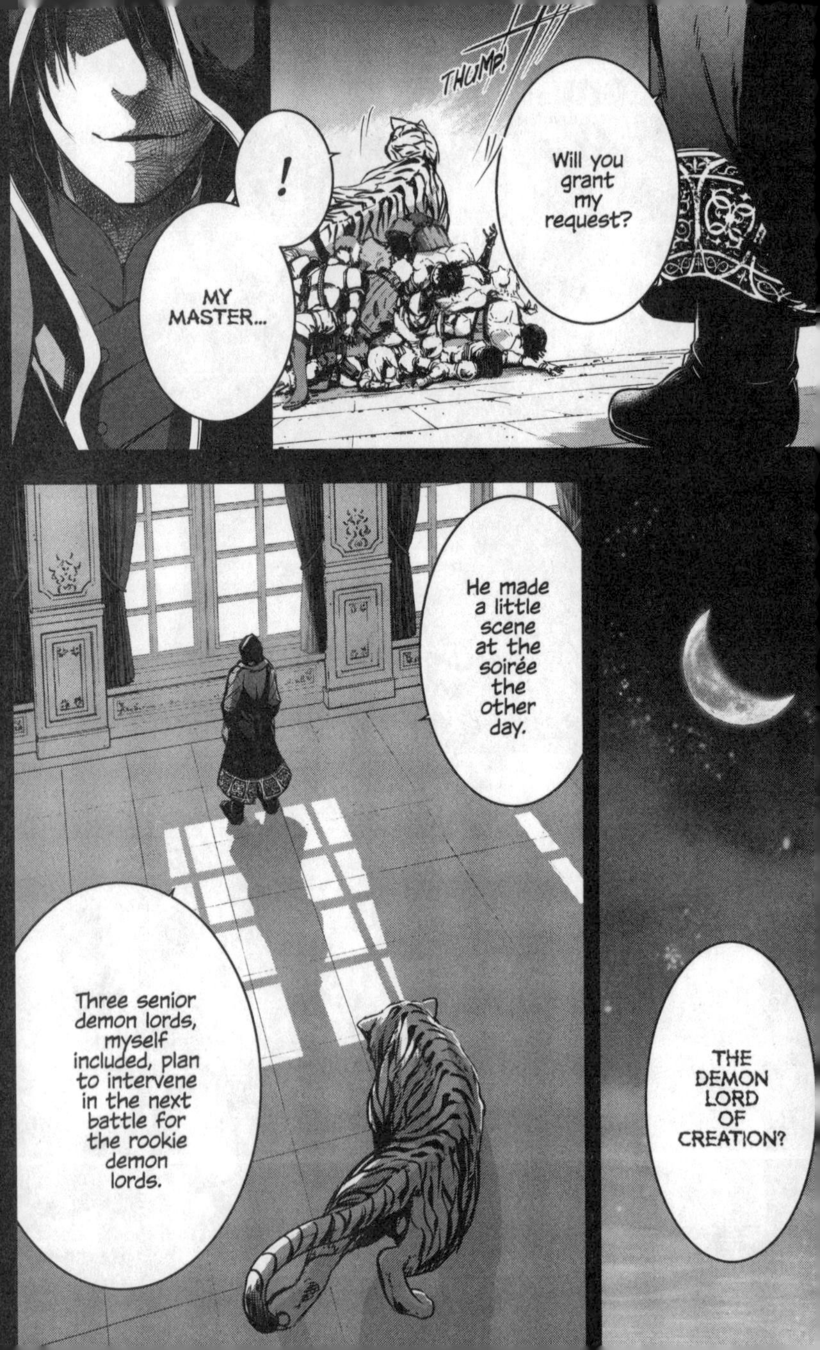
THUMP!
Will you grant my request?
!
MY MASTER...
THE DEMON LORD OF CREATION?
He made a little scene at the soirée the other day.
Three senior demon lords, myself included, plan to intervene in the next battle for the rookie demon lords.

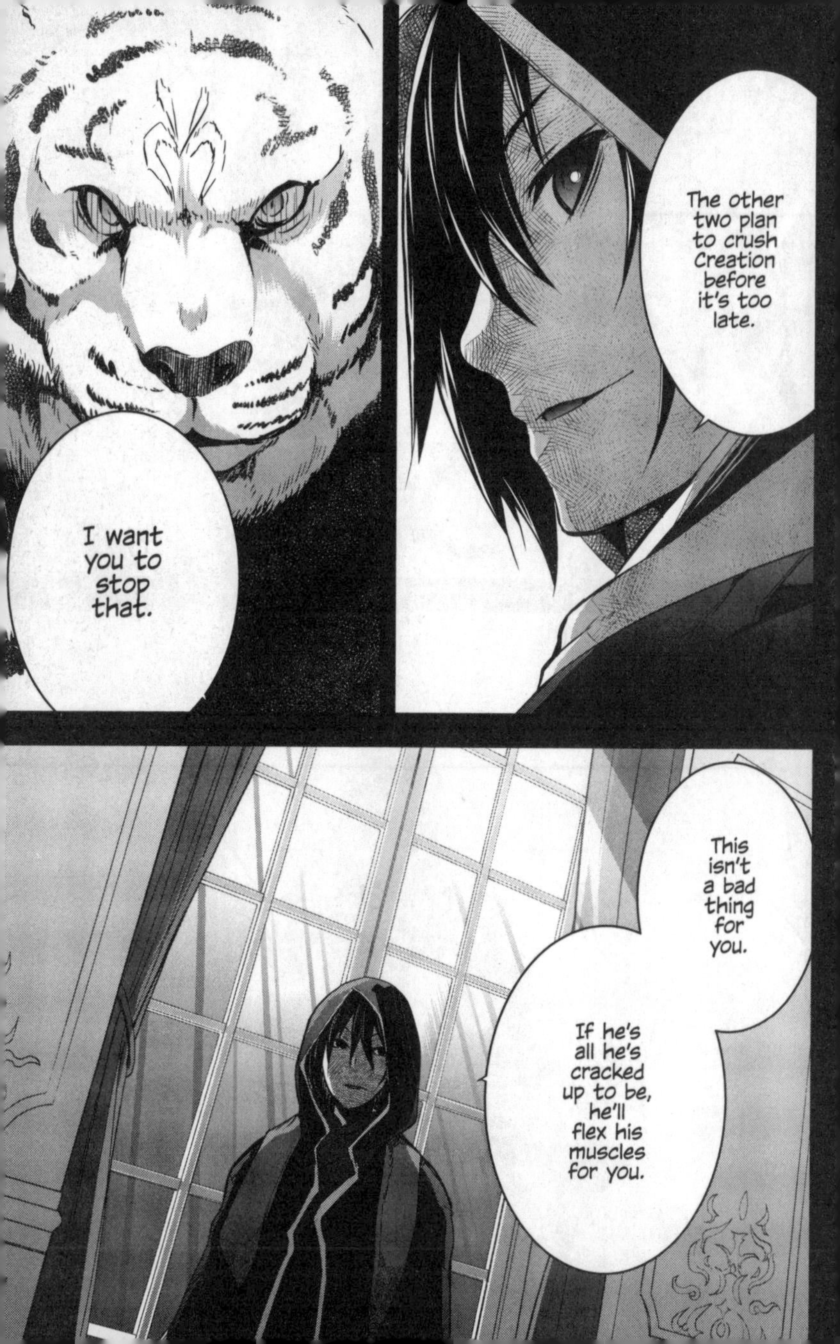
The other two plan to crush Creation before it's too late.
I want you to stop that.
This isn't a bad thing for you.
If he's all he's cracked up to be, he'll flex his muscles for you.

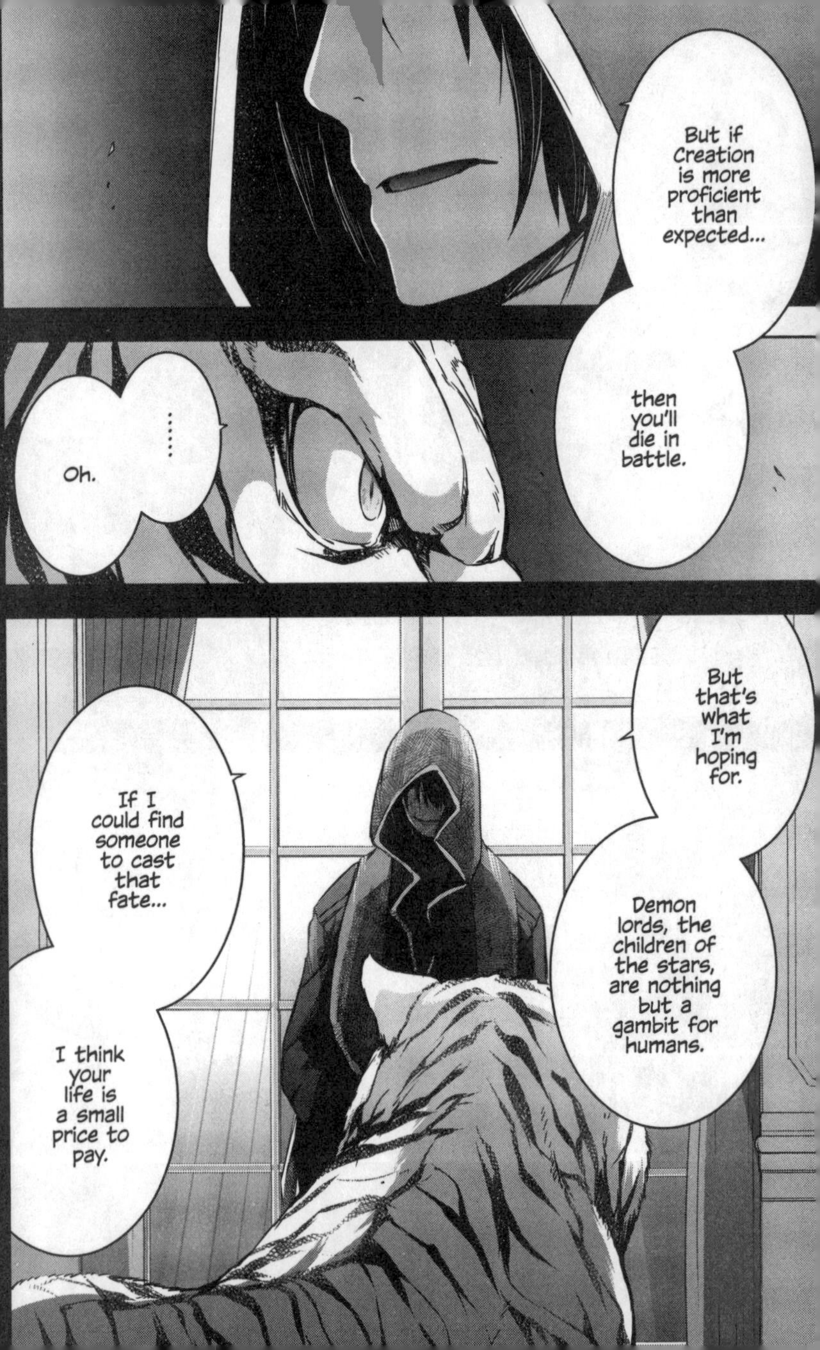
But if Creation is more proficient than expected...
then you'll die in battle.
......
Oh.
But that's what I'm hoping for.
Demon lords, the children of the stars, are nothing but a gambit for humans.
If I could find someone to cast that fate...
I think your life is a small price to pay.

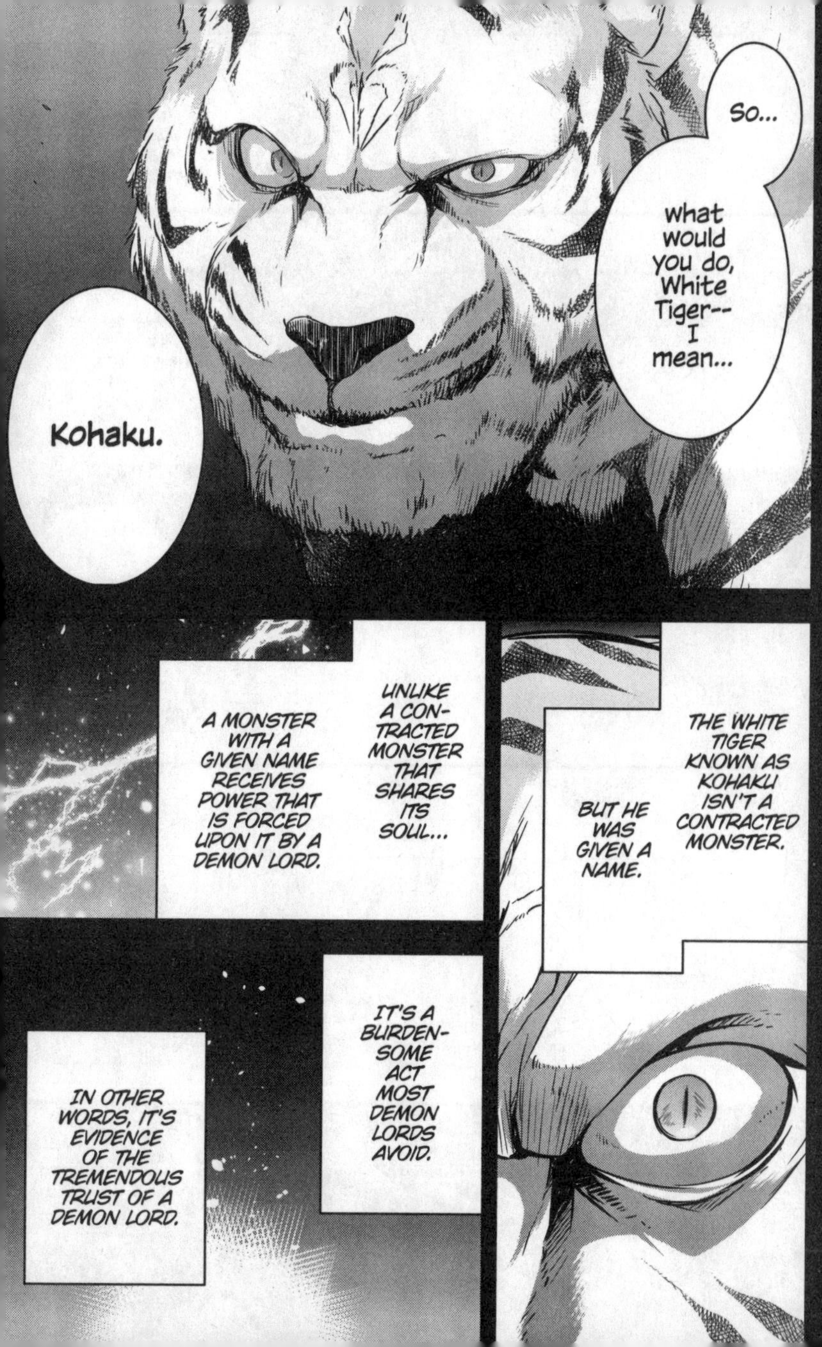
So...
what would you do, White Tiger-- I mean...
Kohaku.
THE WHITE TIGER KNOWN AS KOHAKU ISN'T A CONTRACTED MONSTER.
BUT HE WAS GIVEN A NAME.
UNLIKE A CON-TRACTED MONSTER THAT SHARES ITS SOUL...
A MONSTER WITH A GIVEN NAME RECEIVES POWER THAT IS FORCED UPON IT BY A DEMON LORD.
IT'S A BURDEN-SOME ACT MOST DEMON LORDS AVOID.
IN OTHER WORDS, IT'S EVIDENCE OF THE TREMENDOUS TRUST OF A DEMON LORD.

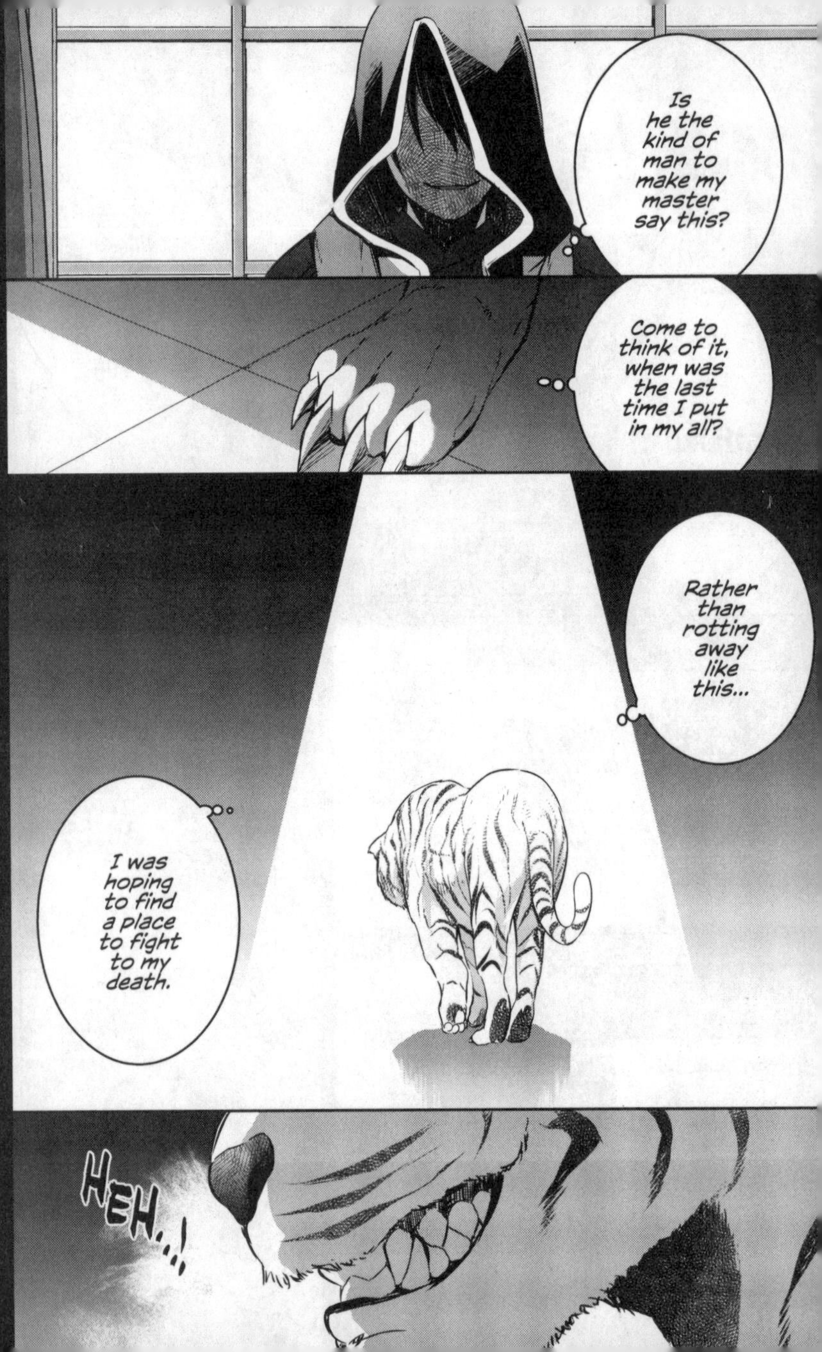
Is he the kind of man to make my master say this?
Come to think of it, when was the last time I put in my all?
Rather than rotting away like this...
I was hoping to find a place to fight to my death.
HEH...!

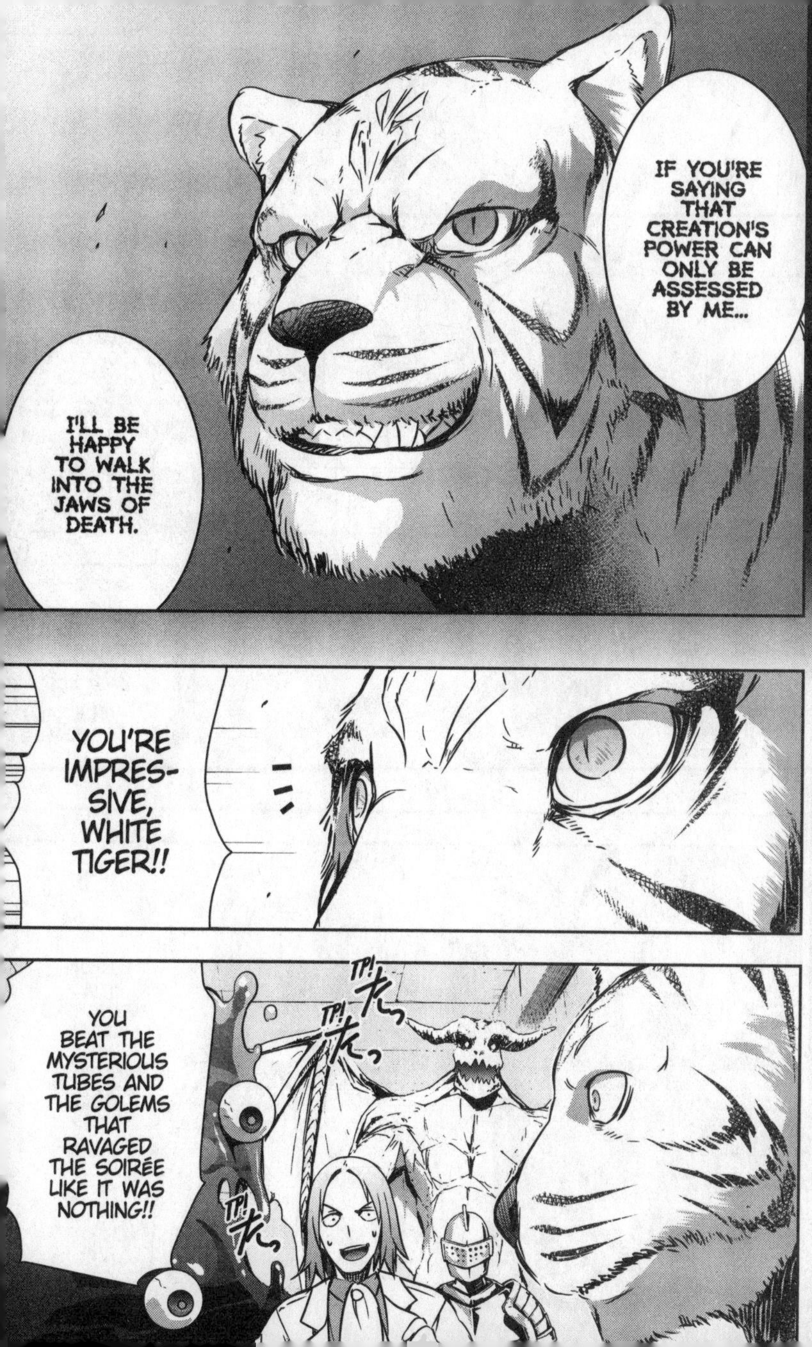
IF YOU'RE SAYING THAT CREATION'S POWER CAN ONLY BE ASSESSED BY ME...
I'LL BE HAPPY TO WALK INTO THE JAWS OF DEATH.
YOU'RE IMPRES-SIVE, WHITE TIGER!!
TP!
TP!
YOU BEAT THE MYSTERIOUS TUBES AND THE GOLEMS THAT RAVAGED THE SOIRÉE LIKE IT WAS NOTHING!!
TP!

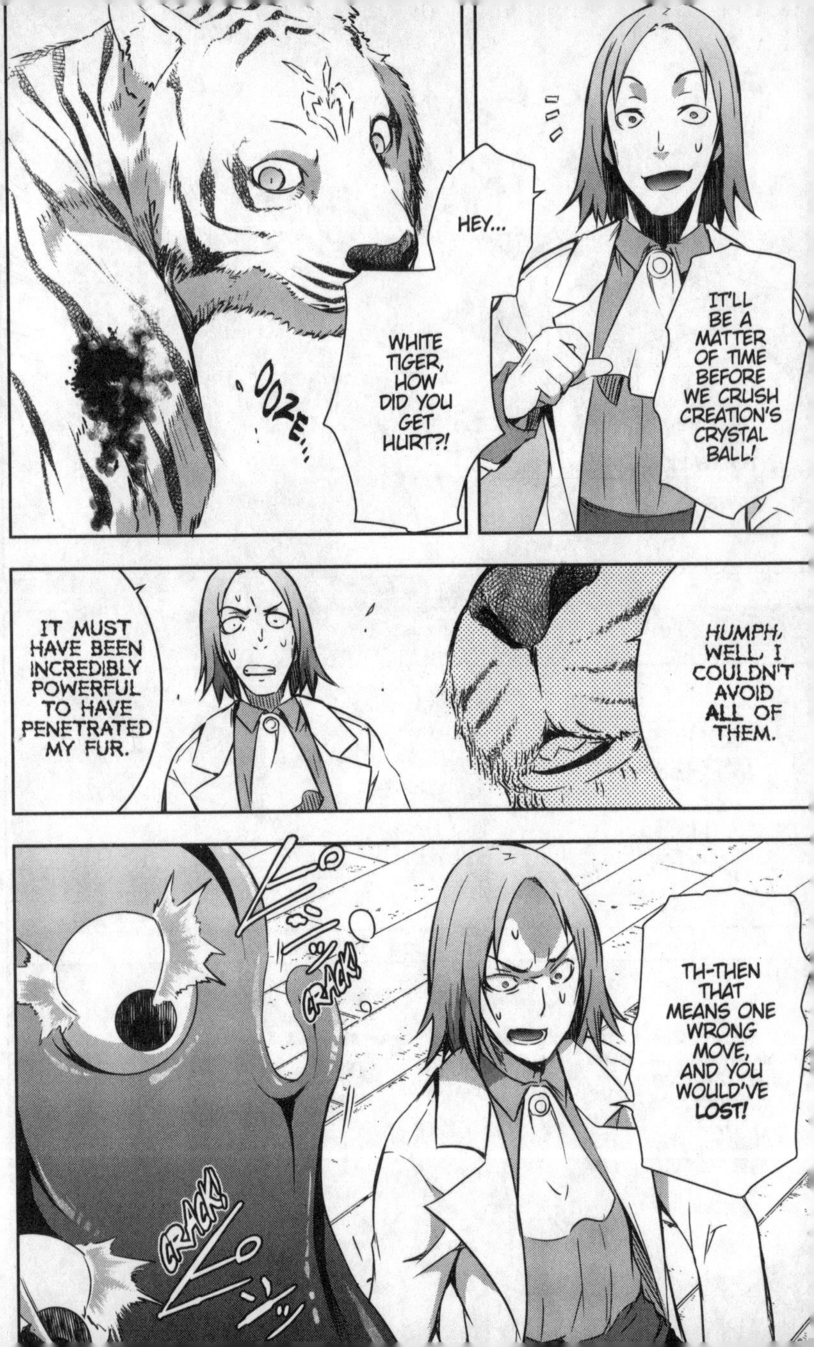
IT'LL BE A MATTER OF TIME BEFORE WE CRUSH CREATION'S CRYSTAL BALL!
HEY... WHITE TIGER, HOW DID YOU GET HURT?!
OOZE...
HUMPH, WELL, I COULDN'T AVOID ALL OF THEM.
IT MUST HAVE BEEN INCREDIBLY POWERFUL TO HAVE PENETRATED MY FUR.
TH-THEN THAT MEANS ONE WRONG MOVE, AND YOU WOULD'VE LOST!
CRACK!
CRACK!

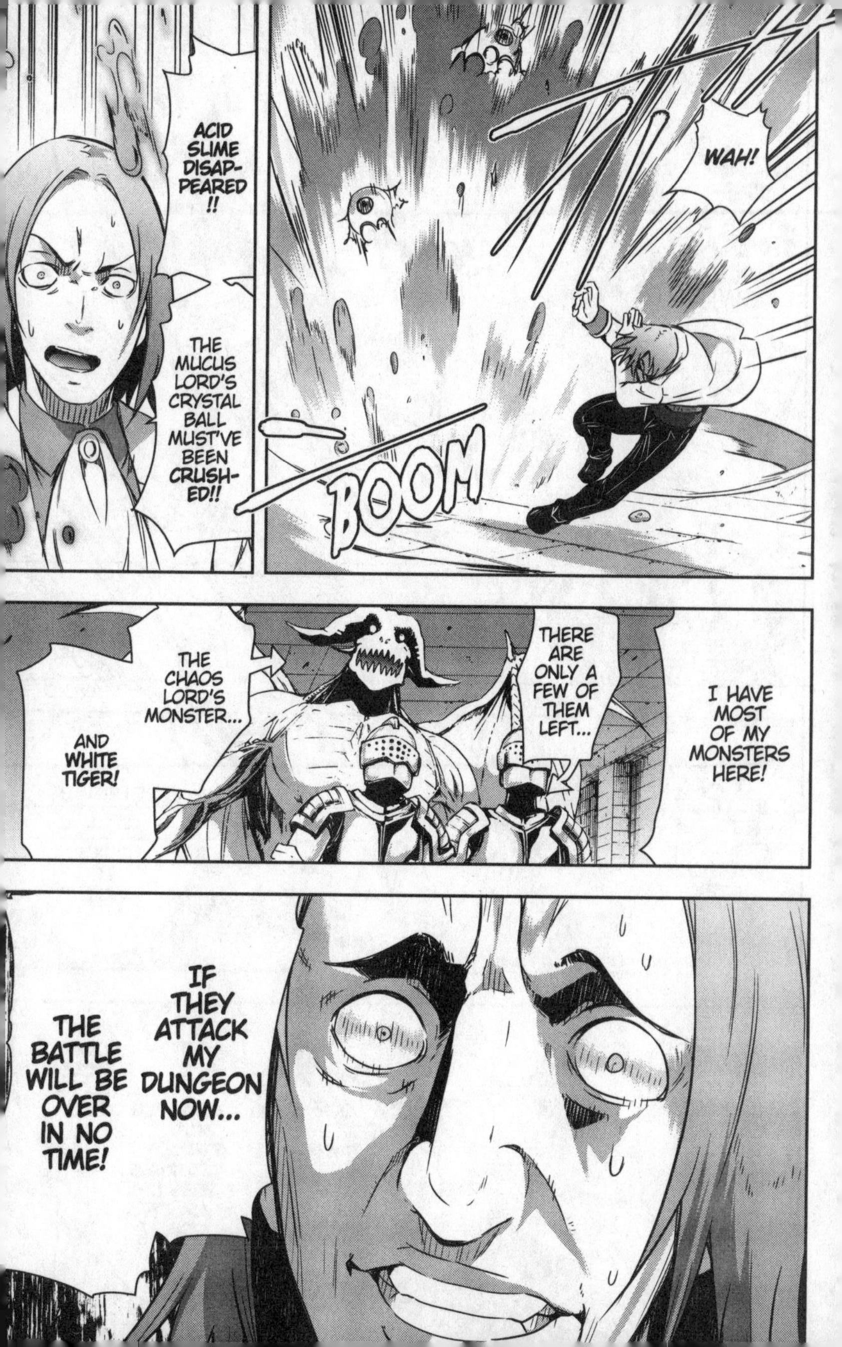
WAH!
BOOM
ACID SLIME DISAPPEARED!!
THE MUCUS LORD'S CRYSTAL BALL MUST'VE BEEN CRUSHED!!
I HAVE MOST OF MY MONSTERS HERE!
THERE ARE ONLY A FEW OF THEM LEFT...
THE CHAOS LORD'S MONSTER...
AND WHITE TIGER!
IF THEY ATTACK MY DUNGEON NOW...
THE BATTLE WILL BE OVER IN NO TIME!

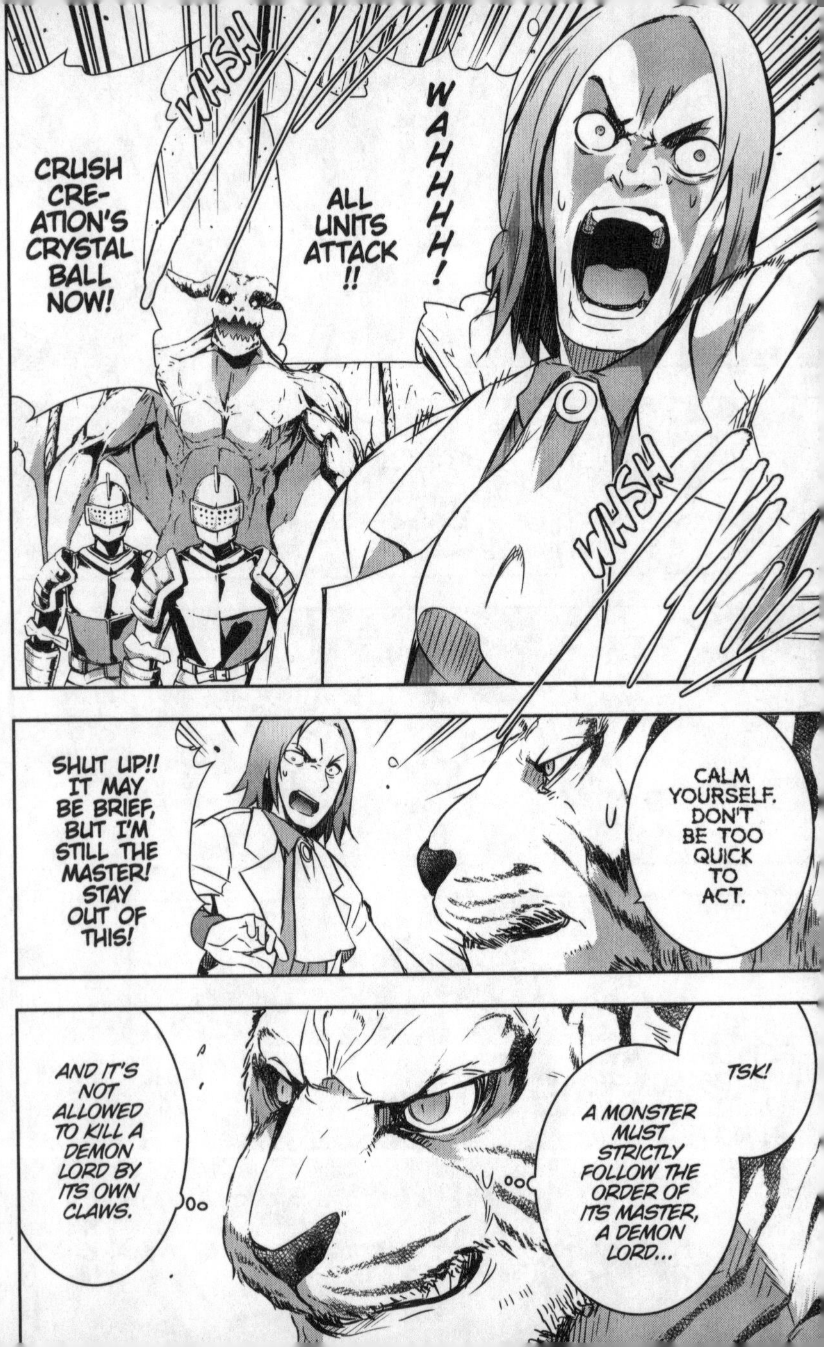
WAHHHHH!
ALL UNITS ATTACK!!
WHSH
CRUSH CRE-ATION'S CRYSTAL BALL NOW!
WHSH
CALM YOURSELF. DON'T BE TOO QUICK TO ACT.
SHUT UP!! IT MAY BE BRIEF, BUT I'M STILL THE MASTER! STAY OUT OF THIS!
TSK!
A MONSTER MUST STRICTLY FOLLOW THE ORDER OF ITS MASTER, A DEMON LORD...
AND IT'S NOT ALLOWED TO KILL A DEMON LORD BY ITS OWN CLAWS.

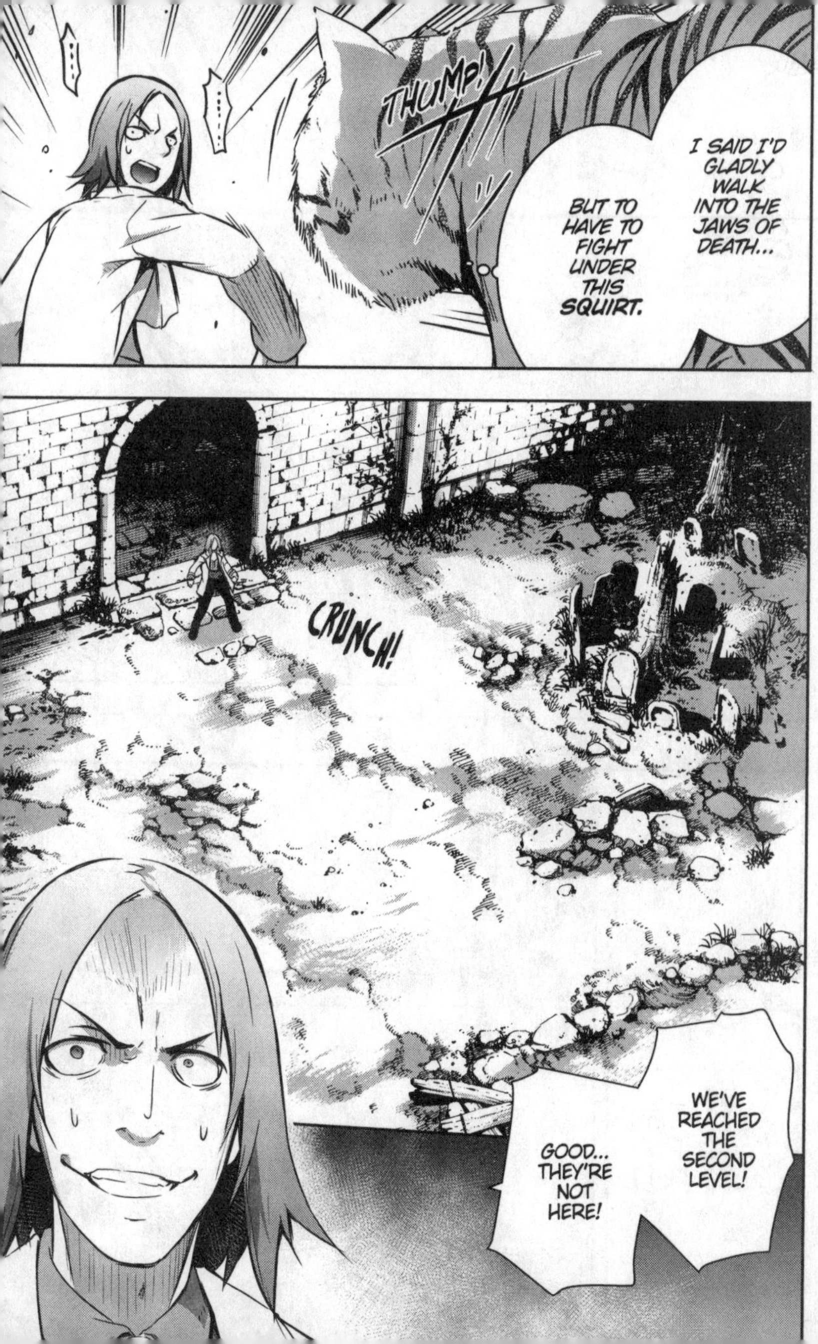
I SAID I'D GLADLY WALK INTO THE JAWS OF DEATH...
BUT TO HAVE TO FIGHT UNDER THIS SQUIRT.
THUMP!
CRUNCH!
WE'VE REACHED THE SECOND LEVEL!
GOOD... THEY'RE NOT HERE!

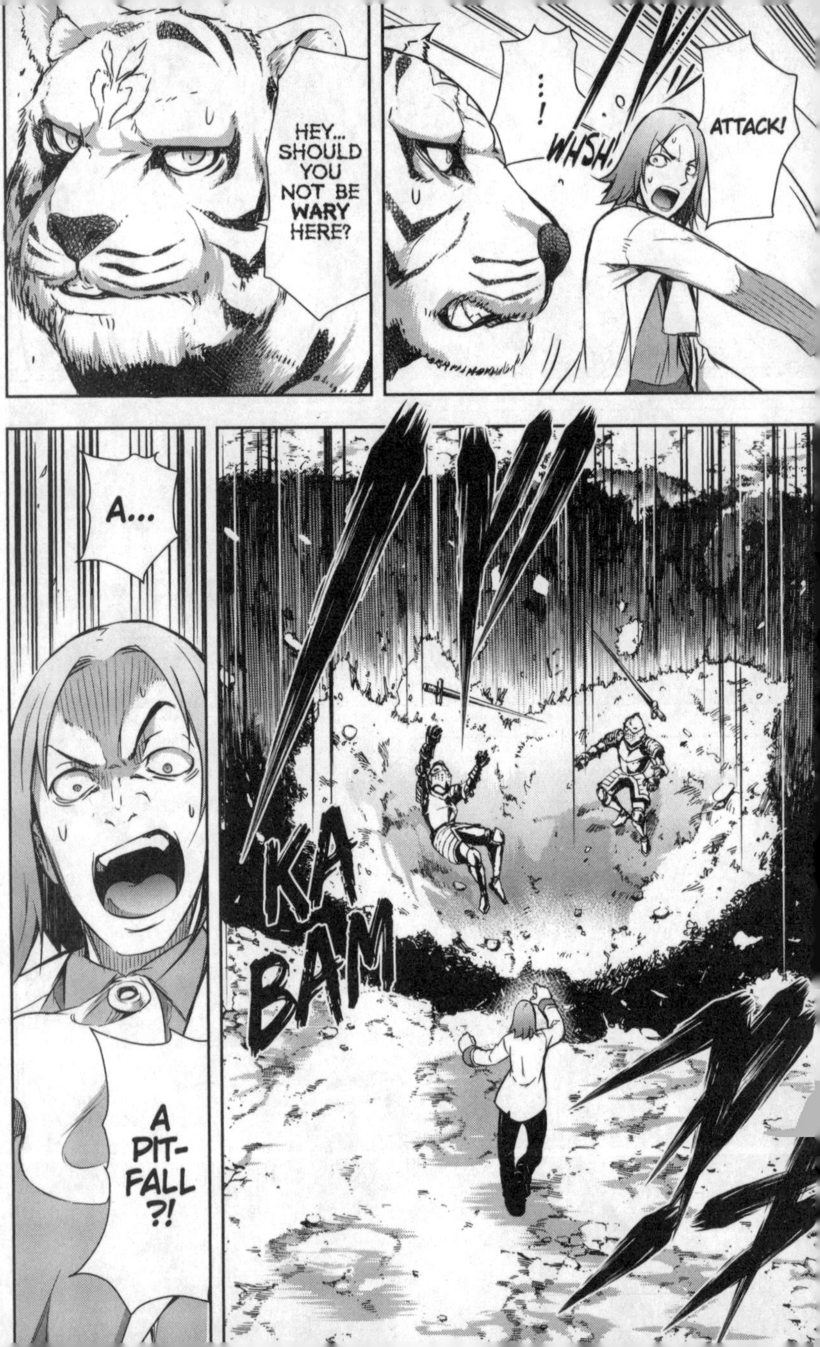
ATTACK!
...!
WHSH!
HEY... SHOULD YOU NOT BE WARY HERE?
KA BAM
A...
A PIT-FALL?!

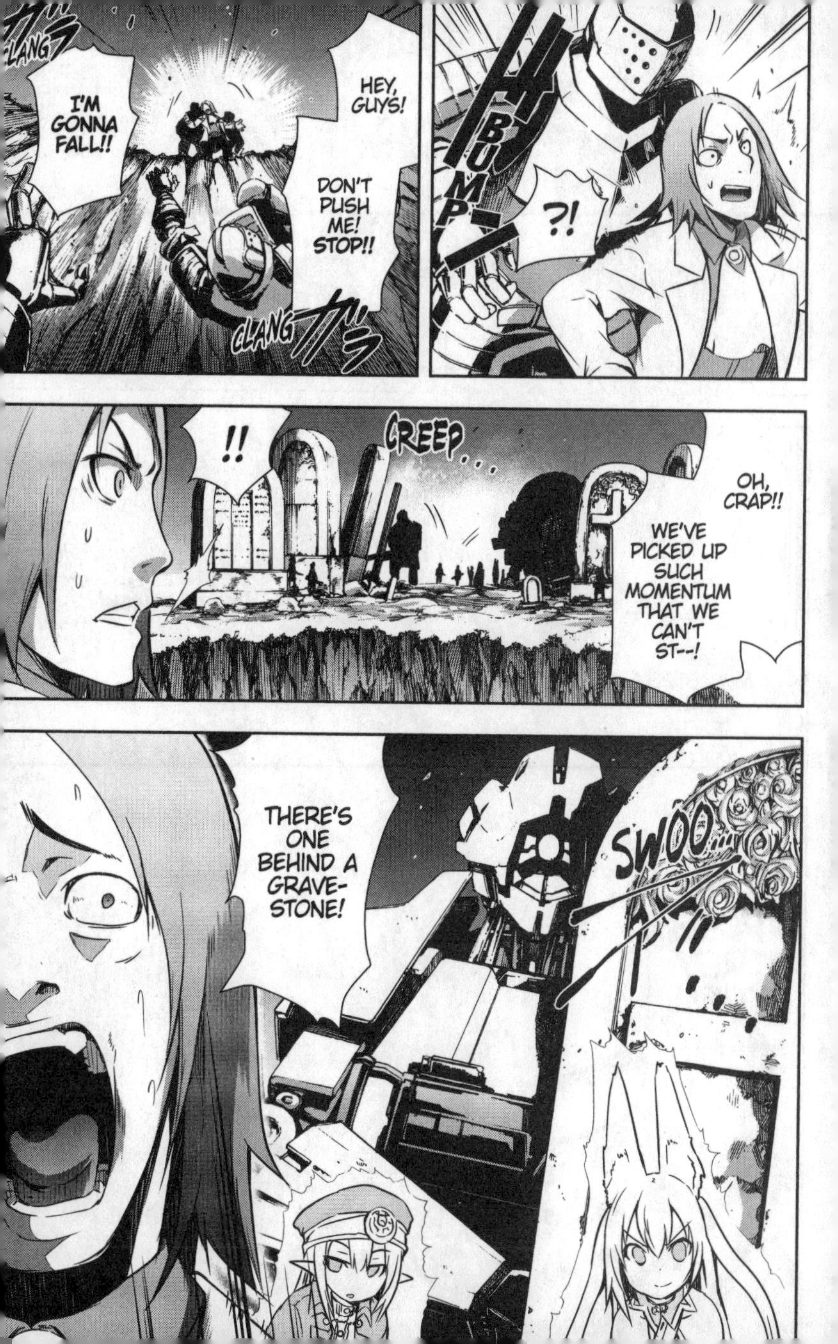
BUMP
?!
HEY, GUYS!
DON'T PUSH ME! STOP!!
I'M GONNA FALL!!
CLANG
CLANG
OH, CRAP!!
WE'VE PICKED UP SUCH MOMENTUM THAT WE CAN'T ST--!
CREEP...
!!
SWOO...
...
THERE'S ONE BEHIND A GRAVE-STONE!

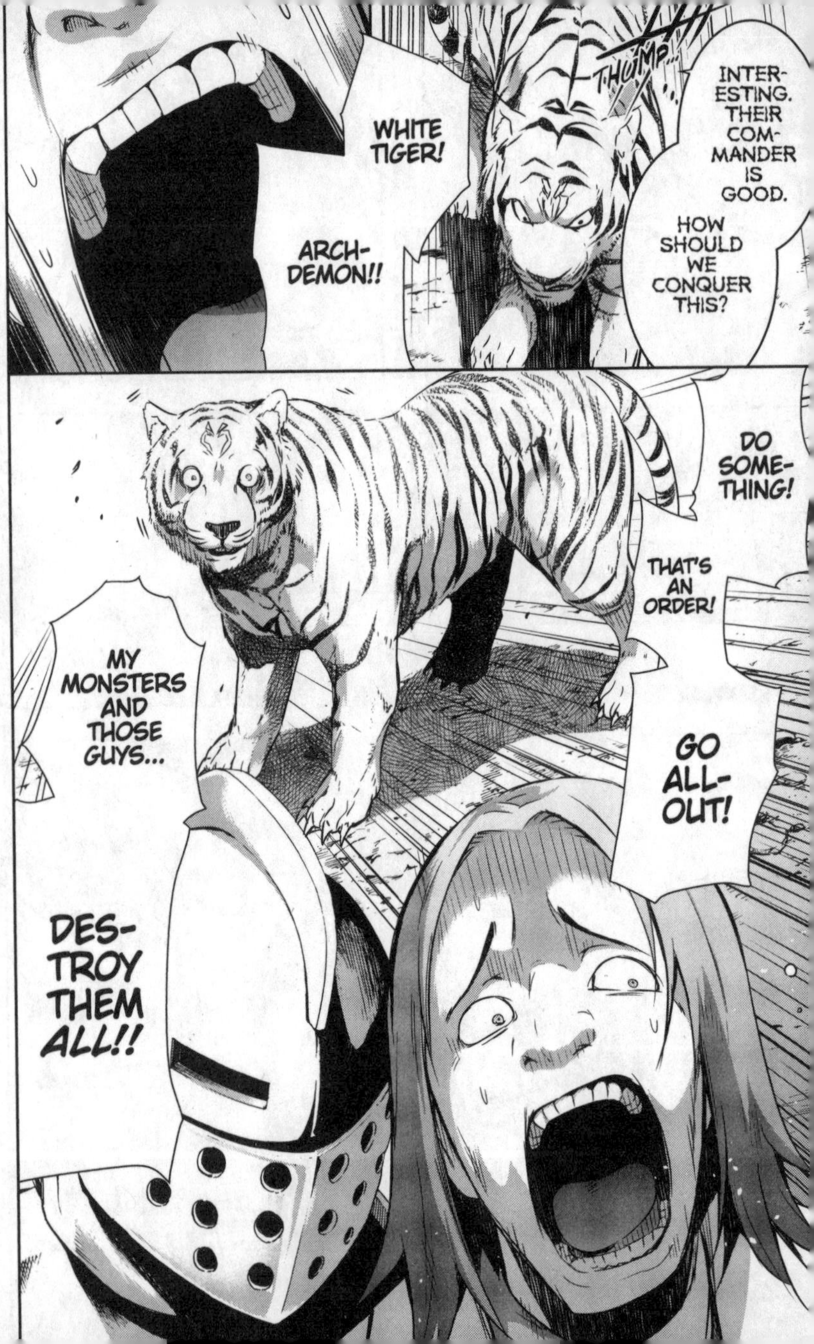
THUMP...
INTER-ESTING. THEIR COM-MANDER IS GOOD.
HOW SHOULD WE CONQUER THIS?
WHITE TIGER!
ARCH-DEMON!!
DO SOME-THING!
THAT'S AN ORDER!
GO ALL-OUT!
MY MONSTERS AND THOSE GUYS...
DES-TROY THEM ALL!!

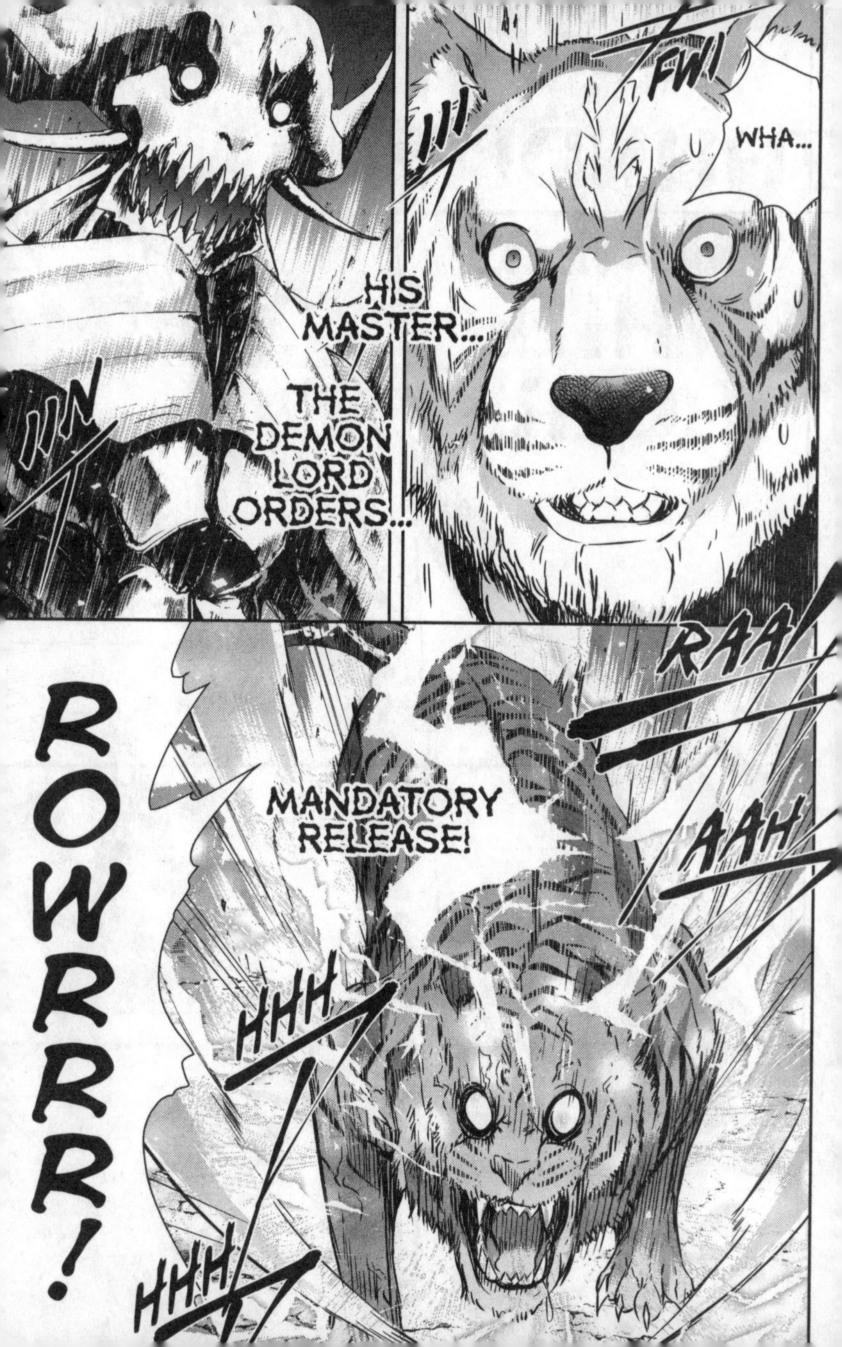

FWI
III
WHA...
HIS MASTER...
THE DEMON LORD ORDERS...
DIN
RAA
AAH
MANDATORY RELEASE!
ROWRRR!
HHH
HHH

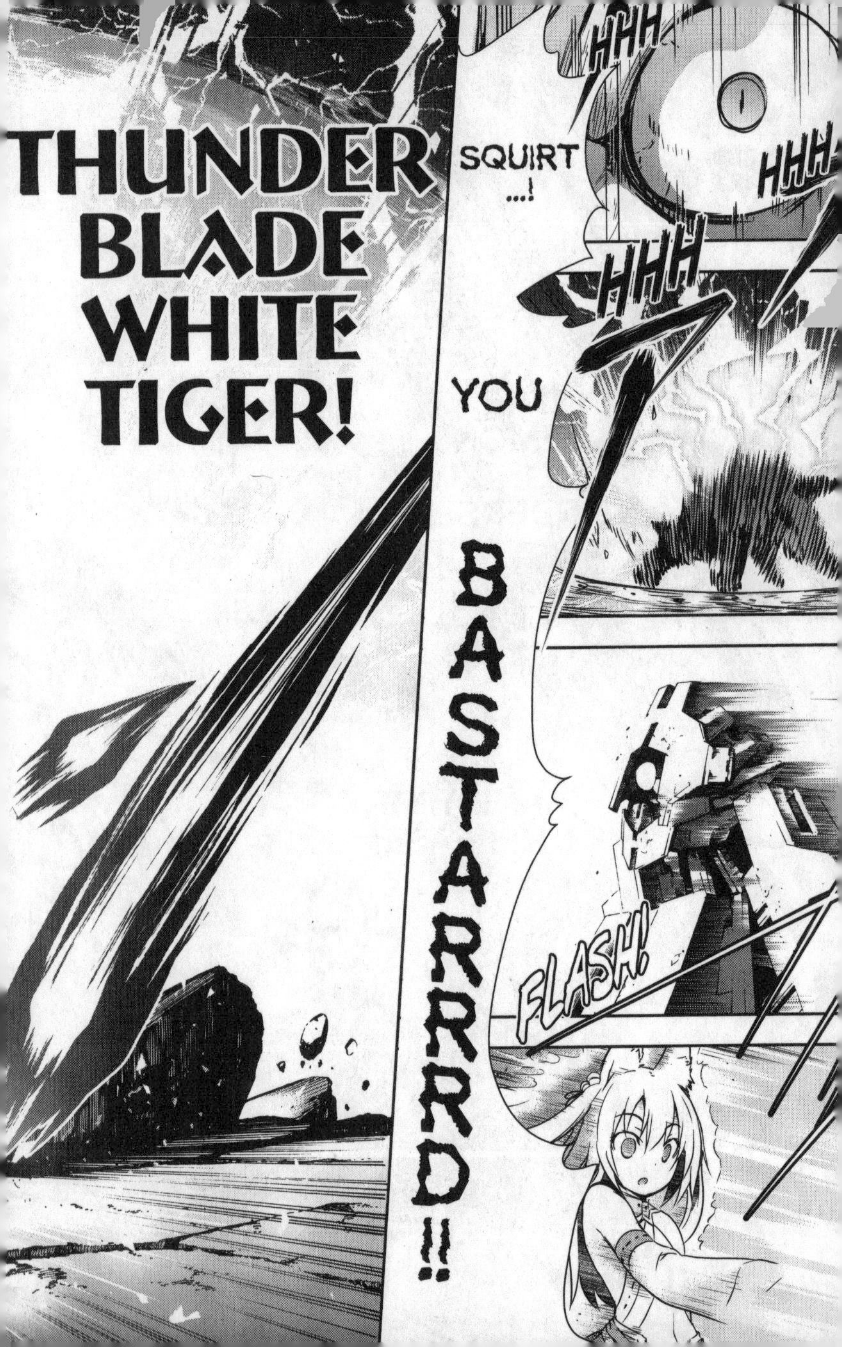
HHH
HHH
SQUIRT
...!
HHH
YOU BASTARRRD!!
FLASH!
THUNDER BLADE WHITE TIGER!

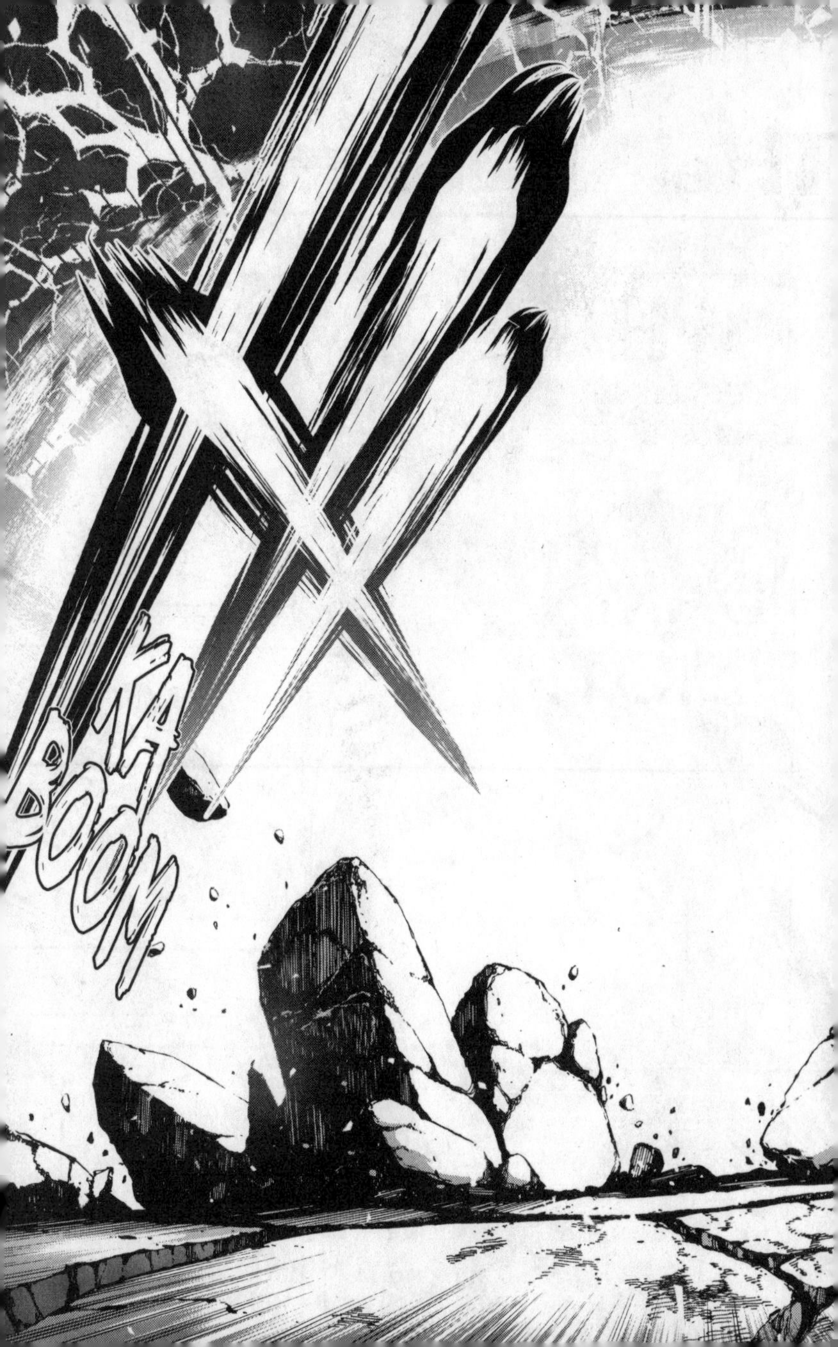
KA-BOOM

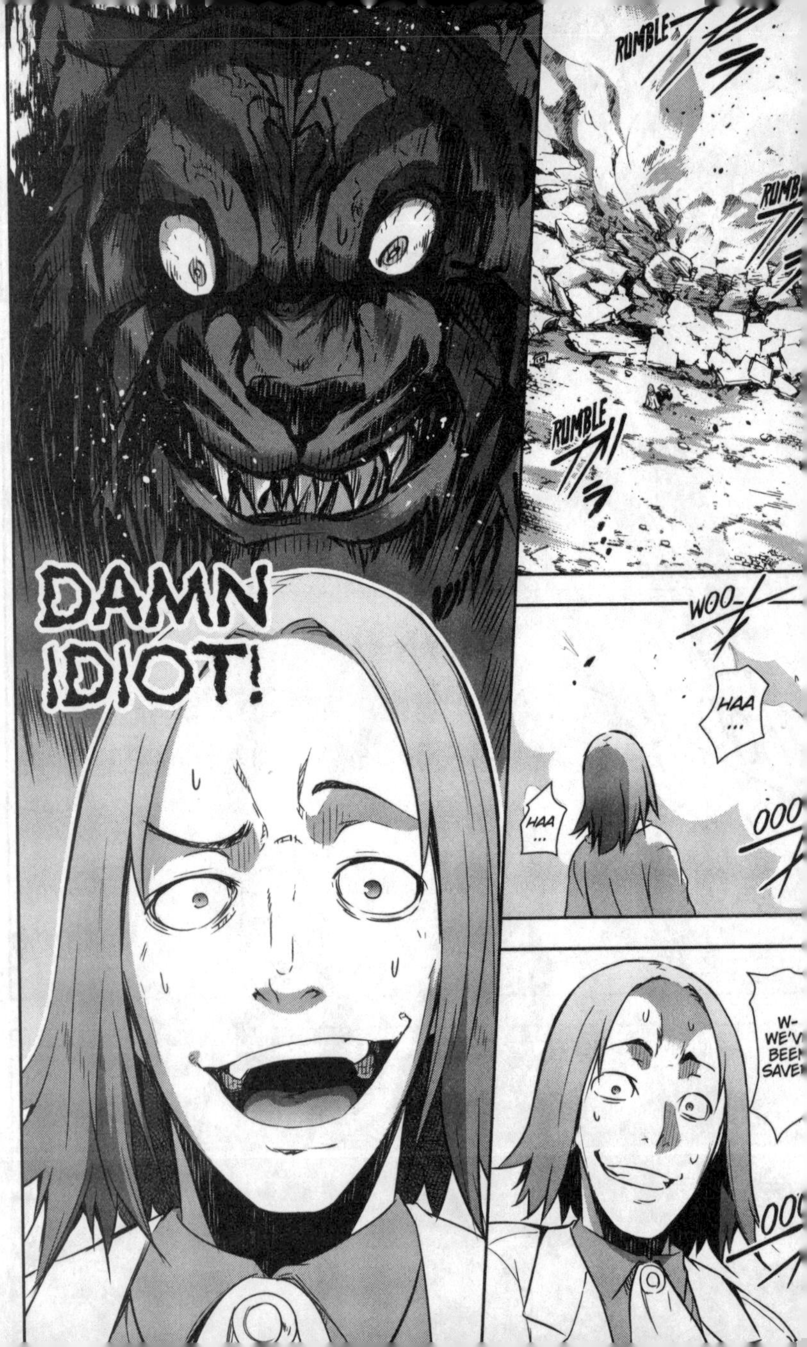
RUMBLE
RUMBL
RUMBLE
WOO-
HAA ...
HAA ...
OOO
W- WE'V BEEN SAVE
OOO
DAMN IDIOT!

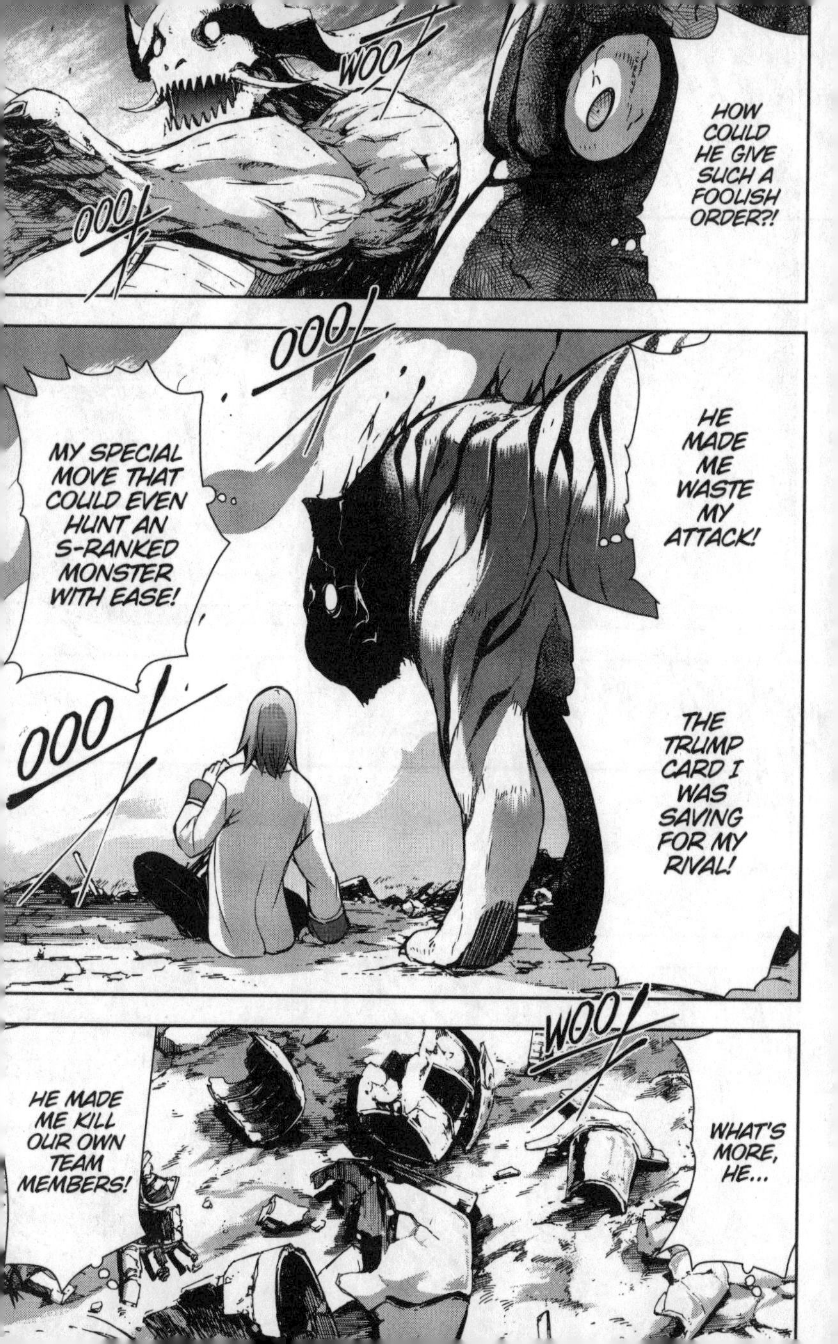
HOW COULD HE GIVE SUCH A FOOLISH ORDER?!
WOO
OOO
HE MADE ME WASTE MY ATTACK!
OOO
MY SPECIAL MOVE THAT COULD EVEN HUNT AN S-RANKED MONSTER WITH EASE!
THE TRUMP CARD I WAS SAVING FOR MY RIVAL!
OOO
WOO
WHAT'S MORE, HE...
HE MADE ME KILL OUR OWN TEAM MEMBERS!

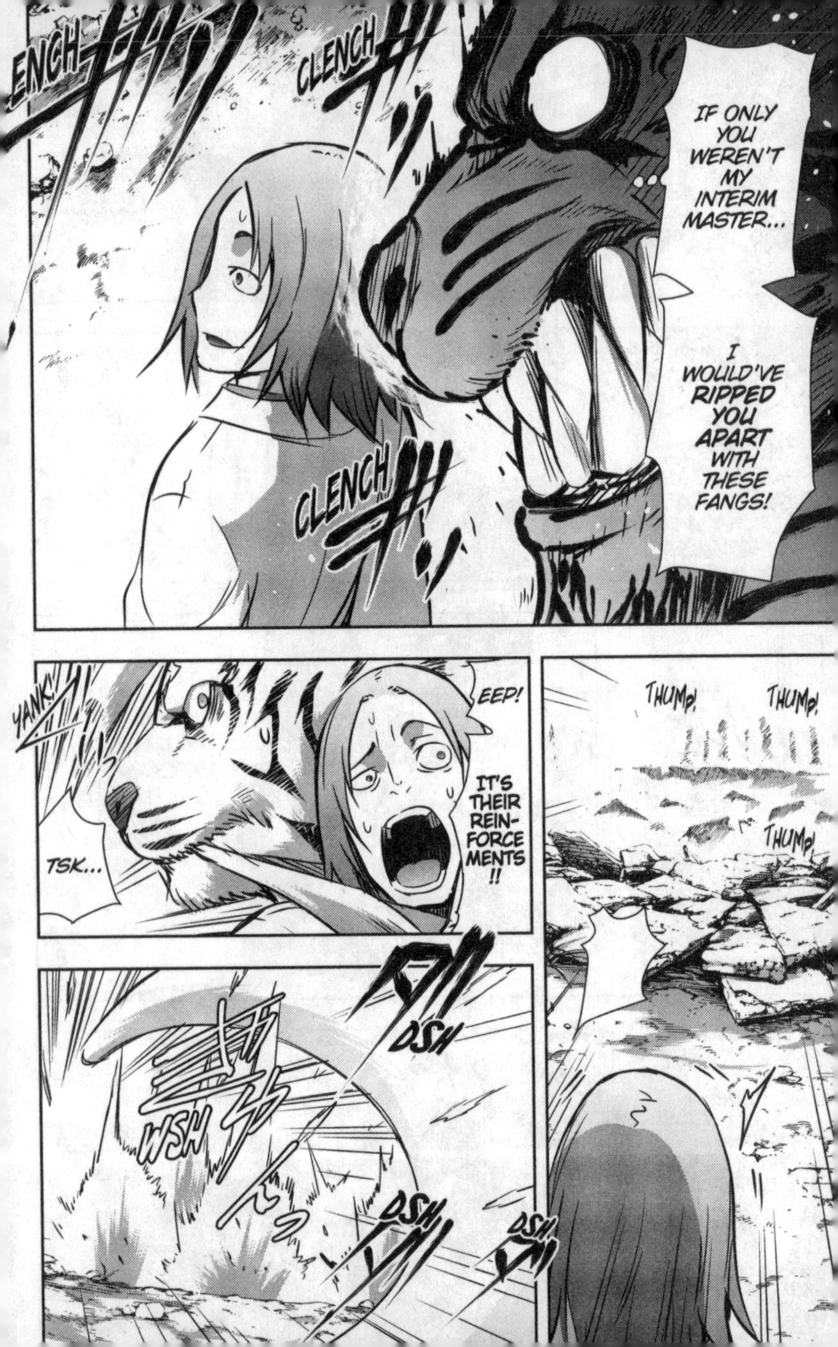

IF ONLY YOU WEREN'T MY INTERIM MASTER...
I WOULD'VE RIPPED YOU APART WITH THESE FANGS!
CLENCH
ENCH
CLENCH
THUMP!
THUMP!
THUMP!
DSH
EEP!
IT'S THEIR REIN-FORCEMENTS!!
YANK!
TSK...
DSH
WSH
DSH

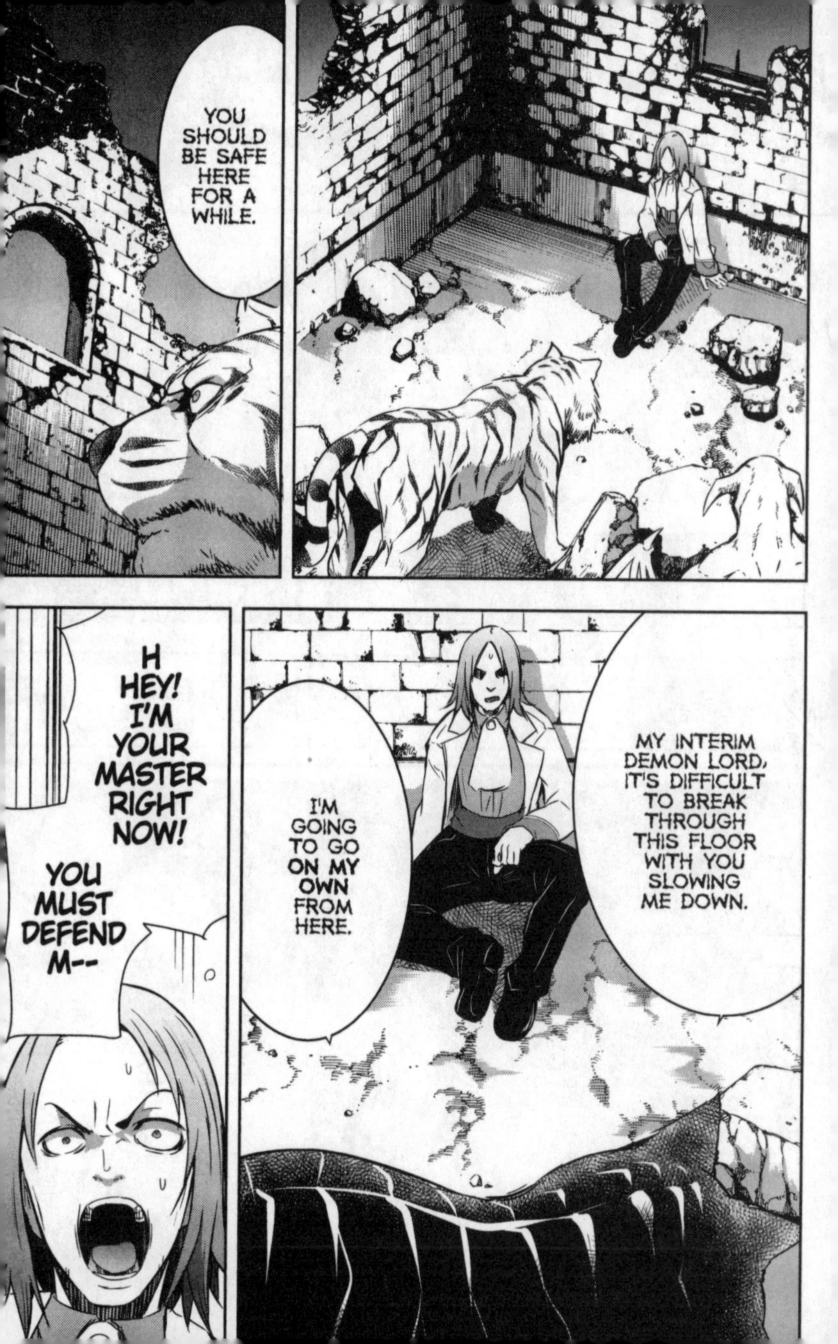
YOU SHOULD BE SAFE HERE FOR A WHILE.
MY INTERIM DEMON LORD, IT'S DIFFICULT TO BREAK THROUGH THIS FLOOR WITH YOU SLOWING ME DOWN.
I'M GOING TO GO ON MY OWN FROM HERE.
H HEY! I'M YOUR MASTER RIGHT NOW!
YOU MUST DEFEND M--

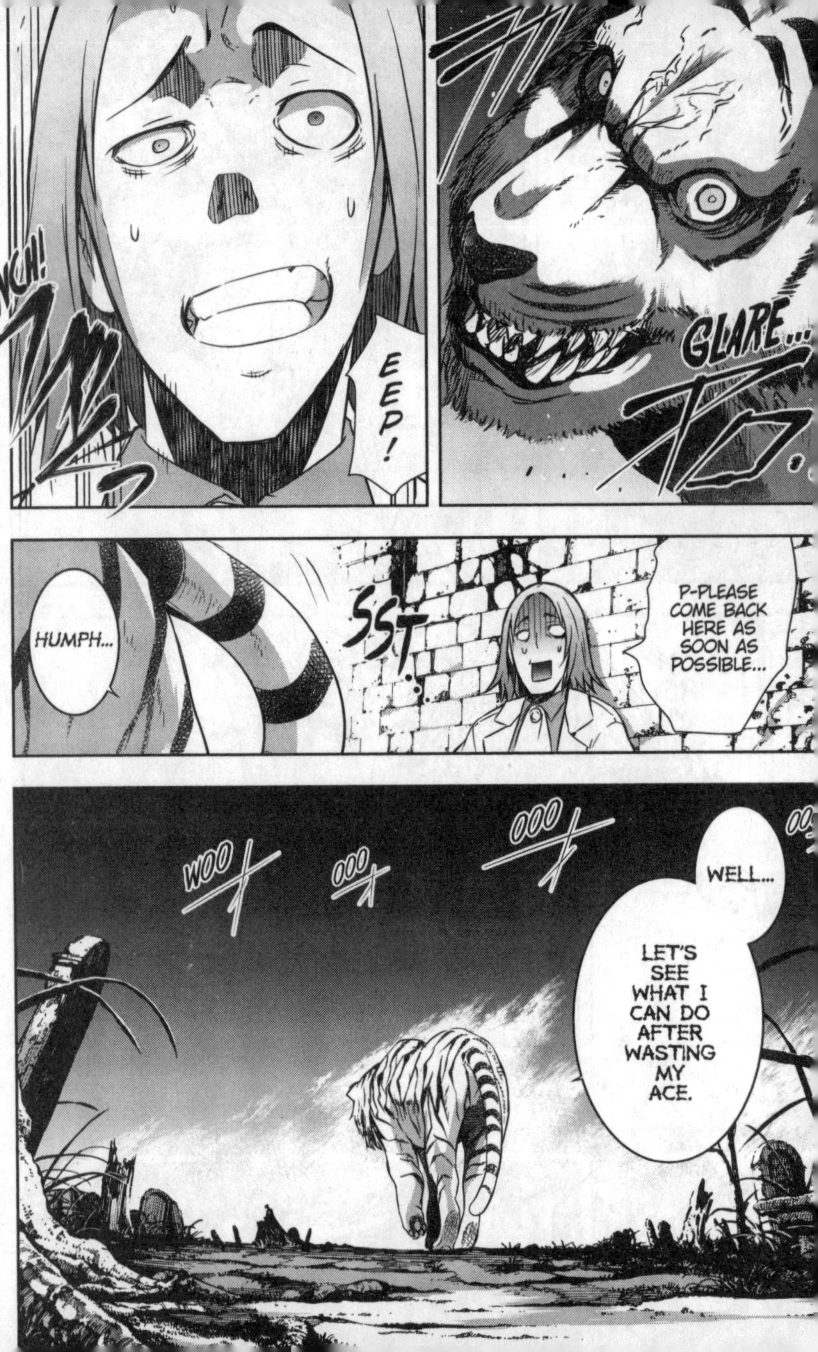
GLARE...
EEP!
INCH!
P-PLEASE COME BACK HERE AS SOON AS POSSIBLE...
SST
HUMPH...
WELL...
LET'S SEE WHAT I CAN DO AFTER WASTING MY ACE.
OOO
OOO
WOO

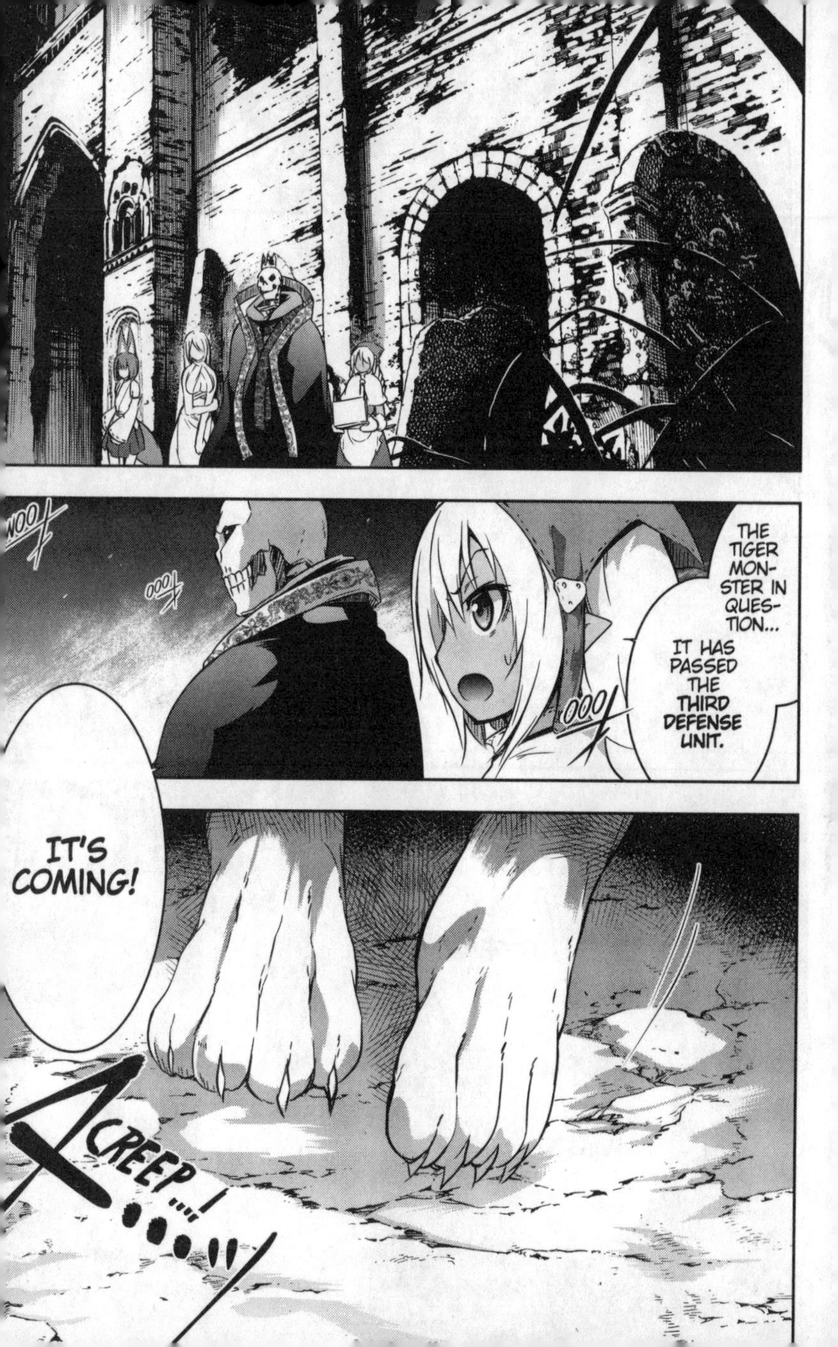
THE TIGER MONSTER IN QUESTION... IT HAS PASSED THE THIRD DEFENSE UNIT.
WOOO
OOO
OOO
IT'S COMING!
CREEP...!
...!!

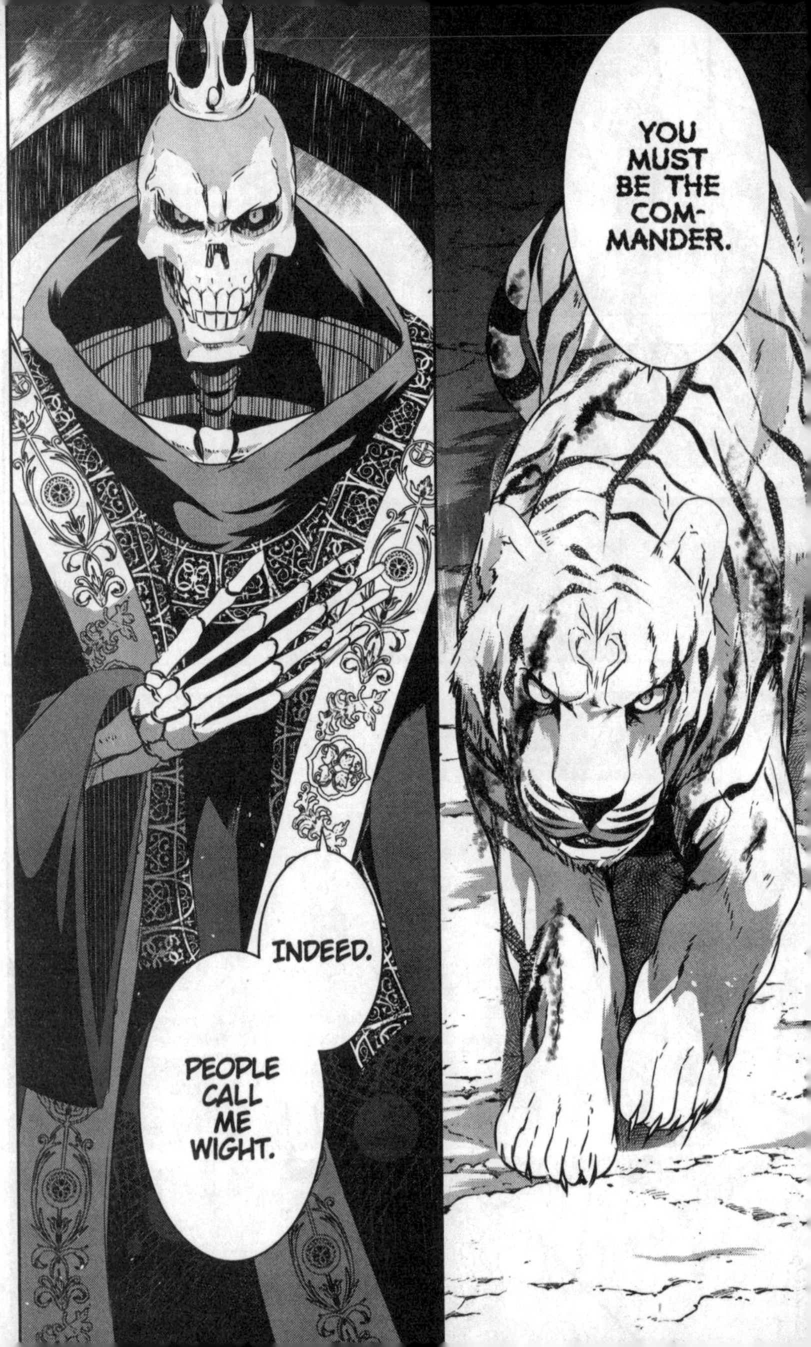
YOU MUST BE THE COM-MANDER.
INDEED.
PEOPLE CALL ME WIGHT.

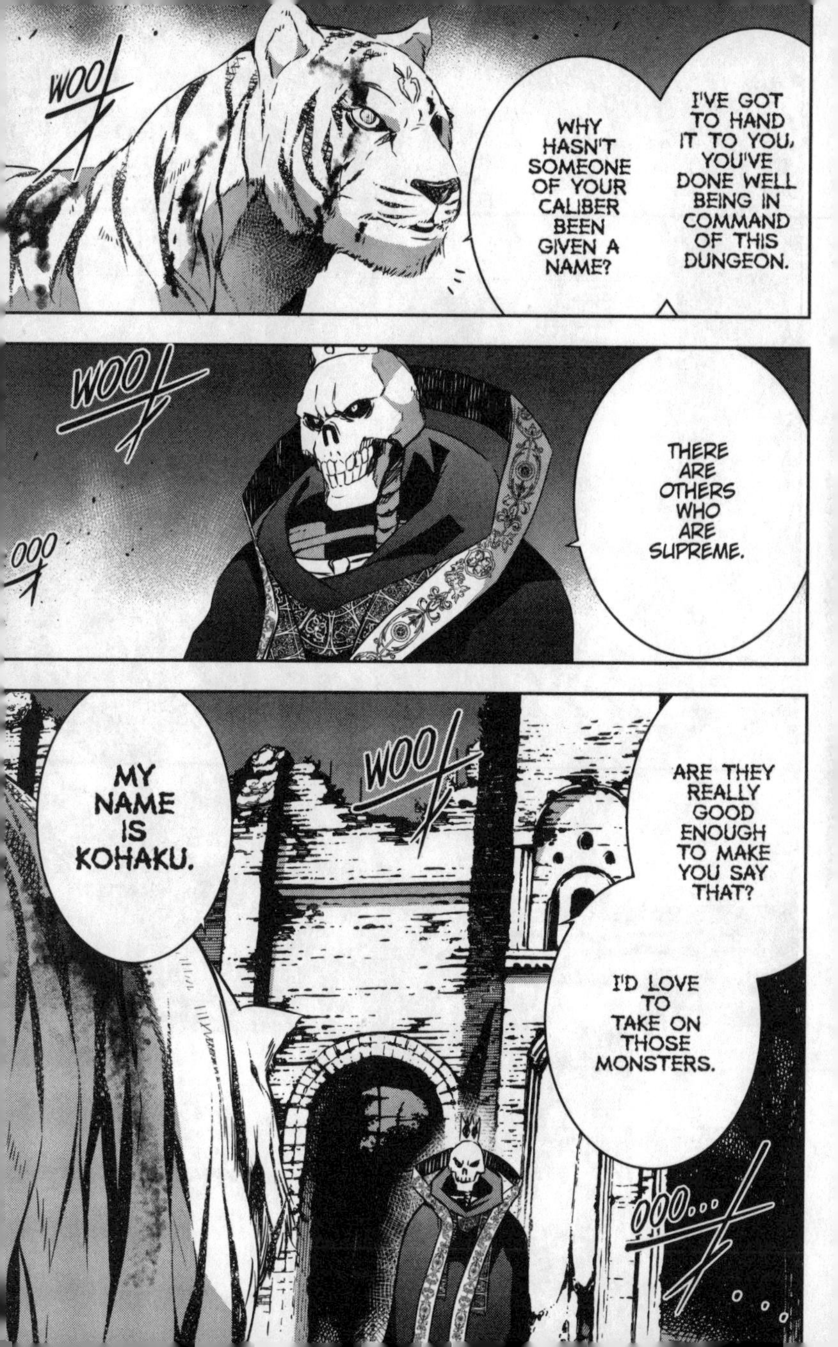
I'VE GOT TO HAND IT TO YOU, YOU'VE DONE WELL BEING IN COMMAND OF THIS DUNGEON.
WHY HASN'T SOMEONE OF YOUR CALIBER BEEN GIVEN A NAME?
WOO
THERE ARE OTHERS WHO ARE SUPREME.
WOO
OOO
ARE THEY REALLY GOOD ENOUGH TO MAKE YOU SAY THAT?
I'D LOVE TO TAKE ON THOSE MONSTERS.
OOO...
WOO
MY NAME IS KOHAKU.

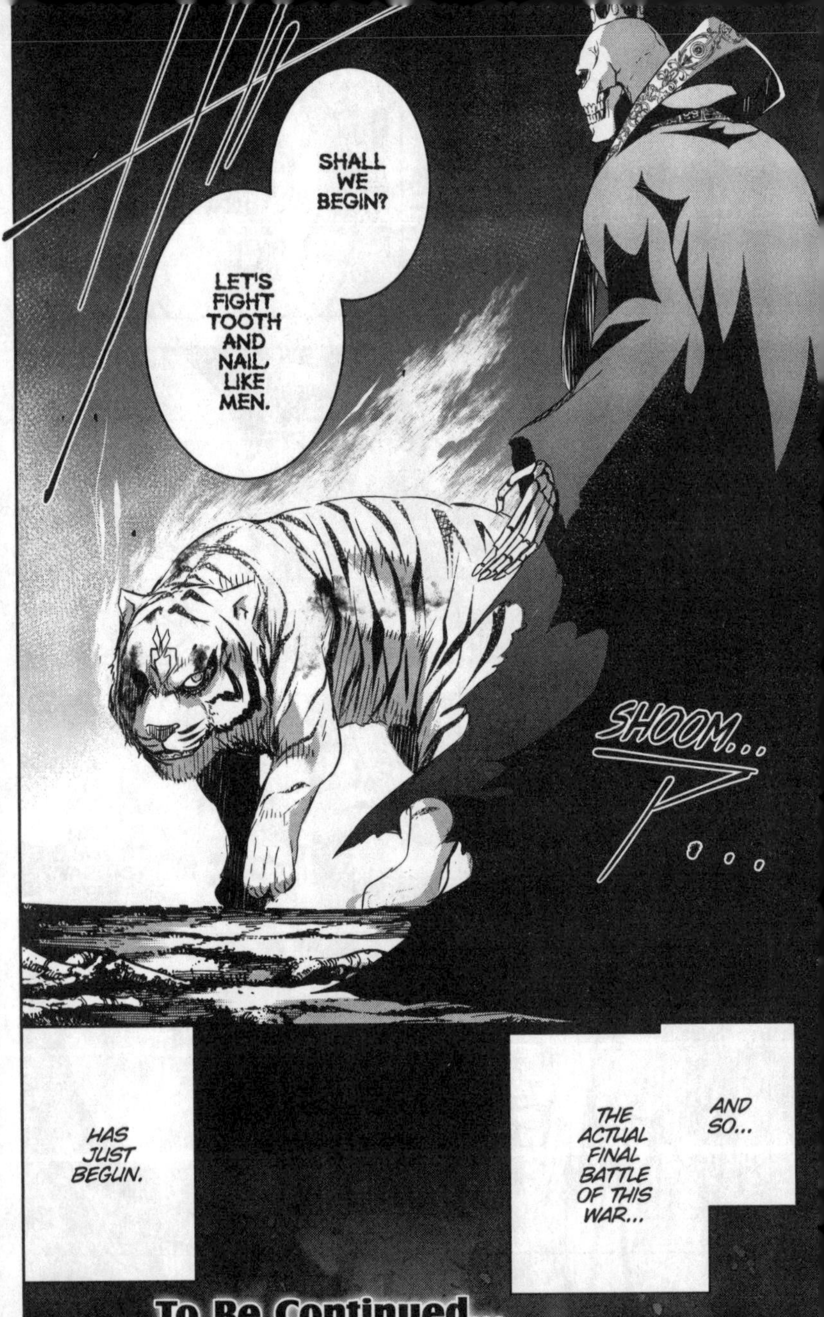
SHALL WE BEGIN?
LET'S FIGHT TOOTH AND NAIL, LIKE MEN.
SHOOM...
P...
AND SO...
THE ACTUAL FINAL BATTLE OF THIS WAR...
HAS JUST BEGUN.

To Be Continued...

Bonus Manga: **That's Not Funny, Aura**

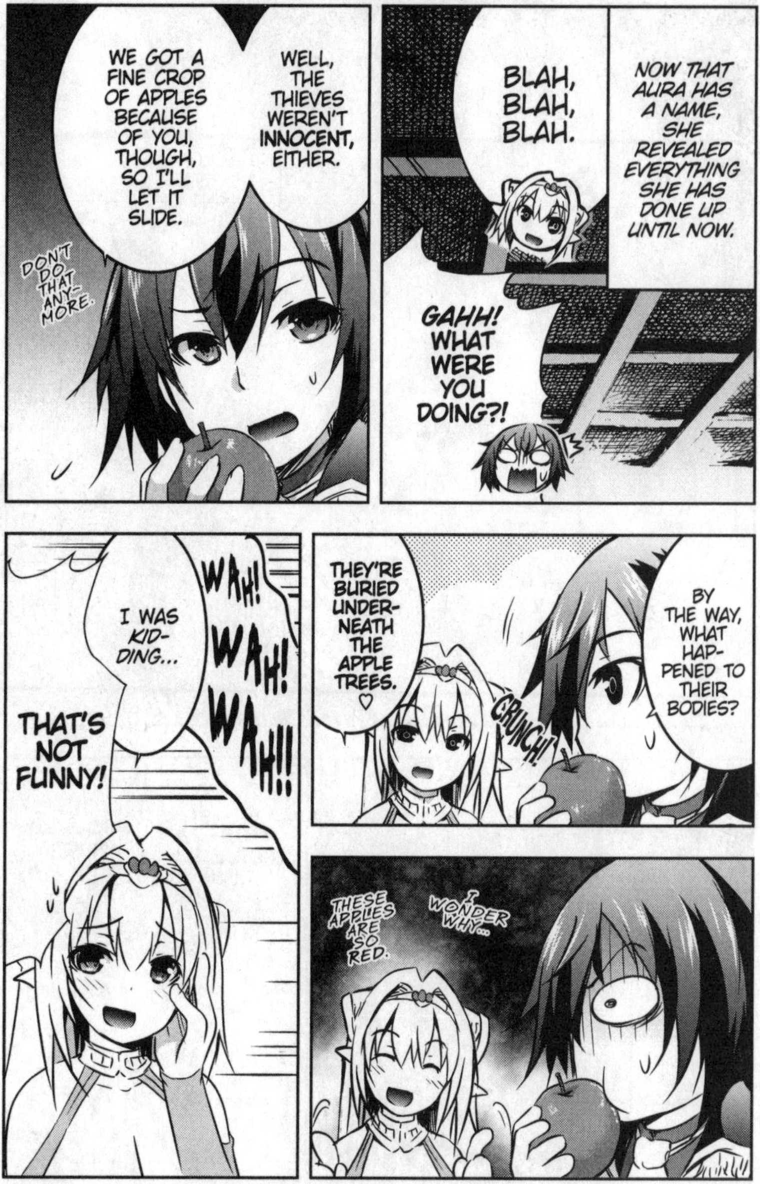

NOW THAT AURA HAS A NAME, SHE REVEALED EVERYTHING SHE HAS DONE UP UNTIL NOW.
BLAH, BLAH, BLAH.
GAHH! WHAT WERE YOU DOING?!
WELL, THE THIEVES WEREN'T INNOCENT, EITHER.
WE GOT A FINE CROP OF APPLES BECAUSE OF YOU, THOUGH, SO I'LL LET IT SLIDE.
DON'T DO THAT ANY-MORE.
BY THE WAY, WHAT HAP-PENED TO THEIR BODIES?
CRUNCH!
THEY'RE BURIED UNDER-NEATH THE APPLE TREES. ♡
I WONDER WHY...
THESE APPLES ARE SO RED.
WAH! WAH! WAH!!
I WAS KID-DING...
THAT'S NOT FUNNY!

Bonus Manga: **Quina is Very Observant**

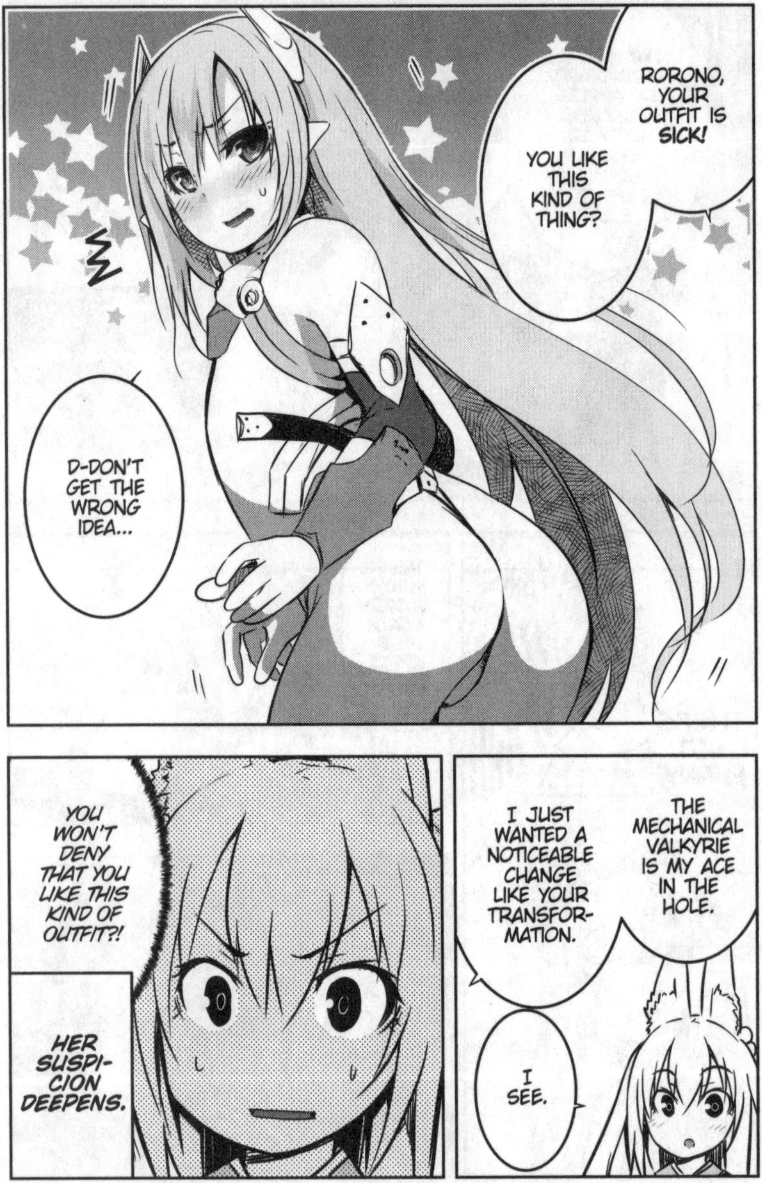
RORONO, YOUR OUTFIT IS SICK!
YOU LIKE THIS KIND OF THING?
D-DON'T GET THE WRONG IDEA...
THE MECHANICAL VALKYRIE IS MY ACE IN THE HOLE.
I JUST WANTED A NOTICEABLE CHANGE LIKE YOUR TRANSFORMATION.
I SEE.
YOU WON'T DENY THAT YOU LIKE THIS KIND OF OUTFIT?!
HER SUSPICION DEEPENS.

Bonus Manga:
The Steel Lord Wants to Take Every Precaution

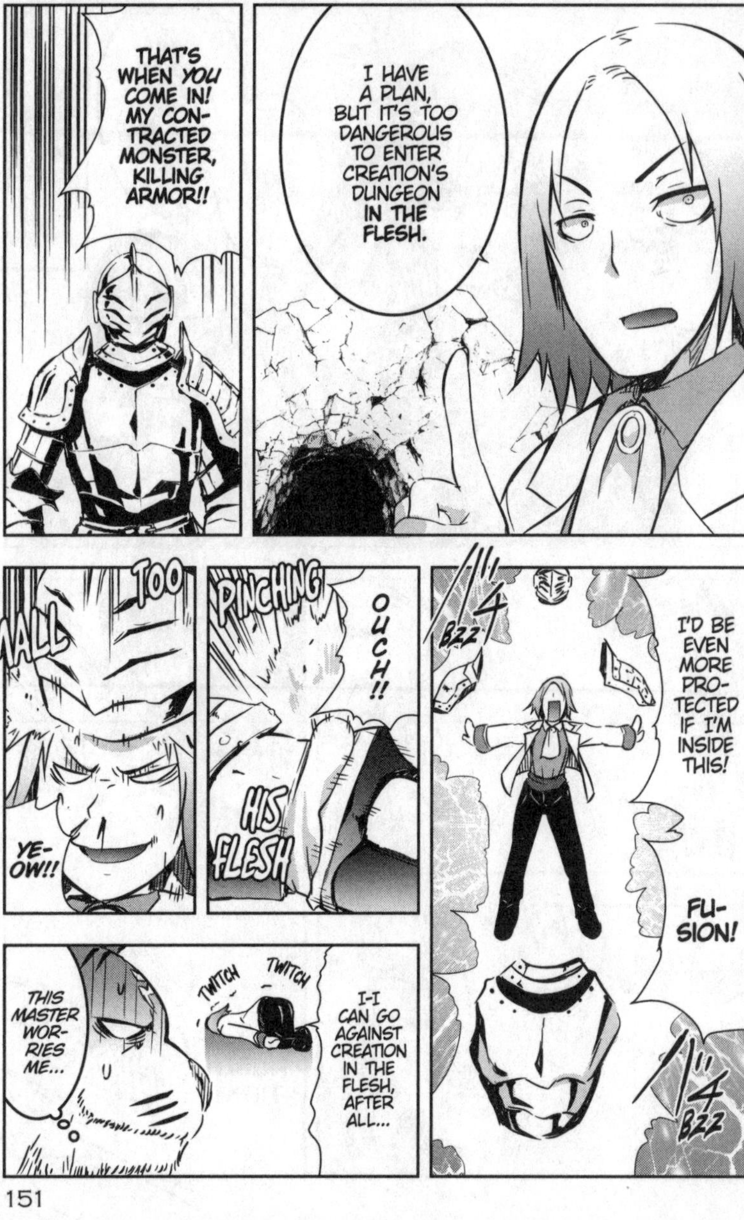
I HAVE A PLAN, BUT IT'S TOO DANGEROUS TO ENTER CREATION'S DUNGEON IN THE FLESH.
THAT'S WHEN *YOU* COME IN! MY CONTRACTED MONSTER, KILLING ARMOR!!
I'D BE EVEN MORE PROTECTED IF I'M INSIDE THIS!
BZZ
FUSION!
BZZ
OUCH!!
PINCHING
HIS FLESH
TOO
SMALL
YE-OW!!
I-I CAN GO AGAINST CREATION IN THE FLESH, AFTER ALL...
TWITCH
TWITCH
THIS MASTER WORRIES ME...

Bonus Manga: **Stolas Noticed It**

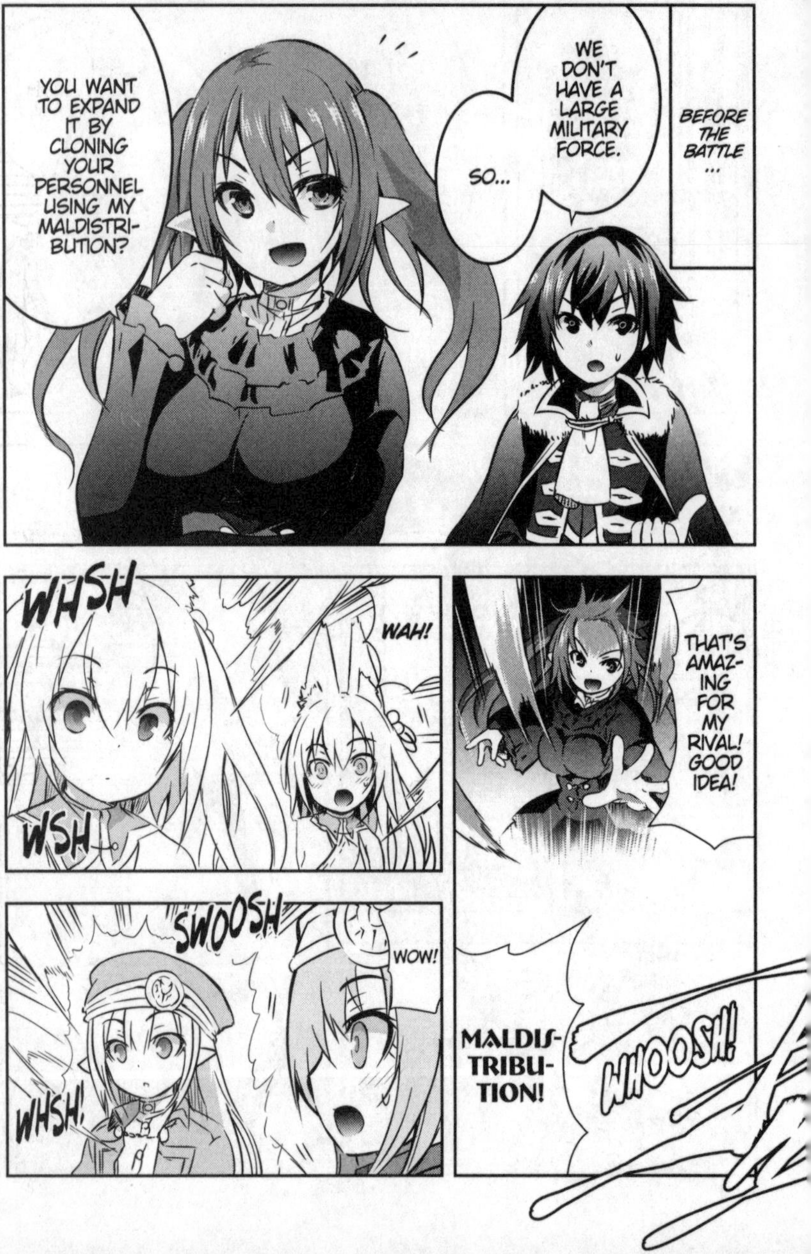

BEFORE THE BATTLE...
WE DON'T HAVE A LARGE MILITARY FORCE.
SO...
YOU WANT TO EXPAND IT BY CLONING YOUR PERSONNEL USING MY MALDISTRIBUTION?
THAT'S AMAZING FOR MY RIVAL! GOOD IDEA!
MALDISTRIBUTION!
WHOOSH!
WAH!
WHSH
WSH
SWOOSH
WOW!
WHSH!

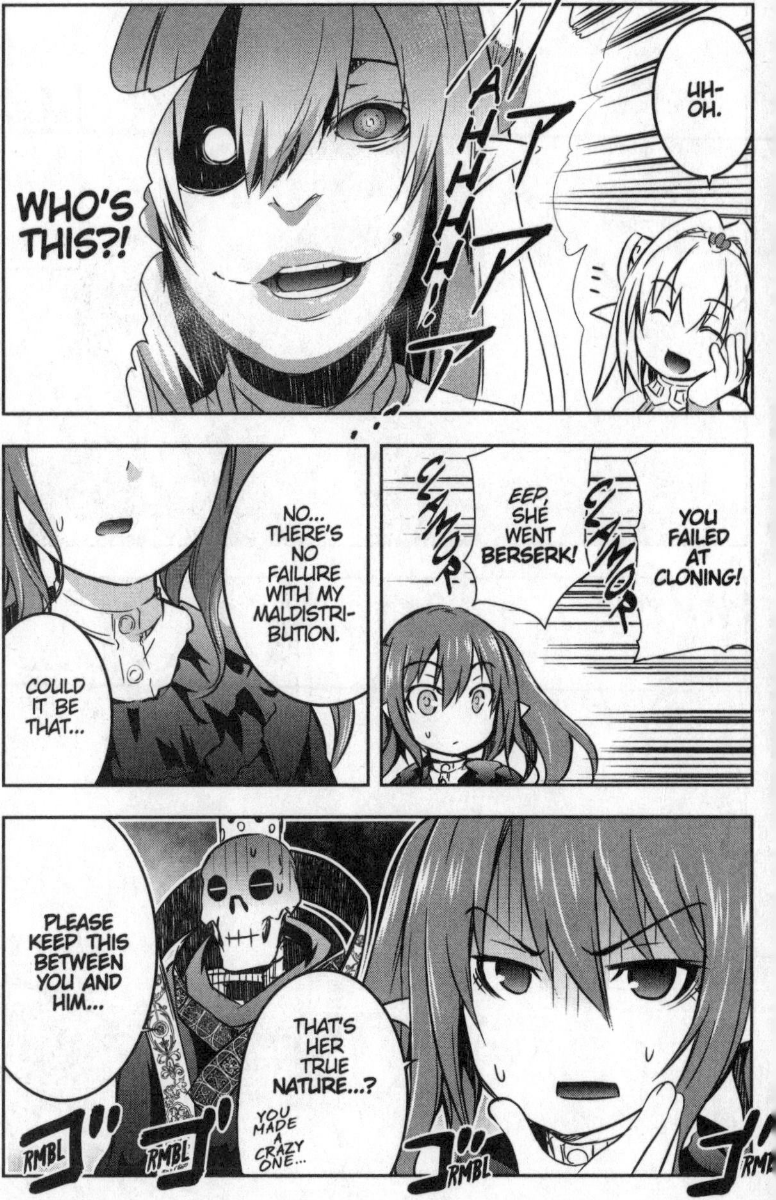
UH-OH.
AHHHHH!!
WHO'S THIS?!
YOU FAILED AT CLONING!
CLAMOR
EEP, SHE WENT BERSERK!
CLAMOR
NO... THERE'S NO FAILURE WITH MY MALDISTRIBUTION.
COULD IT BE THAT...
THAT'S HER TRUE NATURE...?
PLEASE KEEP THIS BETWEEN YOU AND HIM...
YOU MADE A CRAZY ONE...
RMBL
RMBL
RMBL
RMBL

DUNGEON BUILDER:
THE DEMON KING'S LABYRINTH IS A MODERN CITY!

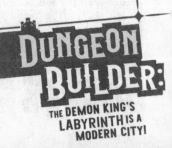

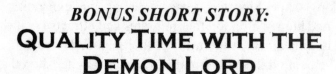

BONUS SHORT STORY:
QUALITY TIME WITH THE DEMON LORD

It's dinner time. Aura, the Ancient Elf, is cooking dinner and humming a song. Most elves are rather slender, but Aura has quite a voluptuous figure. There's something about her cooking in her apron that turns me on.

"Yah, El. It smells so good!" The Tenko, Quina, appears, lured by the smell of the food. Quina's a pretty, lovable, upbeat teen girl with fox ears.

"Hmm? I smell meat, but this is new." The Elder Dwarf, Rorono, shows up after Quina. She and Quina are about the same age, but Rorono is flat-chested, with a cool and relaxed personality.

"The market just got some beef today. It was so unusual that I had to buy it."

"I've never had it before!"

"I know. They raise cattle, but it's so costly and time-consuming that they rarely have beef at the market."

"Really? I can't wait!" A particularly homey air surrounds them, and one would never know that we were a demon lord and his underlings.

We live in a town called Avalon. It's probably the only town in this world where humans and monsters co-exist. This place was built in order to make my dream a reality. What at first seemed like an absurd idea is now slowly taking shape. Monsters have created a town, expanding as one human after another migrates and attracts business to it. This dinner is the fruits of their labors. We're able to have beef on the table because of a fine butcher shop that just opened a new location in town.

"Dinner is ready, let's eat! Lord Procel, I put plenty of love into this meal. I hope you enjoy it." Aura smiles brightly. Love is the greatest ingredient; many may disagree, but I can't deny it. How could I not appreciate the hard work of my sweet girls? Food is meant to be enjoyed with your tastebuds, as well as your heart and mind.

Aura made steaks, as the butcher suggested. He said it was the best way to enjoy the beef. We all began to eat, but Rorono frowned.

"This meat is tough. It tastes okay, but it makes my jaw sore."

"I agree, it's pretty hard to chew."

"Yah, Quina doesn't mind at all! It's yummy!"
Everyone but Quina the Tenko didn't care for it. When I

took a bite, I saw what they meant. It was tough... It must have been an old working cow, all muscular and fibrous. While that made it flavorful, it was like chewing rubber. Quina was able to eat it because Tenkos had strong jaws.

"Quina, you can have mine."

"Yah, Rorono, thank you!" Rorono offers her stake to Quina. She's always had a slight appetite, so she's quick to give it up.

We demon lords and monsters feed off of human emotions and magical power, and ingesting food is only done for entertainment purposes. We can skip a meal, no problem.

But as their demon lord, I couldn't leave my sweet girls disappointed.

"Aura, do we have any meat left?"

"Yes, we do! I bought extra since Quina always has seconds."

"Good. Let me prepare it. I'll make it nice and tender."

"What? You have magic that can do that?!"

"Yeah."

Somehow, a part of me was convinced I could do it. I couldn't explain it, but occasionally I knew things I shouldn't. My unique skill as a demon lord was Creation. It was an ability to generate matter from memory. I was able to create a firearm, which I shouldn't know how to do. Marchosias didn't even know why, and he's a senior demon lord, often counted among the three most powerful chiefs. The method for making meat tender was in that mysterious knowledge of mine, too. Someday I'd find out what was behind this power of mine, but at that moment I just wanted to make my sweet girls happy.

Some time later, I finished making steaks with Aura's help.

"Here, try it now, Rorono."

"Um-hmm, I'm so happy. My lord made this for me... I'll dig in... It's very tender. Tasty... Thank you, Dad." When Rorono got emotional, she called me "Dad" instead of "my lord" without realizing it. Whenever I heard it, I knew I made her happy. It made me so proud.

"This really is tender... It seemed more like a magic trick than cooking. How could it be so tender when all you did was pound it and marinate it with grated onions?" Aura tilted her head.

Rorono's face lit up. This was always a sign she was about to go off on a tangent, mumbling random facts and tidbits. As the supreme subspecies of dwarf, Rorono had a vast depth of knowledge and loved to talk about it.

"I know. He broke down the fiber and cut against the grain of the meat. Onions have an enzyme called protease, which breaks down protein... It's simple logic."

"Wow, that's amazing. Is that true? I just did it the way I knew it would work, but I didn't know the logic behind it."

I noticed Quina was quiet. She should have been

more hyped up about this than anyone.

"You haven't eaten your steak. What's the matter?"

"Unnhhh, I'm so stuffed, I can't eat any more..."

Quina had Aura make her a large piece of steak, and also shared a piece with Rorono.

"But I want to have the steak Dad made for me too." Quina's eyes welled up with tears. I couldn't help but notice how cute she looked. I have her a wry smile as I gently stroked her hair.

"I'll make more tomorrow. The butcher shop is still open. I'll buy more meat."

"Yah, I love you, Dad!" Quina jumped on me and wagged her fox tail. I didn't know what to do with her, sometimes.

"What should we do with the rest of the meat?"

"Let's have it for breakfast. It's already so tender. How about putting it in a sandwich?"

"Oh, that's a great idea. I'll put tomato sauce and lettuce on it too."

"That sounds yummy!" Everyone looked at Quina who, despite being too stuffed to eat, was already excited about tomorrow's food, and laughed. And so our wonderful dinner ended. Quality family time like that is not typical for a demon lord, but I cherish those moments and hope they last forever. Tomorrow I will work hard to make that wish come true.

"Let's all go for a walk and shop for snacks along the way." We had a new shop for such luxuries in Avalon. Most women and children loved the sweet treats, and it seemed no different with monsters—these girls loved them, too.

"Yah! ♫"

"I can't wait."

"*Hehe*, let's go."

We all went together. In the growing town of Avalon, there was sure to be a new snack at every shop.

THE END

Comment by: Rui Tsukiyo
Art by: Hideaki Yoshikawa

Afterword

Thank you for reading *Dungeon Builder!*
The battle is in full swing. I'm starting to miss the part about dungeon building. When this battle ends, the town will go through an evolution. I hope you look forward to it as you enjoy the Battle Arc!

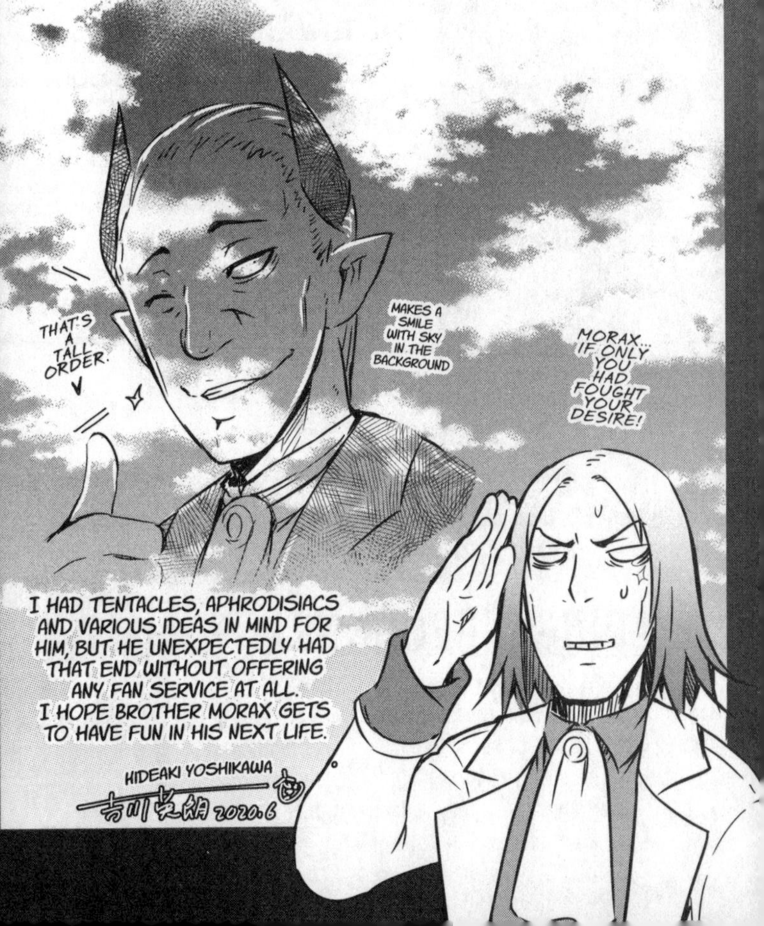
MORAX... IF ONLY YOU HAD FOUGHT YOUR DESIRE!
MAKES A SMILE WITH SKY IN THE BACKGROUND
THAT'S A TALL ORDER.
I HAD TENTACLES, APHRODISIACS AND VARIOUS IDEAS IN MIND FOR HIM, BUT HE UNEXPECTEDLY HAD THAT END WITHOUT OFFERING ANY FAN SERVICE AT ALL. I HOPE BROTHER MORAX GETS TO HAVE FUN IN HIS NEXT LIFE.
HIDEAKI YOSHIKAWA
2020.6

SEVEN SEAS ENTERTAINMENT PRESENTS

DUNGEON BUILDER:
THE DEMON KING'S LABYRINTH IS A MODERN CITY!

story by RUI TSUKIYO   art by HIDEAKI YOSHIKAWA   VOLUME 4

TRANSLATION
Elina Ishikawa

ADAPTATION
Julia Kinsman

LETTERING AND RETOUCH
Roland Amago
Bambi Eloriaga-Amago

COVER DESIGN
Kris Aubin

PROOFREADING
Kurestin Armada, Dawn Davis

EDITOR
Matthew Birkenhauer

PREPRESS TECHNICIAN
Rhiannon Rasmussen-Silverstein

PRODUCTION MANAGER
Lissa Pattillo

MANAGING EDITOR
Julie Davis

ASSOCIATE PUBLISHER
Adam Arnold

PUBLISHER
Jason DeAngelis

MAOU-SAMA NO MACHIZUKURI! SAIKYOU NO DUNGEON WA KINDAI
TOSHI VOL. 4
© 2020 Hideaki Yoshikawa
© Rui Tsukiyo/SB Creative Corp.
First published in Japan in 2020 by OVERLAP Inc., Ltd., Tokyo.
English translation rights arranged with OVERLAP Inc., Ltd., Tokyo.

Seven Seas press and purchase enquiries can be sent to Marketing Manager
Lianne Sentar at press@gomanga.com. Information regarding the distribution
and purchase of digital editions is available from Digital Manager CK Russell
at digital@gomanga.com.

Seven Seas and the Seven Seas logo are trademarks of
Seven Seas Entertainment. All rights reserved.

ISBN: 978-1-64827-213-4

Printed in Canada

First Printing: May 2021

10 9 8 7 6 5 4 3 2 1

FOLLOW US ONLINE: www.sevenseasentertainment.com

READING DIRECTIONS

This book reads from **right to left**, Japanese style.
If this is your first time reading manga, you start
reading from the top right panel on each page and
take it from there. If you get lost, just follow the
numbered diagram here. It may seem backwards at
first, but you'll get the hang of it! Have fun!!

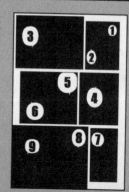